"*Malware, Rootkits & Botnets* is a great of cyber attack. This is a guideline for all information technology persons to have the understanding of today's threat landscape."

—Oscar Chang, Chief Development Officer, Trend Micro, Inc.

"As stated in the *Art of War* by Sun Tzu, if you know your enemies and know yourself, you can win all battles. Christopher Elisan's book systematically demystifies the thought process of both of the malware writers and the anti-malware solution providers. Christopher is generous in sharing his security knowledge and experience in this book. He took a hands-on approach in explaining the industry lingo, common practices, the layered approach to malware analysis, and some of the tools and techniques used by both the 'good guys' and the 'bad guys.' Reading this book is how you get to know your enemies and yourself really well. I would characterize this book as compulsory reading material for all the security professionals responsible for securing hosts, applications, or networks from known and unknown security threats."

—Chee Tan, Director of Business Development, Avira Inc.

"Security is often hard to simplify without sacrificing key points that are critical to the protection of data and systems. Christopher is able to take one of the most complex topics in security and simplify it without sacrifice. This book is a must-read for beginner and advanced users alike."

—Richard Kohn, Sr. Services Product Manager, Symantec

"A fascinating, deep-dive into the work performed by anti-malware vendors and the daunting challenges they face in the never ending cat-and-mouse game with malware authors. Truly great insight into how pervasive and truly frightening today's malware landscape has become."

—David Monaco, Director of Information Security, Radialpoint Inc.

"Computers are our day-to-day tools in this information driven world. Be it smartphones, tablets, or laptops, more and more of our lives depend on the safe use of these life enhancing devices. How are we making sure we protect our information? Christopher explains in easy to understand language one of the most exciting fields of IT: the Anti-Virus world. Read this book to understand how to prepare for that fight. Anyone who wants to take responsibility for their own security must read this book."

—Vasco Duarte, Agile Coach, Avira Operations GmbH

"This is one of the best books on malware today. It explains malware techniques in detail from both sides, attacker and defender, with rich sets of real-world cases. If you are a beginner, this book helps you build a solid knowledge foundation; if you are already a professional, it convinces you that what you have implemented is not good enough and you still have tough challenges ahead; if you are a CIO/IT security manager, it presents you with a clearer picture of why fighting with malware is not easy and why you may have to allocate more budget for it."

—Lixin Lu, CTO, validEDGE

"Malware, Rootkits & Botnets is a great primer on malware and what you can do to protect yourself and your organization from it. If you've been mystified by or apprehensive about learning all of the lingo, rest assured that this book will clearly explain the basics in a way that will empower you to understand the big picture—from the sides of both the bad guys and the good guys. And once you do, you'll be prepared to evaluate your security posture, recognize possible malware threats, and take action!"

—Roger Harrison, Senior Director of WebPulse R&D, Blue Coat Systems

"If you are joining (or want to learn about) the computer security industry, *Malware, Rootkits & Botnets: A Beginner's Guide* is a must-read to quick start your way into learning all the jargon, concepts, and technologies that comprise the Threat Landscape. It accurately explains the history of malware and the work that goes on inside anti-malware labs in creating solutions against computer threats as they evolved."

—Jong Purisima, Antivirus Lab Manager, GFI-VIPRE

"Malware, Rootkits & Botnets: A Beginner's Guide offers an excellent introduction to the art and science of threat intelligence and malicious code analysis. Chris Elisan offers a real world, pragmatic approach that takes the reader (regardless of his or her experience level) through detailed methodology and examples that are sure to enhance the comprehension and expertise of the reader. As threat campaigns become more prevalent and sophisticated— threatening an ever increasing number of organizations globally—the ability to understand the threat landscape fluently will become nonnegotiable."

—Will Gragido, Sr. Manager, RSA Threat Watch and author of
Cyber Crime and Espionage: An Analysis of Subversive Multi-Vector Threats

"Fresh and insightful book outlining all the key elements of Malware analysis process today. A must have."

—Mario Vuksan, CEO, ReversingLabs

Malware, Rootkits & Botnets
A Beginner's Guide

Christopher C. Elisan

New York   Chicago   San Francisco
Lisbon   London   Madrid   Mexico City
Milan   New Delhi   San Juan
Seoul   Singapore   Sydney   Toronto

The McGraw·Hill Companies

Cataloging-in-Publication Data is on file with the Library of Congress

McGraw-Hill books are available at special quantity discounts to use as premiums and sales promotions, or for use in corporate training programs. To contact a representative, please e-mail us at bulksales@mcgraw-hill.com.

Malware, Rootkits & Botnets: A Beginner's Guide

1234567890   DOC DOC   1098765432

ISBN   978-0-07-179206-6
MHID   0-07-179206-6

Sponsoring Editor   Amy Jollymore

Editorial Supervisor   Jody McKenzie

Project Manager   Manisha Singh,
Cenveo Publisher Services

Acquisitions Coordinator   Ryan Willard

Technical Editors   Julio Canto,
Roberto Perdisci

Copy Editor   Lisa McCoy

Proofreader   Carol Shields

Indexer   Jack Lewis

Production Supervisor   James Kussow

Composition   Cenveo Publisher Services

Illustration   Cenveo Publisher Services

Art Director, Cover   Jeff Weeks

Dedicated to my loving wife, Kara, whose support and understanding enabled me to skip my regular honey-do list and write this book; to my two wonderful sons, Sebastian and Noah, who inspire me to be a better person each and every day; and lastly to my parents, Ernesto and Evangeline, and brothers, Butch and Adrian, without whom I would not have been the person I am today.

About the Author

Christopher Elisan is the media's go-to expert when it comes to cybercrime, providing expert opinion about malware, botnets, and advance persistent threats for leading industry and mainstream publications, including *USA Today, San Francisco Chronicle, SC Magazine, InformationWeek, Fox Business,* and *Dark Reading*. He is also a frequent speaker at various security conferences across the United States, including HackerHalted, Toorcon, International Information Systems Security Consortium (ISC)², and B-Sides. Elisan is a seasoned reverse engineer and malware researcher. He is currently the principal malware scientist at RSA NetWitness. Elisan has a long history of digital threat and malware expertise, reversing, research, and product development. He is an early pioneer of Trend Micro's TrendLabs. This is where he started his career as a computer virus researcher and from there held multiple technical and managerial positions. After leaving Trend Micro, Elisan held a manager-researcher role during his years with F-Secure where he established and led F-Secure's Asia R&D and spearheaded multiple projects that include vulnerability discovery, web security, and mobile security. He then joined Damballa, Inc. as a senior threat analyst specializing in malware research. Elisan graduated with a degree in Bachelors of Science in Computer Engineering and holds the following industry certifications: Certified Ethical Hacker, Microsoft Certified Systems Engineer, Microsoft Certified System Administrator, Microsoft Certified Professional, and Certified Scrum Master.

About the Technical Editors

Julio Canto is a senior developer and security consultant at Hispasec Sistemas. He is the original designer and developer of the world-famous virustotal.com multiscanner service. Canto's main focus is on the improvement of the service core, and he also participates in other software development initiatives in Hispasec Sistemas. Canto also has performed consulting, auditing tasks, and online fraud incident handling, especially those related to malware and phishing. He also gives talks about VirusTotal and malware awareness at several locations and events such as FIRST (Forum of Incident Response and Security Teams).

Roberto Perdisci, a recipient of the 2012 National Science Foundation CAREER award, is an assistant professor in the Computer Science Department at the University of Georgia, Athens (UGA) and a faculty member of the UGA Institute for Artificial Intelligence. Before joining UGA, Dr. Perdisci was a postdoctoral fellow at the College of Computing of the Georgia Institute of Technology, working under the supervision of Prof. Wenke Lee. He also worked as principal scientist at Damballa, Inc., and prior to joining Damballa was a research scholar at the Georgia Tech Information Security Center and Ph.D. candidate at the University of Cagliari, Italy, with the Pattern Recognition and Applications Group.

Contents at a Glance

PART III   The Enterprise Strikes Back

PART IV   Final Thoughts

Contents

PART I   Establishing the Foundation

PART II   Welcome to the Jungle

PART III   The Enterprise Strikes Back

Acknowledgments

First, I would like to thank God for this blessing. Second, I would like to give my heartfelt thanks to the people who gave their time and effort in the making of this book and to those who, in one way or another, were affected by or had an influence in the writing of this book: to Amy Jollymore for the opportunity to write this book; to Ryan Willard for making sure I stayed the course; to Melinda Lytle for helping me polish my book artworks; to Joya Anthony for helping to have the first chapter I wrote off the ground; to Mikko Hypponen for writing the foreword of the book even though his schedule was really tight; to Julio Canto and Roberto Perdisci who both took some time off of their busy schedule to technically review the contents of the book; to my colleagues and former colleagues, especially the members of PinGRE (Pinoy Group of Reverse Engineers), for contributing to my professional growth and learning through endless hours of discussion, debate, and exchange of ideas; and to my friends who had to endure endless excuses of not "being there" while I was writing this book (now they know the real reason). Third, I thank the companies I have had and continue to have the pleasure of working with: to Trend Micro for sending out a telegram inviting me for an interview and on-the-spot technical exam and after going through multiple grueling interviews finally deciding to hire me even though I had nothing to show in terms of experience except for my records and achievement in college (Trend Micro laid the foundation for me in terms of malware research and reverse engineering, and for that I will be forever grateful);

to F-Secure, for expanding my horizon and giving me the confidence to do big things that have meaningful impact to those inside and outside the company; to Damballa, for giving me the freedom to research and do exciting things in the realm of digital threats and cybercrime; and to RSA NetWitness, for welcoming me into the team and for opening new doors that lead to new and exciting adventures in fighting cybercrime.

And last but definitely not the least, I give thanks to the person who guided me through life, set me on the right path, and taught me the value of hard work: my mom. None of this would be possible if my mom did not have the will and the courage to send me to the best schools even if the odds seemed insurmountable during those times.

Foreword

The real world isn't like the online world.

In the real world, you only have to worry about the criminals who live in your city. But in the online world, you have to worry about criminals who could be on the other side of the planet. Online crime is always international because the Internet has no borders.

Today computer viruses and other malicious software are no longer written by hobbyist hackers seeking fame and glory among their peers, but by professional criminals who are making millions with their attacks. These criminals want access to your computer, your PayPal passwords, and your credit card numbers.

I spend a big part of my life on the road, and I've visited many of the locations that are considered to be hotspots of online criminal activity. I've been to Moscow, Sao Paolo, Tarto, Vilna, St. Petersburg, Beijing, and Bucharest.

I've met the underground and I've met the cops. And I've learned that things are never as simple as they seem from the surface. One would think that the epicenter for banking attacks, for example, would prioritize fighting them, right?

Right, but dig deeper and complications emerge. A good example is a discussion I had with a cybercrime investigator in Brazil. We spoke about the problems in Brazil and how Sao Paolo has become the largest source of banking Trojans in the world.

The investigator looked at me and said, "Yes. I understand that. But what you need to understand is that Sao Paolo is also one of the murder capitals of the world. People are regularly gunned down on the streets. So where exactly should we put our resources? To fight cybercrime? Or to fight crimes where people die?"

It's all a matter of balancing. When you balance the damage done by cybercrime and compare it to a loss of life, it's pretty obvious what's more important.

National police forces and legal systems are finding it extremely difficult to keep up with the rapid growth of online crime. They have limited resources and expertise to investigate online criminal activity. The victims, police, prosecutors, and judges rarely uncover the full scope of the crimes that often take place across international boundaries. Action against the criminals is too slow, the arrests are few and far between, and too often the penalties are very light, especially compared with those attached to real-world crimes.

Because of the low prioritization for prosecuting cybercriminals and the delays in launching effective cybercrime penalties, we are thereby sending the wrong message to the criminals and that's why online crime is growing so fast. Right now would-be online criminals can see that the likelihood of their getting caught and punished is vanishingly small, yet the profits are great.

The reality for those in positions such as the Sao Paolo investigator is that they must balance both fiscal constraints and resource limitations. They simply cannot, organizationally, respond to every type of threat. If we are to keep up with the cybercriminals, the key is cooperation. The good news is that the computer security industry is quite unique in the way direct competitors help each other. It's not publicly known, but security companies help each other out all the time.

On the surface, computer security vendors are direct competitors. And in fact, the competition is fierce on the sales and marketing side. But on the technical side, we're actually very friendly to each other. It seems that everyone knows everyone else. After all, there are only a few hundred top-level antivirus analysts in the whole world.

These analysts meet in face-to-face private meetings, closed workshops, and at security conferences. We run encrypted and closed mailing lists. We chat in secure online systems. And in these venues we exchange information on what's happening.

On the surface, this doesn't seem to make sense. Why do we cooperate with our competitors to such a large extent? I believe it's because we have a common enemy.

You see, normal software companies do not have enemies, just competitors. In our business, it's different. Obviously we have competitors, but they are not our main problem. Our main problem is the virus writers, the bot authors, the spammers, and the phishers. They hate us. They often attack us directly. And it's our job to try to keep them at bay and do what we can to protect our customers from them.

In this job, all the vendors are in the same boat. This is why we help each other.

And we need all the help we can get to keep up with the changing landscape of online attacks.

All this is happening right now, during our generation. We were the first generation that got online. We should do what we can to secure the 'Net so that it will be there for future generations to enjoy.

Mikko Hypponen
Chief Research Officer,
F-Secure

Introduction

Why This Book?

This book is a good springboard into malware, rootkits, and botnets. The concepts presented and discussed in the book peel away the complexity of the topics and present them in a very easy-to-read and easy-to-understand format. And after reading this book, you will be able to carry a very intelligent conversation about malware, rootkits, and botnets with your peers and industry experts.

Who Should Read This Book

This book is written for self-guided IT professionals who are responsible for securing enterprise networks and systems; security professionals who need a refresher; students who are taking technology courses; and computer users who are simply interested in educating themselves about malware, rootkits, and botnets.

What This Book Covers

This book covers concepts and topics about malware, rootkits, and botnets. What are these threats? What makes them dangerous? And what are the technologies they use to achieve their malicious goal? The book also looks at the cybercriminals that use these malicious creations to perform an attack on a desired target. Who they are? What roles does each of them play in the world of cybercrime? And how do they prosper and have money flow into their pockets?

But this book is not all about the dark side of computing. The book also covers and discusses ways of protecting an organization's network by proposing practical steps and procedures to improve the security posture of an organization.

How to Use This Book

The book can be read from cover to cover. This will give the reader the most benefit because the book is written in such a way that the succeeding chapters build on top of the previous chapters. But this does not mean that this is the only way to read the book. Although the chapters are interrelated, they can be read separately without reading the previous or the next one and still have the chapter's main idea and concept understood. Each chapter can stand on its own independently, but also enjoys interdependency with the other chapters. Therefore, if a reader is already familiar with a specific chapter's subject matter, that chapter can be skipped without sacrificing the book's continuity. And since the chapters are independent of each other, this book can be used as a reference as well.

How This Book Is Organized

The book consists of 12 chapters divided into four parts:

- Part I: Establishing the Foundation
- Part II: Welcome to the Jungle
- Part III: The Enterprise Strikes Back
- Part IV: Final Thoughts

Part I

Part I gives the reader the needed foundation in understanding the threats we face today. It introduces the usual culprits in cyberattacks and gives the reader sufficient understanding of malware, rootkits, and botnets. Part I consist of four chapters:

- Chapter 1 – Getting in Gear
- Chapter 2 – A Brief History of Malware
- Chapter 3 – Cloak of the Rootkit
- Chapter 4 – Rise of the Botnets

Chapter 1 gets the reader in gear. It serves as a brief introduction to the current threat landscape and a short discussion on the threat malware poses in our daily lives. It is aimed at getting us started on our journey into the world of malware, rootkits, and botnets.

Chapter 2 introduces the reader to the wonderful world of malware. A historical background is presented, concentrating on the most significant advances in malware technology and how it affected and changed the digital world and our view of computing in general. A primer on malware classification is also presented describing the nature of each malware based on behavior and intent.

Chapter 3 takes a look at the most common rootkit techniques malware uses to gain control of a target system that enable it to hide its presence.

Chapter 4 is all about botnets. It defines what a botnet is, its major components, the different methods it uses to communicate to the attacker, and the common network evasion techniques it uses to avoid detection and take-down by the authorities.

Part II

Armed with a strong foundation and sufficient understanding of the threats, Part II takes the reader into the heart of the action. The reader is given an "over-the-shoulder" view of how the attackers operate; organize as a cybercrime entity; and use existing technologies to create, deploy, and manage the malware and botnets under their control. The reader is taken on a journey of the whole threat life cycle: from malware creation, to target selection, to deployment through different infection vectors, to system infection, and ultimately to the execution of the malware payload. The second part also sheds light on how regular people unwittingly become participants of the cybercrime organization and how the attackers profit from this malicious endeavor. Part II consists of four chapters:

- Chapter 5 – The Threat Ecosystem

- Chapter 6 – The Malware Factory

- Chapter 7 – Infection Vectors

- Chapter 8 – The Compromised System

Chapter 5 introduces the reader to the concept of the threat ecosystem and the different elements that make it up. This chapter not only discusses the elements that make up an advance persistent threat, but also the criminals behind it. A closer look is given at how these criminals make money by digging deeper into how they monetize the amount of infected machines under their control, how they sell stolen data, and how they are able to launder money coming to them by using, among others, regular people as money mules.

Chapter 6 delves into what is really behind the growing number of malware samples seen per day, from a mere handful of samples from yesteryears to the five-digit figures we see today. This chapter looks at the different attacker tools and methods that make possible not just the creation of an army of malware, but also the ability to make them virtually undetectable by antivirus products. And to better understand how these tools and methods evade antivirus detection, an overview of the most common detection technologies used by antivirus products is explained. The chapter then takes the reader inside the malware factory, an assembly-line approach of mass-producing malware.

Chapter 7 answers the question of how malware got into the system. Different methods and techniques used by malware to get into the system, also known as infection vectors, are enumerated and dissected for further understanding.

Chapter 8 shows what happens after the successful deployment of malware. The chapter mainly discusses how malware infects a system and how it behaves once the system is compromised.

Part III

With a newfound awareness of how malware, rootkits, and botnets are used by cybercrime organizations to maliciously attack systems, Part III guides the reader on how to deal with these attack threats and improve the security posture of systems under the reader's watch. The third part introduces practical ways of understanding the existing security posture of a system, identifying a possible threat to that system, and mitigating a known or identified threat through the use of industry best practices and tools. Part III consists of three chapters:

- Chapter 9 – Protecting the Organization
- Chapter 10 – Detecting the Threat
- Chapter 11 – Mitigating the Threat

Chapter 9 introduces concepts on how to protect an organization's computer systems by exploring the value of each system and how it contributes to each system becoming a high-value target for the attackers, and how to handle and overcome a possible attack through the introduction of an incident response plan that takes into consideration the system's value and the current security posture of the organization's network.

Chapter 10 discusses how to detect and identify a possible threat based on anomalies in the network and in the host, and then have this detected threat classified based on its attack directive so the threatened systems can be protected and the proper mitigation techniques can be applied.

Chapter 11 is all about threat mitigation, from the immediate response an organization can take to mitigate the threat to the more proactive approach of mitigation that includes different preventive measures, such as putting in place regular audits and user education.

Part IV

The fourth and final part of the book offers my view of where the threat landscape is going. Part IV tackles the future of malware, rootkits, and botnets based on current trends, near- and long-term technology development, and advances in malware technology. It also makes the readers aware of ongoing research work on the antimalware front and how this is becoming a never-ending race between the good guys and the attackers. Part IV consists of one chapter, two appendices, and a glossary:

- Chapter 12 – The Neverending Race
- Appendix A – The Bootup Process
- Appendix B – Useful Links
- Glossary

Chapter 12 takes a look back at what has been discussed throughout the book and my take on the future of malware, rootkits, and botnets.

Appendix A describes the BIOS-based and EFI-based bootup process.

Appendix B contains links that the reader will find useful when dealing with malware, rootkits and botnets.

The **Glossary** contains a collection of security-related definitions and terms that the reader can use as reference while reading the book.

About the Series

I worked with the publisher to develop several special editorial elements for this series, which I hope you'll find helpful while navigating the book—and furthering your career.

Lingo

The Lingo boxes are designed to help you familiarize yourself with common security terminology so that you're never held back by an unfamiliar word or expression.

IMHO

When you come across IMHO (In My Humble Opinion), you'll be reading my frank, personal opinion based on experiences in the security industry.

Budget Note

The Budget Notes are designed to help increase your ease while discussing security budget needs within your organization, and provide tips and ideas for initiating successful, informed conversations about budgets.

In Actual Practice

Theory might teach us smart tactics for business, but there are in-the-trenches exceptions to every rule. The In Actual Practice feature highlights how things actually get done in the real world at times, exceptions to the rule, and why.

Your Plan

The Your Plan feature offers strategic ideas that can be helpful to review as you get into planning mode, as you refine a plan outline, and as you are embarking on a final course of action.

Into Action

The Into Action lists are get-going tips to support you in taking action on the job. These lists contain steps, tips, and ideas to help you plan, prioritize, and work as effectively as possible.

PART I

Establishing the Foundation

CHAPTER 1

Getting In Gear

We'll Cover

- A brief overview of the current threat landscape
- Malware as a threat to national security

This chapter serves as a brief introduction to get us started into our journey into malware, rootkits, and botnets. To get us in gear, I will discuss my first encounter with malware that triggered a curiosity in me that still continues today in my career as a reverse engineer and a malware researcher. Then the chapter gives a brief overview of the current threat landscape and a short discussion on the threat malware poses to our national security.

A Malware Encounter

In one way or another, our lives have been affected by malware. Each one of us probably still remembers our first encounter with these malicious digital creations. Mine came when I got my first IBM-compatible PC. It was an 80386SX, 256 MB hard drive with 4 MB of RAM. It had three floppy disk drives that supported two 5¼ and one 3½ floppy disks. I also had a 14-inch paper-white VGA monitor and an Epson dot matrix printer. My operating system was DOS 6.22, and I was running Windows 3.11 on top of that. That PC served me well. It was where I honed my Pascal, C, and assembly-language programming skills.

Occasionally, I would cross paths with floppy disks infected with viruses the likes of STONED, Jerusalem, and Brain. But it was nothing my McAfee Antivirus scanner couldn't handle. Life with my PC was good. I was turning in well-formatted reports courtesy of WordPerfect and I was enjoying playing PC games with MIDI sound effects. But then one day while I was running Windows 3.11, the computer started going haywire. Nothing was working. All I got was a series of software error messages. I restarted my PC and inserted my McAfee scanner. It detected nothing. I ran WIN.COM to start Windows 3.11 but after a minute or so, I experienced the same error. I reinstalled Windows 3.11 using around ten 3½ floppies, but still the problem persisted. Not knowing what to do, the next day I brought my PC tower to a friend who owns a computer shop. He started scanning my PC using his own McAfee scanner, but with an updated SCAN.DAT. Then a virus was found. It was the DIE-HARD 2 virus. It infected Windows 3.11 executables and components. And since Windows 3.11 is a different format than DIE-HARD 2, which is a DOS virus, the virus essentially destroyed the Windows 3.11 components, hence, the software error messages.

LINGO
SCAN.DAT is McAfee's virus signature file also known as a version 1 DAT file.

This experience started me on the path of becoming more curious and interested about viruses, their nature, and how they work. My hobby of modifying and patching DOS's COMMAND.COM to display funny error messages and playing around with Norton Utilities was replaced by an unceasing curiosity about viruses until it eventually became my profession. I was recruited by Trend Micro fresh out of college, after getting my bachelor's of science degree in computer engineering, for my assembly-language skills and from then on I was in the forefront in the fight against malware.

Joining Trend Micro and seeing how the advancement of virus and malicious software technology play out was an eye-opener for me. It made me aware about the serious impact viruses were having on individuals, businesses, and even law enforcement agencies. Here I was working with a team of experts solving the malware problems facing the world, one malware at a time. It's a very exciting gig. The threat landscape is changing so fast that the only way to keep up is to learn and adapt. Otherwise, you will be left behind. Continuous learning is a must. And the familiarity of the threat landscape is a major requirement.

A Brief Overview of the Threat Landscape

Malware is still a force to be reckoned with, and advances in technology did not slow it down. Malware actually rode the improving technology and made it its tool and ally. For example, e-mail, which revolutionized the way we send messages to anywhere in the world, was utilized as a fast method of spreading malware globally. Social network postings became a space to point users into a malicious website that specializes in the automatic installation of malware in the systems of unsuspecting users. And as I have demonstrated in my previous conference talks, Twitter is being abused to control malware residing in compromised systems. And on top of all this, malware is becoming better at protecting itself. The development of technologies that enable malware to evade detection and analysis made it virtually unstoppable in infiltrating its high-value targets. It's not just new malware protection technologies that are making it difficult to stop malware, but the staggering number by which new malware is being produced on a daily basis, as I have also demonstrated in my previous conference talks. This is made possible by new technologies that enable the assembly-line approach to creating new malware and recycling old ones.

Also, the always-online state of systems today made it possible for attackers to communicate with malware residing in a compromised system. What started as a one-is-to-one ratio became a one-is-to-many. An attacker now has the ability to control thousands of infected machines all at once, making it possible to conduct a coordinated attack. This is known as a botnet, a main component of advanced persistent threats.

Behind all of these threats are not the rival malware writing groups in a pissing contest, but rather highly motivated and well-funded cybercriminals. Plus targets of advanced persistent threats are high-value targets carefully selected, either because of what they are or based on the attack sponsor's directive.

> **LINGO**
> A **coordinated attack** is a term used to describe an attack coming from multiple infected machines acting on a single directive.

Cybercriminals recognize the profitability of malware; that investment in this space gave rise to an underground malware economy. The malware's shift from nuisance to threat redefined the threat landscape in a very sinister manner, and now malware is being taken seriously by law enforcement agencies not just here in the United States but worldwide as well.

The malware also did not limit itself to the PC. It ventured out to devices that have the ability to run software. Among them is the mobile phone. With mobile phones packing more computing power and faster connectivity, they have become mini-PCs. But what makes mobile phones so attractive and popular is that almost everyone has one, plus it holds data that can be monetized by the attackers. This is why mobile malware is on the rise again.

Unfortunately, most antimalware products did not advance as fast as malware technology did. Some solutions are still stuck in the malware stone-age. Those that still rely on signatures are bound to get whooped by malware. And some even contribute to a false sense of security for misinformed users. Some think that if their security products do not detect anything that they are secure already and do not need to keep up with what's going on in the threat landscape. It has to be understood early on that malware today is stealthier than the malware of yesteryears. It is not as boisterous as the early generations, when it always announced its presence and dominance in a compromised system. Today, malware conceals its presence more than ever. It is like the devil. It goes to great lengths to convince the victimized user that it does not exist.

The problem has become so serious that the dangers of malware are not confined to fiction anymore. We can see it play out in the news more and more on a regular basis. Businesses are starting to take serious notice more than ever, and they are making security a major part of their budget allocation. Even the government is starting to consider malware a threat to national security.

Threat to National Security

Cybercrime will eclipse terrorism. That was the statement given by FBI Director Robert Mueller at the 2012 RSA conference in San Francisco [1]. Although terrorism does remain the FBI's top priority, they recognize and anticipate that in the not-too-distant future, cybercrime will pose the greatest threat to the United States—especially now that cybercrime is not perpetrated anymore by rival malware writer groups but powered by highly motivated and well-funded cybercriminals, some of which are state sponsored.

There are names of certain countries floating around that have the will and capability to perform a cyberattack on the United States in the event of a conflict. It is also believed that some of them are doing it now in the form of cyberespionage by gathering intelligence and trade secrets that they can use to their advantage. This may include information on their possible targets, including critical infrastructure like smart grids. Imagine the damage a cyberattack on critical infrastructure could cause. For example, an attack on the U.S. smart power grids could potentially affect millions of residents. It could result in higher bills or even loss of power, which could result in failure of some critical systems or infrastructure relying on a continuous flow of electricity with minimal power interruptions.

Since most of our infrastructure today is online and has many possible points of attacks, the need to secure it is more important than ever before. A disruption in any of these points can cause chaos or even have deadly consequences. An attack on the computer infrastructure that powers Wall Street trading could cause financial chaos. An attack on systems controlling the thousands of flights across the United States could put the lives of thousands of travelers on the line. There are more deadly scenarios if a system goes haywire as result of an attack. What seems to be far fetched a couple of decades ago is now a possibility.

But this is not the only threat we are facing today. Loose groups like Anonymous and Lulzsec have risen to prominence as a result of their recent high-profile attack campaigns that targeted commercial and governmental entities. These hacktivist groups are fueled by an ideology that, if crossed, the offending entity will be subject to attack.

To address this growing threat the FBI has dedicated a team of cybersecurity experts in each of its 56 field offices and has 1000 dedicated agents and analysts monitoring the Web. They focus on three key threat groups: terrorists, organized crime rings, and state-sponsored cyberespionage [1].

Starting the Journey

It is evident in what we see today that the malware problem will not go away. It will simply evolve. New threats will be unleashed and new technology will be developed to stop them. Sometimes they will work and sometimes they won't. It will take a lot of effort from different sectors of society to confront it. The research community, the security industry, private and public entities, and law enforcement agencies have their own way of addressing the malware problem. Some work actively together while some work on their own silos.

But one thing is certain; we have our work cut out for us. It's challenging, but it's fun. And as an individual and a self-guided professional, there is one thing that can be done. You are doing it now. And that is to educate yourself. This book will start you on that journey into learning more about malware, rootkits, and botnets.

We've Covered

- A brief overview of the current threat landscape
  - Malware technology improves and adapts to technology changes
  - Malware evolved from a lone-wolf type of attack to a coordinated form of attack
  - Attacks are profit-driven
  - Malware threat is multi-device and multi-platform
  - Antivirus solutions still rely on signature-based detection
- Malware as a threat to national security
  - Critical infrastructure that is online runs the risk of being attacked
  - Other governments have capabilities to conduct a cyberattack against the United States
  - The FBI is recognizing the problem and is taking steps in addressing it

References

1. http://money.cnn.com/2012/03/02/technology/fbi_cybersecurity/index.htm?iid=Lead.

CHAPTER 2

A Brief History of Malware

We'll Cover

- Different types of computer viruses

- Early challenges of computer viruses

- Different types of malware

- The most significant areas of malware evolution

- Different types of riskware

- Malware creation kits

The popularity of the IBM-based PC made it the platform of choice for malware. It became a hotbed for malicious programs. As the PC evolved, so did malware. The malware grew almost hand in hand with the developing microcomputer technology and the operating system developed for it. The level of interconnectivity that we have been enjoying for some time now also made malware much more dangerous. The convenience and the speed of data and information exchange removed the geographic boundaries of malware. It gave the malware the capability to infect a system half a world away in seconds.

This chapter introduces the reader to the wonderful world of malware. A brief history of malware from its early beginnings as a computer virus to the different types of malware we see today, including significant areas of malware evolution, is presented. A primer on the different types of riskware is also discussed to make the reader aware of how malicious intention and the user reaction to such software can be dangerous. The chapter then ends with the introduction of malware creation kits and how this technology has significantly changed the playing field and given attackers a very powerful arsenal.

Malware can be found in almost all platforms and operating systems, but in this chapter we will concentrate mainly on malware written for IBM PCs running DOS and Windows.

Computer Viruses

Before Yisrael Radai coined the word "malware" in 1990, malicious programs were collectively called computer viruses. Computer viruses are self-replicating programs that spread from one host to another. This is because the early malicious programs were mostly file infectors and self-replicators. When the first computer virus known as ELK Cloner, written by then ninth-grader Rich Skrenta in Pittsburgh, Pennsylvania, appeared in 1982 in a mass-produced microcomputer, the Apple II, nobody knew what to call it. This situation would remain until 1984, when Dr. Frederick Cohen introduced the term "computer viruses" in his research paper titled "Computer Viruses – Theory and Experiments." From then on, malicious programs were called computer viruses, a very appropriate name for a program that spreads through infection.

Classification of Computer Viruses

Computer viruses are usually classified based on the object they infect. The three types of virus are the following:

- File infectors
- Boot-sector viruses
- Multipartite viruses

File Infectors

File infectors defined the computer virus era. They were the reason the term computer virus was coined.

There are two types of file infectors:

- Direct infectors
- Memory-resident viruses

Direct Infectors   Direct infectors are computer viruses that immediately infect files as soon as they are executed. They actively search for the files that they are able to infect. The search parameter for files to infect varies depending on the virus. It can be limited to files located in the same folder where the virus is located or can include all the files in the disk.

Direct infectors can be divided into the following types:

- Overwriting viruses
- Companion viruses
- Parasitic infectors

Overwriting viruses, as the name suggests, overwrite the host files they infect with their own malware code. Figure 2-1 shows the results of an overwriting virus infection.

An infection from an overwriting virus results in the total destruction of the host file because the host file's code is completely overwritten with the virus code. This is why overwriting viruses are considered the first destructive computer virus. There is no way

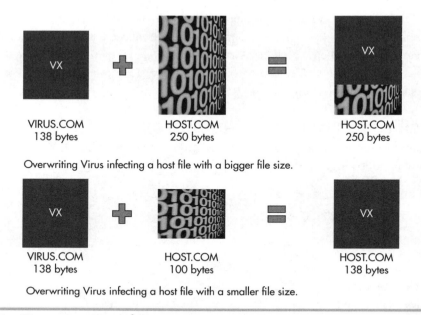

Overwriting Virus infecting a host file with a bigger file size.

Overwriting Virus infecting a host file with a smaller file size.

Figure 2-1   Overwriting virus infection scenarios

to recover from this infection. If the host file's size is bigger than the overwriting virus, the resulting file is the overwriting virus plus the remaining bytes at the end of the host file not overwritten by the virus. If the host file's size is equal to or smaller than the overwriting virus, the resulting file is the overwriting virus itself because it has completely overwritten the host file. The result is an equivalent image of the overwriting virus with the name of the now-overwritten host file.

For performance reasons, some overwriting viruses simply replace the host file with its own copy. Therefore, regardless of the file size, the resulting file is equivalent to the overwriting virus with the name of the host file. This method only needs a few lines of code, making the malware smaller and faster. And during those days, the smaller the virus, the better it was when it came to performance. The drawback of simply replacing the host files with a copy of the virus means that it was easy to detect the virus's presence just by listing the files in the directory. For example, if a 138-byte overwriting virus is executed in a folder with 100 files having varying file sizes, the result of the infection will show those 100 files all having a 138-byte file size. Also, if the overwriting virus does not have a routine to retain the original date of the infected host files, the directory listing will also show all files having the same dates, which is usually the time when the host files were infected. These telltale signs are so obvious that detection through optical inspection makes it easy to spot the virus.

Another telltale sign of an overwriting virus infection is that every time a host file is executed, it will not function as expected because the overwriting virus is the one executed instead, which is often silent. As far as the user is concerned, nothing happened. This will raise the level of suspicion that something is amiss.

The second type of direct infectors is known as companion viruses. *Companion viruses* operate by renaming the host file's extension and then creating a copy of itself with the name of the host file. The renamed host file is also given a hidden attribute so it will not show up in directory listings. Figure 2-2 shows the result of a companion virus infection.

A host program with a COM extension is renamed to host.con and is given a hidden attribute. The virus takes on the name host.com so when the user executes host.com, the virus is the one being executed. After the malware executes, it passes control to host.con so the host program gets executed.

In DOS, there is a hierarchy when it comes to execution based on file extensions. The order of execution based on filename is COM, EXE, and then BAT. For example, if you have three files named HELLO.BAT, HELLO.EXE, and HELLO.COM and they are located in the same directory, typing HELLO in the command prompt will execute HELLO.COM. If you delete HELLO.COM and type HELLO in the command prompt again, HELLO.EXE will be executed. The virus utilizes this hierarchy by using COM as its extension when infecting EXE files as seen in Figure 2-3. So instead of hiding the host program as in the first scenario, it hides itself. Since it has a COM extension, it will get executed first when the user types the host program name in the command prompt. After which, it will pass control back to the host with the EXE extension. But there's an issue with this technique: If the user types the whole filename, including the EXE extension of the host program, the virus will not be executed. This is why it became a practice to type the whole filename when executing a program using the command prompt.

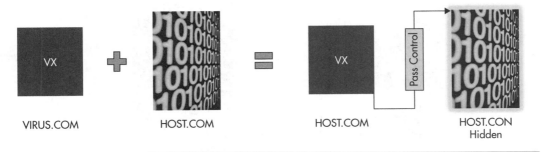

Figure 2-2   Typical companion virus infection

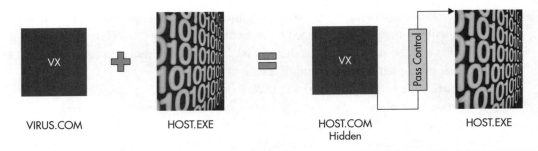

Figure 2-3   Companion virus infecting an EXE file

Tip
When executing programs in a DOS command line, it is always advisable to type the whole filename including the extension.

Another type of direct infectors is the parasitic virus. *Parasitic viruses* attach themselves to the host file during infection. This is the classic form of file infection. Parasitic viruses take control of the host file's first instruction to point to the virus code. After the virus execution concludes, control is passed to the host program.

There are two types of parasitic viruses, as shown in Figure 2-4. They are

- Prepending
- Appending

A prepending parasitic virus attaches itself to the top of the host file, while an appending parasitic virus attaches itself to the end of the host file. Since a prepending

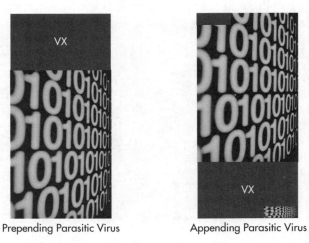

Prepending Parasitic Virus   Appending Parasitic Virus

Figure 2-4   Parasitic virus infection

virus is at the top of the file, its instructions get executed first. As for an appending virus, it hijacks the host program's first instruction to point to its virus code. After virus execution, it passes control back to the host program. The virus is able to do this by saving the location of the first instruction of the host program.

Memory-Resident Viruses   Memory-resident viruses, unlike direct infectors, do not infect files directly upon execution, but instead hide and wait in memory until a host program is executed and infect it. This virus achieves memory residency by utilizing DOS's TSR (Terminate but Stay Resident) system call.

A memory-resident virus utilizes the same infection strategy as direct infectors. They can overwrite a host program, they can be a companion virus, and they can also use parasitic techniques to infect host programs. The only difference is when the host program infection occurs. Direct infectors infect host programs when the virus or an infected host is executed, while memory-resident viruses infect host programs when the host programs are executed.

Note
There is nothing stopping memory-resident viruses from infecting other programs even before they go in memory, but with the goal of minimizing code size and improving performance, this is not done by most memory-resident viruses.

Boot-Sector Viruses

A boot-sector virus infects the boot sector of a disk to get control of the computer system's execution flow even before the operating system. A boot-sector virus works by hijacking the first instruction in the boot sector to point to itself, and then passes control back to the boot sector code after virus execution. Since a boot sector only contains 512 bytes of code, a boot-sector virus often utilizes other sectors of the disk to hide its code.

A boot-sector virus spreads from one machine to another via an infected floppy disk boot-sector. In the DOS days, the main mode of data exchange and storage was removable floppies. The risk of getting infected was higher if the floppy disk was not write-protected and was inserted in a system where a boot-sector virus was active. This method of spreading to different machines via infected floppy disk boot sector is more effective compared to executable file infections being copied from one computer to another via floppy disks, because most of these disks carry documents and other files that are not necessarily executable.

For machines with hard drives, a boot-sector virus, if it supports it, will infect the hard drive's master boot record (MBR). The MBR is 512 bytes in size and is located at the first sector of the device. It contains the boot code and the partition table. The partition table contains the location of a bootable partition. The boot-sector virus can hijack the boot code in the MBR or use it to find the boot sector of the bootable partition and hijack that instead.

Multipartite Viruses

In the context of DOS computer viruses, multipartite viruses are viruses that infect both boot sector and files. This virus has a boot-sector component and a file infector component. When executed, the virus looks for files to infect and then looks for the presence of disks in drives and infects their boot sectors. If it supports MBR infection, it looks for a fixed drive and attempts to infect that as well. The infection method does not need to be in any particular order.

LINGO
Multipartite is a term used to refer to viruses that are capable of multiplatform infection.

Early Challenges

The limited hardware resources of the existing systems during the DOS era and the number of antivirus (AV) solutions coming out of the woodwork, both from commercial companies and hobbyists, was a major challenge for virus writers. For their creation to thrive, it must withstand these challenges:

- Performance challenges
- Antivirus challenges

Performance Challenges

Unlike today, where memory, storage, and computing power are cheap, these resources were limited during the DOS days. This is the main reason why virus optimization is imperative. The virus must be able to function without affecting system performance that will raise suspicion from the user. To maintain a level of nondisruptive performance, the virus writers employed two things:

- Code optimization
- Double-infection checking

Code Optimization   Each central processing unit (CPU) cycle is precious, which is why the most resource-efficient computer viruses were written in assembly. Each assembly instruction takes a certain amount of CPU cycles. The lesser the CPU cycle, the faster the program will be. Also, register dependencies have to be taken into account when it comes to optimization. For example, the assembly code MOV AX,0 and XOR AX; AX will result in the same value of AX, which is zero. Each instruction also consumes one CPU cycle. But the main difference is in register dependency. XOR takes up less space; therefore, it has less lag resulting from register dependency.

Code optimization also calls for less code without sacrificing virus functionality. The aim is to make computer viruses that are smaller in size, but highly effective. In terms of virus optimization, size does matter—the smaller, the better. Optimized viruses are small in size, so they use less memory when executed. In DOS, COM executables, which is what most viruses are, appear the same on disk and in memory. Therefore, the smaller the virus, the fewer footprints it has on the system so as not to affect system performance. And as stated, that is one thing the computer virus always tries to preserve to avoid raising any suspicion of its presence.

Double-infection Checking   Having an optimized virus with no double-infection checking can affect system performance significantly. Imagine a host file infected multiple times by the same virus. Before the control is passed to the host program, the virus will execute multiple times. This means more system resources are consumed and more delay before the host program performs its function. This delay in the host program execution, if significant, might raise suspicion. Which is why most computer viruses check whether a host is already infected or not. If it is already infected, the virus skips that host and goes to the next one.

Double-infection checking only works for infection by the same virus. It does not work for multiple infections resulting from different computer virus families. If this is the case, it is very likely that the user will suspect something because program execution will slow down to a crawl.

Antivirus Challenges

Computer viruses were easy to detect using signatures in those days. Almost everyone who had knowledge of assembly could create a virus scanner and cleaner. So if the virus wants to survive, it has to evolve. Since detection via signatures is their primary enemy, the virus writers introduced virus encryption to beat signature detection. The development in virus encryption, including polymorphism and metamorphism, is discussed further in Chapter 6 of this book.

Another technology computer viruses used aside from the aforementioned is packers. A packer is a tool that compresses and encrypts an executable to save space and hide its code. The result is a self-executing compressed and encrypted file. Although packers became very infamous after the DOS era, virus writers were already utilizing them during the DOS days. The most utilized packer was PKLite. Real-time packers are discussed further in Chapter 6 of the book.

Malware

During the heyday of computer viruses, there were already malicious programs written that did not necessarily infect other files. During those days, they were also called viruses. It was like that for some time until the term malware was coined. Malware, short for malicious software, became the de facto term for everything malicious, including computer viruses.

Classification of Malware

There are many ways to classify malware. Some classify them based on behavior, based on their target platform, or based on their attack directive. In this section, we will classify malware based on their behavior, with the exception of mobile malware, wherein we will treat it as a specific class of malware that infects mobile devices, a classification based on its target platform.

The different classes of malware are

- Infectors
- Network worms
- Trojan horse
- Backdoors
- Remote access Trojans
- Information stealers
- Ransomware
- Mobile malware

In Actual Practice

If a malware exhibits more than one behavior, such as it is a file infector and is a network worm at the same time, the classification is made based on the hierarchy of behaviors. The order is usually infector, network worm, Trojan, and backdoor, so in this case, the malware will be classified as infector malware.

Infectors

File infectors are computer viruses. As new operating systems are introduced and new software with application-specific programming support started to emerge, the file infectors were right there with them. With these new platforms and capability, file infectors branched out into different types. They include

- Executables
- Macros
- Scripts

Executable Viruses   Computer viruses continued to flourish as platforms changed. When Microsoft introduced Windows and shipped the first version on November 20, 1985, it opened a new world in computing. Instead of DOS command lines, the user was presented with different program boxes or windows that the user could work on using a click of a mouse. This also marked a change in file format. Although Windows 1.0 to 3.xx still ran on top of DOS, it used a different file format when it came to executables running under the new Windows environment. This new file format was called New Executable or NewEXE (NE). It was the successor to the old DOS MZ format.

The old DOS viruses did not work in Windows. But since Windows runs on top of DOS, it is at risk of being infected. And since the file format is different, this results in the corruption of Windows or the component that got infected. I remember my first run-in with the DIE_HARD 2 virus. It ended up corrupting my Windows 3.11 installation, resulting in numerous software error messages every time I ran Windows. But it didn't take long for computer viruses to emerge in this new file format. The same thing happened with the introduction of Windows 95, which sported a new file format known as Portable Executable (PE). There was even a belief before that this new OS, with its new memory structure and new file format, would be the end of computer viruses, but we all know that was not the case.

Microsoft Windows is not only the platform where computer viruses can be found, although it is often the most targeted platform because of its popularity and user base. Other operating systems such as Linux and Mac also have their share of computer viruses, but the number is not as staggering as those attacking Windows.

Macro Viruses   A macro is a set of instructions that performs a specific task automatically. It can be a series of mouse movements, clicks, and keystrokes that follow a specific pattern that can be repeated over and over again without the user having to perform the task manually. Macros can also be constructed using an application-specific macro language. A macro language is a form of scripting that enables a user to program tasks to run automatically. This is especially useful in word processors and spreadsheets to automate text formatting and crunching numbers. And since a macro language is essentially a programming language, the virus writers saw its potential as a new platform for their creation. This resulted in a new form of file infectors called macro viruses. Macro viruses are computer viruses that are created using an application-specific macro language.

Although macros were not confined to Microsoft Office alone, it has become the main platform for macro viruses. The first macro virus, named Document Macro Virus (DMV), targeting WinWord appeared in December 1994 written by Joel McNamara. DMV was written as a proof of concept to show that it is possible to spread a virus using data files. Before that, it was believed that viruses were only possible in executable files.

LINGO
In-the-wild is a term used to describe malware that is found or captured in multiple infected machines found in different geographical locations. This means that the malware has already spread and did what it was supposed to do.

A few months after the creation of DMV, a new macro virus named Concept (detected as WM/Concept by most AV vendors) appeared in-the-wild. Many more came after that, infecting different Microsoft Office documents resulting in the following macro viruses:

- Word macro virus
- Excel macro virus
- Access macro virus
- PowerPoint macro virus
- Cross-platform macro virus

This prompted Microsoft to introduce a macro warning in Office 97 that an Office file has an embedded macro. Figure 2-5 shows a warning when an Excel file containing macros is opened. And for versions prior to Office 97 that do not have the macro warning feature, Microsoft provided the Microsoft Virus Protection Tool, aka ScanProt. It only detects and removes the Concept macro virus; it does not detect any other viruses. It is still useful, however, because it installs macros that will warn a user if the file being opened contains macros.

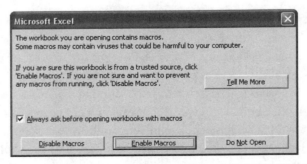

Figure 2-5   Office 97 macro warning in Excel

It is also worth mentioning that macro viruses are OS independent. It means that if the application with macro capability runs in Windows and in Mac, the macro virus will still spread because its main dependency is not in the OS but in the application-specific macro language.

A *Word macro virus* infects Word documents and templates. The usual target is the infection of Normal.dot, which is Word's default template. This results in the infection of all other Word documents that are opened and those that are newly created.

Note

The infamous Melissa worm is a Word macro virus and is also considered a network worm because of its spreading capability.

It was July 1996 when the first *Excel macro virus* came out. Its name is Laroux (detected as XM/Laroux by most AV vendors). As with the Concept Word macro virus, this is a nondestructive macro virus. It was written to prove a concept.

Excel macro viruses usually target templates or drop infected workbooks in the Excel startup folder, also known as the XLstart folder. This is the location for Excel templates, and anything that is placed in it gets loaded every time Excel is started. The effect of having an Excel macro virus in this folder is analogous to having an infected Normal.dot in Word. This results in the infection of all other Excel documents that are opened and those that are newly created.

The first *Access macro virus* was found in March 1998. It's called by many aliases. Among them are Jerk1N (the author), AccessiV (function name), and JetDB. This is also a nondestructive macro virus. Its main goal is to simply spread.

To be able to launch a macro virus in Access, the AutoExec script, which is analogous to DOS's autoexec.bat, is modified to include the Access macro virus code so that it gets activated every time a new database is opened.

In December 1998, the first *PowerPoint macro virus* was discovered. Its name is Attach (detected as P97M/Attach by most vendors). This virus's main goal is to infect PowerPoint files located in the user's documents folder. It did not have any destructive payload or routine.

PowerPoint macro viruses usually target Blank.pot, which is PowerPoint's default template. It gets loaded every time a PowerPoint slide is opened or created, resulting in the infection of these files.

Since Visual Basic for Applications (VBA) is the macro language across Office documents, it was expected that sooner or later a *cross-platform macro virus* would be created. The first one, discovered in January 1998, came in the form of a cross between a

Word and an Access macro virus called Cross.Poppy written by VicodinES. The second one is a cross between Word and Excel called StrangeDays written by Reptile/29A. It was discovered in June 1998.

Cross-platform macro viruses utilize the same techniques as specific platform macro viruses. For example, if a Word document infected with a cross-platform macro virus is opened, the virus will look for other Word documents and templates to infect, including Normal.dot, and it will also drop an infected Excel template in the XLstart folder so the next Excel sheet that is opened will result in an infection. The same thing happens if the initial file that is opened is an Excel workbook. The virus will look for other Excel workbooks and templates to infect and it will also modify Normal.dot so that Word documents that are opened and created will become infected.

> **LINGO**
> **29A** is a hexadecimal number equivalent to 666 in decimal. 29A is a virus writing group responsible for introducing some of the most interesting malware concepts and technologies.

Script Viruses   As stated in the previous section, a macro language is a form of scripting. Macro viruses showed the malicious possibilities of scripts—that it was a no-brainer to make script viruses that are not embedded in a data file like macro viruses are.

Office 95 used WordBasic as its macro language. In Office 97, Microsoft changed it to VBA. The familiarity with VBA helped the virus writers transition to VBS (Visual Basic Script) as the scripting language of choice for their script viruses. Plus, Windows already supports it, so no special dependencies needed to be satisfied.

Note

The infamous ILoveYou worm is a script virus written in VBS.

JavaScript is also another scripting language that is utilized to create script viruses. But unlike VBS, JavaScript works as part of an application such as a web browser and a Portable Document File (PDF) document. Therefore, for it to function as intended by the virus writer without revealing its true nature to the user, it needs to take advantage of vulnerabilities present in the application where the JavaScript is implemented.

Network Worms

A network worm is malware that replicates itself to multiple systems in the network with little or no user intervention using widely used network services such as browsing, e-mail, and chat. Early worms usually relied on social engineering to spread, while the most advanced worms exploit software vulnerabilities to infect other systems. A network worm

knows no boundaries. Everyone connected
to the Internet is a potential victim. Before
network worms, the infection coverage of
any malware was very limited. Given that
early infectors spread only through files

LINGO
Network worms are also known as computer worms.

and removable media, the infection was limited to a single or a few geographic locations.
But network worms changed that. The proliferation of network worms and the speed by
which they spread across the network gave new meaning to the term malware outbreak.
What took days or even months for typical malware to spread across different geographic
locations only took seconds for a network worm to accomplish.

The first known network worm appeared in November 2, 1998, written by Robert
Morris Jr., a computer science graduate student at Cornell. The worm was for educational
and experimental purposes, but its network-propagating capabilities led it to spread much
faster than he thought it would after unleashing it on the Internet.

Network worms are usually classified based on their network-propagating features, as
follows:

- Mass mailers
- File-sharing worms
- Instant messaging worms
- Internet Relay Chat (IRC) worms
- Local network worms
- Internet worms

Mass Mailers   Mass mailers are worms that spread via e-mail. Usually, this type of
worm uses social engineering techniques to fool the user into opening the e-mail and
clicking the link or the attachment that comes with it. Mass mailers utilize the victim's
address book to spread. This type of worm became so rampant that e-mail security and
antispam solutions became really hot in the industry.

File-sharing Worms   File-sharing worms are worms that spread by adding copies
of themselves to publicly facing file-sharing folders using enticing names like
"MSOfficeCrack.EXE," "StarwarsOnlineKeyGen.EXE," etc. The main idea here is that
they get picked up by other users of the file-sharing peer-to-peer program, downloaded on
their machines and then executed.

Instant Messaging Worms   Instant messaging (IM) worms use IM software as the
main vector of infection. Machines infected with this worm send out instant messages to

the infected user's contact list containing a malicious link that results in the downloading and installation of the worm in the target systems. Some IM worms also initiate file transfers to target victims. Since it is coming from a known contact and the file has a very enticing name, there is a big chance that the file transfer request will be accepted. The social engineering ingredient also helps in convincing the target to execute the file received from the infected user.

IRC Worms   IRC worms spread through IRC channels by sending messages containing malicious links or instructions that the receiver should type in return for "free software" or "get ops channel privilege." The links obviously point to a website that serves the worm, while the instruction that a user is being socially engineered to type results in a series of commands that can result in infection not just of the user's system, but the other users in the channel as well.

IRC worms also send DCC (direct client to client) file transfer requests to users joining the channel. These files, like any other socially engineered malicious files, have enticing names to increase their chances of being executed.

Local Network Worms   Local network worms are worms that spread within the confines of a local area network (LAN). A typical way of spreading is by scanning for writeable shared folders in hosts connected to the network and copying itself in those folders. The worm also searches for public folders in the network to drop a copy of itself there. The copies take on enticing names similar to those used by file-sharing worms. Another way the local network worm spreads is by exploiting vulnerabilities found in the OS or in software used in the corporate environment.

Internet Worms   Internet worms spread to other systems by scanning the Internet for vulnerable machines. Some also use vulnerable browsers to infiltrate target systems. This is why it is often advised to have a system hardened first before connecting it online.

Unfortunately, some needed patches, software updates, and host security updates can only be downloaded from the Internet. Therefore, connecting online before the machine has been hardened is sometimes inevitable. Systems that go online have a certain "survival time" before they become victims. The Internet Storm Center has a very good write-up on this, which can be found at http://isc.sans .edu/survivaltime.html.

LINGO
A **hardened system** is a system that has been deemed secure and resistant against infection and attack by installing security software, applying software updates and security patches, and configuring the system with the most secure settings.

In Actual Practice

Most enterprise organizations download needed patches and other updates periodically and have them available on the network for use by newly set-up machines so they are hardened before connecting online or even before joining the corporate network.

Trojan Horse

The Trojan horse, also known simply as a Trojan, is malware in disguise. It passes itself as a harmless, legitimate program such as a game or a tool, easily convincing the user to execute it.

LINGO
The **Trojan horse** was named after the wooden horse the Greeks used to infiltrate the city of Troy.

A Trojan's main purpose is destruction. It can be a destruction of files, software, or the operating system itself. The only way to recover from a Trojan is through reinstallation and restoration from backup.

Notes
The name Trojan has been attached to different classes of malware. Some of them are banking Trojans, keylogging Trojans, password stealing Trojans, and backdoor Trojans. In the strictest technical sense, this is inaccurate. The adding of "Trojan" to these other classes of malware originated in the heyday of computer viruses. The term was added to denote that the malicious application is not a virus or a nonreplicating program. Some circles will argue that these are still Trojans and that the class represents the Trojan's payload. But if this is the case, then this means that there are only two types of malware: the replicating kind (aka viruses) and the nonreplicating kind (aka Trojans). This is up for debate. And an exciting debate this is, especially if you get stuck on a plane ride with a fellow security researcher.

Backdoors

Backdoors enable an attacker to gain access to a compromised system, bypassing any form of safeguards and authentication, usually through the use of undocumented OS and network functions. The access can be in the form of a shell with root permission. A backdoor usually operates in stealth mode because its success lies in it being undetected. A backdoor can be embedded in software or it can be a stand-alone executable.

Tip
Be wary of programs whose source code is publicly available. Some are modified by the attackers to have backdoor functionality.

Remote Access Trojans

A remote access Trojan (RAT) is a malicious administrative tool that has backdoor capabilities, enabling an attacker to gain root access to the compromised machine. The main difference between a RAT and a traditional backdoor is that the RAT has a user interface, the client component, which the attacker can use to issue commands to the server component residing in the compromised machine. This gives the attackers control over compromised machines on a one-is-to-one ratio. Imagine what they can do if they can control thousands of compromised machines. This will be explored further in Chapter 4 of this book.

> **LINGO**
> **Remote access Trojans** are also known as remote administration Trojans, remote access tools, and remote administration tools.

A RAT usually gives the attackers the capability to do almost anything to the compromised machine. It is only limited by its feature set. The most dangerous RATs give attackers the ability to install other programs in, steal information from, and destroy the compromised machine.

Three of the most popular RATs came out in the late 1990s. NetBus, created by Swedish programmer Carl-Fredrick Neikter, appeared in March 1998. BackOrifice then followed in August 1998. Its creator, Sir Dystic, a member of the hacker group Cult of the Dead Cow, revealed it in DefCon 6. Then in May 1999, mobman released SubSeven, one of the versions of which is seen in Figure 2-6.

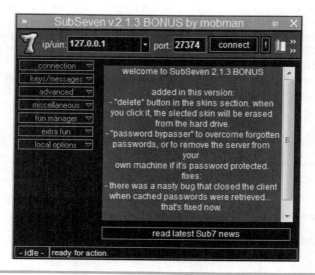

Figure 2-6   SubSeven by mobman

Information Stealers

Information stealers are exactly that. They steal information. The information can be a password, financial credentials, proprietary data, private information, or anything that the attackers can use to their advantage or monetize.

The most common information stealers are the following:

- Keyloggers
- Desktop recorders
- Memory scrapers

Keyloggers   Keyloggers capture keystrokes and log them. This type of information stealer records keypresses and stores them locally for later retrieval, or sends them to a remote server that the attacker has access to.

Note

Keyloggers are not confined to software alone. There are also hardware implementations of keyloggers.

Desktop Recorders   Desktop recorders work by taking a screenshot of the desktop or the active window on a predefined time interval or when triggered by an event such as a mouse click or the pressing of the return key. This is especially useful for password stealers to get around virtual keyboards utilized by some online banks.

One drawback of this type of information stealer is the amount of data that results from its operation. The file size of each screenshot quickly adds up.

Memory Scrapers   Memory scrapers steal information in memory while it is being processed. Data that is processed in memory is unencrypted. This is why this is the best place to grab data.

LINGO
Memory scrapers are also known as RAM scrapers.

Ransomware

Ransomware is a malicious program that holds data or access to systems or resources containing that data hostage unless the user pays a ransom. Ransomware is a form of virtual extortion that can be any of the following:

- Encryption of data
- Trojan threat of destruction
- User lockout

Encryption of Data   In this scenario, the malware encrypts specific data (e.g., all document files, picture files, or files with specific extensions), specific folders, or a disk partition. The main idea here is to prevent access to data. To have access restored, the user needs to pay a ransom, after which the data will be decrypted by the malware or the user will be provided with a decryption tool and key. Or the criminal can just take the money and not bother anymore, leaving the user with the encrypted data and a hole in his pocket.

Tip
Always back up important data.

Trojan Threat of Destruction   Provide payment in the next 24 hours or your hard drive will be reformatted. This is the main theme in this scenario. Some of these are simply scare tactics. But for some novice users, it might work well enough for them to open their wallets. See discussion about scareware in Part II of the book for more information.

User Lockout   In this scenario, the user is locked out and denied log-in access to a system. Same as the others, the main idea is to extort money from the user in exchange for the login password.

Mobile Malware

Malware does not confine itself to the PC alone. The popularity of mobile devices and the information they contain is enough reason for malware writers to invade mobile devices. In June 2004, the first mobile virus, as seen in Figure 2-7, named Caribe-VZ/29a appeared. This mobile virus affects Nokia's SymbianOS and spreads itself via Bluetooth.

Copyright F-Secure Corp. 2004

Figure 2-7   Screenshot of Caribe-VZ/29a from F-Secure Labs

The targets of early mobile malware were Nokia's SymbianOS and Microsoft's Windows Mobile OS. These were the two popular mobile OSs during that time. Fast forward eight years to 2012, and we now have Apple's iOS and Google Android, and the mobile devices are much more powerful and more robust compared to their predecessors. Plus, there is an expanding market of apps supported by a talented pool of mobile developers. Microsoft Windows Mobile is still around, but SymbianOS is being phased out by Nokia in favor of Windows Mobile.

We are already seeing a growing number of malware attacks on these mobile platforms, most of which are coming from third-party mobile application sources. Although it is not yet comparable to the amount of malware seen in computer systems, it's only a matter of time before they catch up number-wise.

Evolution of Malware

As technology evolves, so does malware. To thrive, the malware has to adapt to new technologies and find much more effective ways of achieving its main goal.

The following are the most significant areas of malware evolution:

- Infection methods and vectors
- Persistency
- Protective mechanisms
- Directive
- Interaction with the attacker

Infection Methods and Vectors

File or system infection was done solely by the malware. Click a virus or an infector, and it will search for files to infect or go resident and wait for files to infect. Most are straight-up infectors. But users wised up, operating systems changed, and the Internet boomed. The malware adapted. Its infection method and target changed from files to systems, and the way it is delivered to the target user evolved from the slow physical media to the cyberspeed of e-mail and other network infection vectors. A more detailed discussion about infection vectors is found in Part II of this book.

Malware routines, including the infection method and payload, among others, were all coded together in one file. This is still true in modern malware, but most advanced malware is modular. Each function or routine is coded in a separate file. In Windows, it can be another executable or a DLL file.

Persistency

To achieve persistency, the malware must survive system shutdown and reboot. Therefore, as critical functions and executables needed to startup every bootup to support the operating system, the malware must also be able to do the same. It must be able to autostart.

The ability to become persistent evolved together with the operating system. The malware used what is available in the current version of the operating system to autostart. To show the evolution, the discussion will concentrate on persistency in DOS and in modern Windows.

Persistency in DOS   In DOS, the malware did mostly the following three things to achieve persistency:

- Hijack the boot sector
- Add itself in Autoexec.bat
- Infect system files

Hijacking the boot sector, or the master boot record if the drive is fixed, is a good way to gain control even before the operating system. Every time a system is rebooted, the malware is immediately executed after the basic input/output system (BIOS). For malware that does not have a boot component and still wants to be persistent, another way to achieve persistency is to add itself in Autoexec.bat. This is especially useful for noninfecting malware such as backdoors and some information stealers. Although this is not a good method because optical investigation of an infection by opening an Autoexec .bat will immediately identify the malware, it is still utilized, especially if the malware file has a name that is similar to a popular program. But the most common method of achieving persistency in DOS is by infecting system files that the operating system executes every bootup. In DOS, the often targeted file is Command.com.

Persistency in Windows   In Windows, the malware is presented with lots of options to autostart, including similar methods used in DOS such as hijacking the boot sector and infecting system files. Although these two methods are still applicable, the twist here is that the boot-sector code and file-infecting mechanism must conform to Windows. A boot virus that is written for DOS will not work on modern Windows. The same goes for infection routines.

Autoexec.bat is not utilized anymore in Windows. The equivalent of this is the StartUp folder where executables and links to executables are placed if they are needed to autostart. Windows also has a Task Scheduler that a malware can utilize. The Microsoft Task Scheduler enables a user to schedule tasks to automate periodic execution of a desired program such as the Disk Defragmenter, which can be scheduled to run every

Sunday at 3:00 A.M. Malware utilizes this by setting itself up as a scheduled task. The malware can then choose to run every bootup; upon logon; one time only; or on a periodic basis like daily, weekly, or monthly.

Aside from all of these available options to autostart, especially by noninfecting malware, the malware can also utilize key configuration settings found in the Windows registry. As defined by Microsoft, the registry is a database where Windows stores its configuration information. It contains profiles for each user of the computer and information about system hardware, installed programs, and property settings. Windows continually references this information during its operation. So for Windows malware to autostart every bootup, it needs to modify some entries in the Windows registry to achieve persistency. The malware modifies the registry by adding its own registry value under a specific registry key to achieve the result it wants.

> **LINGO**
> A **registry** has two basic elements: the keys, which are similar to folders, that contain other keys (aka subkeys); and values, which contain the actual data such as a pointer to an executable file.

Depending on the nature of the malware and how it wants to operate, the registry offers the following commonly used options that enable the malware to set when or how it will start up:

- Boot execution
  - HKLM\System\CurrentControlSet\Control\Session Manager
- Loading of driver and services
  - HKLM\System\CurrentControlSet\Services
- Upon logon
  - HKLM\Software\Microsoft\Windows\CurrentVersion\Run
  - HKLM\Software\Microsoft\Windows\CurrentVersion\RunOnce
  - HKLM\Software\Microsoft\Active Setup\Installed Components
- Loading of Explorer shell extensions
  - HKLM\Software\Classes*\ShellEx\ContextMenuHandlers
  - HKLM\Software\Classes\Directory\ShellEx\ContextMenuHandlers
  - HKLM\Software\Classes\Directory\ShellEx\DragDropHandlers
  - HKLM\Software\Classes\Folder\ShellEx\ContextMenuHandlers
  - HKLM\Software\Classes\Folder\ShellEx\DragDropHandlers

- Loading of browser extensions
  - HKLM\Software\Microsoft\Windows\CurrentVersion\Explorer\Browser Helper Objects
  - HKLM\Software\Microsoft\Internet Explorer\Extensions

Tip
These are just some of the common entries used by malware. There are more. A good way to determine other autostart mechanisms and to identify the programs, including malware, that utilize them is by running Microsoft's Autoruns tool.

Protective Mechanisms

For malware to continue functioning unimpeded in the compromised machine, it must be able to protect itself from the prying eyes of researchers and the detection capability of security solutions. Malware employs two things:

- Presence concealment
- Code protection

Presence Concealment   Hiding its presence is always the first order of business for malware that wants to thrive. It utilizes different techniques to give the sense that it does not exist in the compromised system; therefore, no effort to remove it will be applied. The malware technology of presence concealment evolved from simple stealth techniques to a more sophisticated utilization of rootkit technology. This is further discussed in Chapter 3.

Code Protection   Eventually the hidden malware will be found, and if this happens, its code will be exposed to researchers. The malware addressed this by introducing technologies that enable it to protect its code. These technologies evolved from a simple XOR encryption to a more sophisticated metamorphic protection that enables the malware to change its form every infection. The malware also utilized tools such as real-time packers to hide its code, making reversing and malware detection much more challenging. Further discussion about malware code protection is found in Part II of this book.

Directive

Early malware were proof of concept to show the possibility of infection and operating system subversion. Most were experiments out of curiosity and a show of operating system and programming mastery. The payloads were mostly texts or message pop-ups announcing the presence of the malware. The fancier ones played sounds or displayed graphics, while the nastiest ones performed some sort of computer vandalism and small-scale destruction of data.

Modern malware is totally different. If the intention before of creating sophisticated malware was for fun and bragging rights, now it is for profit. Its initial directive of proving a concept and to show wit and creativity in programming is now replaced with information stealing, sabotage, and destruction. It has become an essential tool for cybercrime. Malware has evolved from simply being a nuisance to being a real threat.

Interaction with the Attacker

Early malware had no way of communicating with its handlers. It was simply deployed into the wild to do its thing. That changed when the first server-client malware was introduced in the form of a remote access Trojan. This gave the attacker the ability to control a compromised system. The attack became interactive. This interaction and the ability to control a compromised machine evolved further with the introduction of botnets. The ratio is not one-is-to-one anymore but one-is-to-many. The topic of botnets is discussed further in Chapter 4.

Riskware

As with other things in life, there are no absolutes. There's always something in the middle that can either be good or bad depending on the circumstances surrounding it. The same is true in software. As there are benign and malicious programs, there are also programs that are walking a thin line between the two. They are called riskware.

Riskware are computer programs that possess features that have the potential to be dangerous. What makes this software dangerous lies in the motivation of the person behind it and/or its possible effect on the user.

Think of a gun. If a person's motivation is to use that gun to kill someone then that gun becomes a dangerous weapon, but in the hands of the police, it becomes an effective tool to maintain peace and order. We all know that when a gun is used, its effect on the one being shot might be deadly. Also, just brandishing or pointing the gun will already have an effect. A person at the end of the barrel might react in a way that will prove to be detrimental.

LINGO
Riskware is also known as greyware.

Classification of Riskware

Riskware is usually classified based on its function or behavior. The following are the common types of riskware:

- Spyware
- Adware
- Hacker tools
- Joke

Spyware

Spyware is software that collects information without the victim's knowledge. It can easily be classified as an information stealer because of its functionality. But the main difference it has with malicious information stealers is that spyware is packaged as commercial software. It is purchased and used by someone who has physical access to or owns the computer system where it is installed. For example, it can be used by a parent who wants to monitor a child's activity while on the computer or by someone who wants to spy on a spouse's online activities.

The use of spyware clearly violates the victim's privacy, and in some states, this is illegal. But in some cases, the use of spyware is acceptable as long as the monitored user is aware of this. An example of this is an office setting wherein the employees are made aware that their online and offline activities are being recorded by the company every time they use company systems.

Adware

Adware is riskware that displays ads in the form of pop-ups. Some adware comes preloaded with ads to be displayed, while some track users' online browsing behavior and displays ads based on their tracked behavior.

Aside from it being a nuisance because of the number of pop-up ads that appear, causing disruption to the user, it invades the privacy of the users by monitoring online activities to produce targeted ads.

Hacker Tools

Hacker tools are system admin tools in the wrong hands. For example, network security tools used to map and secure the network can be used by hackers to map a target network. Again, going back to the gun analogy, it is the motive behind the use of the tools.

Joke

A joke program is a program that is not really malicious but its effect on the user is what makes it dangerous. It might cause the user to do something damaging to the system. For example, a joke program that displays a message saying that the computer has been destroyed and needs formatting might convince the user enough to actually format the drive. It sounds funny but the effect can be significant, especially if the system being formatted contains important data or is a critical system within the company.

Another classic example is Microsoft Sysinternal's Blue Screen of Death (BSOD) screensaver on a server. If someone had no idea that it is just a screen saver and saw it in a server, that sys admin might be alarmed and reboot the server in an attempt to fix it.

Malware Creation Kits

Malware creation kits, or do-it-yourself
(DiY) malware kits, made the creation
of malware accessible to individuals
with zero programming skills. The kits
gave them the ability to create malware

LINGO
Malware creation kits were known
as virus generators or virus code
generators in the early days of computer
viruses.

using a graphical user interface (GUI) or simple command lines. Depending on the kit's
features, its price can range in the thousands of dollars. It has become an essential tool of
cybercriminals as discussed in Part II of the book.

Two of the early malware creation kits are Virus Creation Labs (VCL) and Phalcon/
Skism Mass-Produced Code Generator (PSMPC). VCL, seen in Figure 2-8, appeared in
July 1992. VCL enabled the production of a companion or overwriting virus. The user
can also generate a Trojan and define the payload trigger conditions. It was created by
Nowhere Man of the American virus writing group NuKE.

PSMPC, seen in Figure 2-9, was created by Dark Angel of the American virus writing
group Phalcon-Skism in response to Nowhere Man's VCL. Although not as robust as
VCL, it features encryption, which makes the viruses it produces a challenge to detect,
given the current technology of its era.

So we had two competing malware kit creators in the 1990s. This will further escalate
to the point that one kit has the ability to remove the creation of the competing kit from an
infected system. This will be further discussed in Part II of the book.

Figure 2-8 Virus Creation Labs virus generator

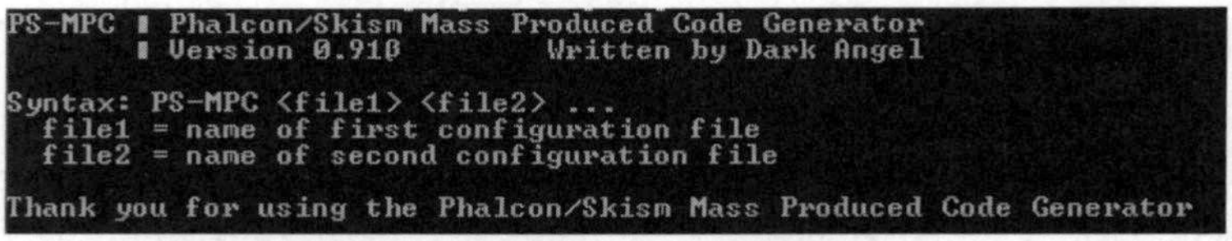

```
PS-MPC ▌ Phalcon/Skism Mass Produced Code Generator
       ▌ Version 0.91β        Written by Dark Angel

Syntax: PS-MPC <file1> <file2> ...
    file1 = name of first configuration file
    file2 = name of second configuration file

Thank you for using the Phalcon/Skism Mass Produced Code Generator
```

Figure 2-9 Phalcon/Skism Mass-Produced Code Generator

The Impact of Malware

From its humble beginnings as a proof of concept to a dangerous threat backed by sinister cybercriminals, malware has become part of computing. It will always be around. As long as there is the ability to program and there is potential value for the attackers, malware is never far behind.

The impact of malware is undeniable and will be obvious in the forthcoming chapters. Businesses are crippled, individuals are seeing their money stolen, and the bad guys seem to be always one step ahead of the good guys. But it has also become a job creator. It spurred a multibillion-dollar antivirus and Internet security industry.

We've Covered

- Different types of computer viruses
- Early challenges of computer viruses
  - File infectors
  - Boot-sector viruses
  - Multipartite viruses
- Different types of malware
  - Infectors
  - Network worms
  - Trojan horse
  - Backdoors
  - Remote access Trojans
  - Information stealers
  - Ransomware
  - Mobile malware

- The most significant areas of malware evolution
  - Infection methods and vectors
  - Persistency
  - Protective mechanisms
  - Directive
  - Interaction with the attacker
- Different types of riskware
  - Spyware
  - Adware
  - Hacker tools
  - Joke
- Malware creation kits

CHAPTER 3

Cloak of the Rootkit

We'll Cover

● What is a rootkit?

● The different privilege levels

● Mechanics of switching from user mode to kernel mode

● The types of rootkits

● The common rootkit techniques

● Popular tools that aid in the detection of rootkits

Chapter 2 introduced us to the wonderful world of malware from its early beginnings as a computer virus to the more dangerous and sophisticated threat we see today. But for malware to thrive, it must remain undetected. It must be able to hide from the prying eyes of antivirus (AV) researchers and from the different detection technologies employed by AV products.

In this chapter, we will take a look at the most common rootkit techniques malware uses to gain control of an application's execution flow and to even undermine the operating system that enables it to hide its presence. The chapter will also discuss the mechanics of the environment the rootkit operates in to lay down the foundation on the discussion of common rootkit techniques. And then finally, a few words on how rootkits are usually tackled.

What Is a Rootkit?

The term rootkit is a compound word formed from the two words, root and kit. Root is a term used to describe the most privileged user on a computer. A kit, on the other hand, is defined by *Merriam-Webster* as a set of tools or implements. Therefore, a rootkit is a set of tools that enables root- or administrator-level access on a computer system. But in the realm of malicious software, we will define rootkit as a set of techniques coded

LINGO
The term **rootkit** has become synonymous with malware and is used to describe malware with rootkit capabilities. In the strictest sense, rootkit is not malware; it is a technology utilized by malware to its advantage. The same technology is used by legitimate programs. The only difference is the intent. Malware uses it for malicious purposes.

into malware to gain root access and complete control of the operating system and its underlying hardware. As a result of this control, the malware is able to accomplish one important thing that is vital to its survival or persistency, and that is to hide its presence in the system.

Environment Mechanics

Before delving more into rootkits, it is important to understand the mechanics of the environment in which the rootkit operates in. In our case, we will concentrate on systems powered by an Intel processor running Windows operating system.

The Operating System Kernel

The kernel is the main component of the operating system. It serves as the bridge between applications and the hardware. It is responsible for managing system resources and processing requests from applications.

The Windows kernel has been designed with flexibility in mind. Therefore, it can be modified or extended. The kernel is modified through the use of loadable kernel modules (LKM). An LKM is code that can be loaded into the kernel and then unloaded after use. It extends the kernel's functionality, such as by adding support for new hardware, file systems, and/or system calls without the need to reboot the system. One common kernel module is a device driver. It allows the kernel to access the specific hardware the driver is written for. For example, if the user wants to access and use the built-in laptop webcam, the appropriate driver for the webcam must be installed or loaded for it to work.

Without the use of loadable kernel modules, the operating system developers must anticipate all needed functionality the kernel must support. This is already a tall order. Plus, building or compiling them into the kernel will result in a bigger kernel that will eat up a lot of memory, because all of these functionalities will be loaded into memory even if they are not used. Another disadvantage of this approach is that the kernel has to be rebuilt and rebooted every time a new functionality needs to be added that was not covered in the initial design.

Note

NTOSKRNL.exe is the Windows kernel. On systems with physical address extension (PAE) support, it is NTKRNLPA.exe.

User Mode and Kernel Mode

The Windows kernel code runs in the highest privileged level in the system, aptly called the kernel mode. Since not all software needs to manipulate system resources and hardware, a lower-privileged-level mode exists, known as the user mode, where these applications run. The difference between the two is that the kernel mode has unrestricted access to all the system resources and the underlying hardware. Its process space is also system wide. This is why kernel mode is reserved for the most trusted and stable functions, because if something goes wrong the whole system can crash. The user mode, meanwhile, is more limited and has no direct access to any system resources and hardware. Access to these resources is provided by the Windows application programming interface (API). Applications running in user mode have their own private virtual address space and private handle table. Since its process space is private and not global like kernel mode, a crash will only affect that application. Other applications that run in user mode will not be affected as well, and most importantly a user-mode application crash does not crash the whole system.

Rings

The enforcement of which mode programs can run in is not provided by the operating system. Instead, the Intel x86 processor provides the mechanism for access control. It does this through the use of rings. There are four rings, as seen in Figure 3-1.

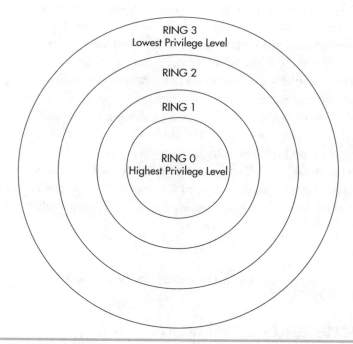

Figure 3-1   The Intel x86 processor rings

Ring zero is the highest privileged level, and ring three is the lowest. In this concept, a code can access rings that are equal to or greater than the number assigned to it. Therefore, a code that is ring three cannot access code or memory in ring zero. This ensures process separation and restricts a code that is not trusted or that does not have the proper privilege level to access resources that are only reserved for higher-privileged-level code to preserve system integrity and stability. Although the Intel x86 processor has four rings, Windows only uses two rings: ring zero and ring three. Ring zero is where the Windows kernel runs; hence, it is also referred to as kernel mode, while ring three is where most user applications run; hence, the name user mode.

Note

Windows does not use rings one and two because of compatibility reasons. It is possible that not all hardware has four privilege levels.

Switching from User Mode to Kernel Mode

User mode and kernel mode in an Intel x86 processor are defined in the privilege level of the code segment of the program that is currently running. This is because there is really no kernel mode in the x86 processor. Unlike other processors that have it built in and defined by a flag in the processor's status register whether a program is currently executing in privileged mode or not, in an x86 processor, one of the properties of the code segment that is running determines it.

Each code segment of a program that is currently running is defined by an eight-byte data structure called a segment descriptor. A segment descriptor contains metadata of a code segment. Among them are the code segment's start address, length, and privilege level. The privilege level is the ring where the code segment is executing; that is, a privilege level of zero is ring zero and a privilege level of three is ring three. Based on this arrangement, it is obvious that the privilege level of a code segment is an attribute of the code segment as defined in its segment descriptor and not really of the processor. The processor relies on the information provided in the segment descriptor on what privilege level the code will be permitted to run in. Therefore, an x86 processor will only allow execution in ring zero if the code segment's segment descriptor shows it with a privilege level of zero.

Segment descriptors are stored in two tables loaded in the system's main memory. They are the global descriptor table (GDT) and the local descriptor table (LDT). There is only one GDT, and it is created by the operating system during bootup. It contains segment descriptors pertaining to operating system code and data segments. The GDT can be shared by all tasks. An LDT on the other hand, is used by a single task or a number of related tasks. Unlike the GDT, an LDT is not mandatory. The pointer to the base address and the size of each descriptor tables are contained in the global descriptor table register (GDTR) and local descriptor table register (LDTR), respectively.

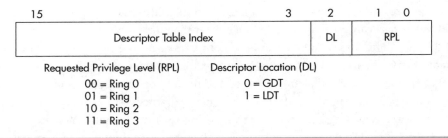

Figure 3-2 The segment selector

To determine which descriptor tables a code segment's segment descriptor resides in, a segment selector is used. A segment selector, seen in Figure 3-2, has three fields.

As seen in the figure, the two fields that are most important are the descriptor location and the requested privilege level (RPL). If the descriptor location is set to zero, the index is located in the GDT. If it is one, it is located in the LDT. The requested privilege level field describes the privilege level of the calling code. These two fields go hand-in-hand with each other. This means if the descriptor location is in GDT, the requested privilege level must be zero. Otherwise, a general fault error occurs.

So if a code segment in user mode or with an RPL of ring three cannot call code in kernel mode or ring zero, how is it possible to switch from user mode to kernel mode? This is done through the following system calls:

- INT 2E
- SYSENTER/SYSCALL

INT 2E

Intel x86 processors have a feature called an interrupt gate. An interrupt gate is a gateway from user mode to kernel mode. To explain further, let's look at how interrupts work. An interrupt is handled by an interrupt service routine (ISR). In DOS, which operates in real mode, the pointers to the ISR are contained in an interrupt vector table (IVT). In Windows, which operates in protected mode, the IVT, which is now called an interrupt descriptor table (IDT), contains interrupt gate descriptors (IGDs). The IGD contains the ISR's code segment location and its base address in the code segment. So instead of the IVT pointing directly to the ISR, as in real mode, the IDT in protected mode uses a middle man or a gate in the form of the IGD. This is a security feature of the processor or CPU that limits user mode code from directly calling kernel mode functions. It does this by checking the privilege level in the IGD's segment selector for the code segment that contains the ISR.

To initiate switching to kernel mode, INT 2E is executed. INT 2E basically is a call to the KiSystemService ISR. KiSystemService is a kernel function that provides system services. The processor then executes a software interrupt by going into the IDT at entry number 2E. The IGD at that location is read. Remember that the IGD contains the ISR's code segment location and its base address in the code segment. It also contains the segment selector for the code segment that contains the ISR. Based on the information contained in the segment selector, the processor loads the appropriate segment descriptor and ultimately the ISR code in kernel mode. But before execution, the processor needs to switch from user-mode stack to kernel-mode stack. This ensures enough stack space for the kernel-mode function and also as a precaution against user-mode stack modification. As a consequence of this switching, the user mode application's stack segment (SS), stack pointer (ESP), code segment (CS), instruction pointer (EIP), and EFLAGS registers are saved on the kernel-mode stack. The KiSystemService then copies the call parameters pushed into the user-mode stack before INT 2E was called. The ISR looks at the value in the EAX register, which is included in the call parameters copied by the KiSystemService to the kernel-mode stack. This value represents the system function the user-mode code wants to be executed in kernel mode. As Microsoft puts it, KiSystemService uses the system service number in EAX as an index into the system service dispatch table, which contains the address of the routine in the operating system to call. This prevents an application from calling any random address in the system. An application can only call those routines that are listed in the system service dispatch table. If everything is in order, the system service is executed in kernel mode just how the user-mode code intended it to be.

After successful execution of the system service, the code execution reverts back to user mode and the processor restores everything back to how it was before INT 2E was invoked by the user-mode code. The original registers are restored, and the instruction pointer points to the instruction after the INT 2E call.

SYSENTER/SYSCALL

INT 2E is slow since it carries with it all the overhead that comes with interrupt handling. In the case of INT 2E, the processor loads both an interrupt gate and segment descriptor to determine which ISR to call, perform privilege-level checking, and do several memory read cycles. This operation is needed because the location of the kernel-mode code segment changes and the sequence of events described in the previous section determines where it actually is. Remember that the kernel-mode code segment contains the ISR.

This causes overhead. With the introduction of faster CPUs, starting in Pentium II and AMD K7, support for a faster way of going to kernel mode is made possible. Instead of using INT 2E, SYSENTER/SYSCALL is used.

Looking at the INT 2E calling operation, the location of the kernel-mode segment changes; hence, the additional memory operations that cause overhead. It would be faster if the location of the system service is hard-coded. There will be no memory operations or loading to determine where the system call should point to. Instead the processor knows where to switch since the kernel-mode code segment is in the same location. This exactly describes how the fast system call instruction works. So SYSENTER uses a fixed-location segment descriptor defining the target code segment hard-coded into the processor. Although the target code segment is hard-coded, the address of the function, analogous to the ISR within the code segment in the INT 2E calling procedure, is not hard-coded. This function is the KiFastCallEntry. SYSENTER is basically a call to KiFastCallEntry. KiFastCallEntry enables user-mode code to access native functions in the system service dispatch table (SSDT). To determine the address of the KiFastCallEntry function, the processor uses the model-specific registers (MSRs), as seen in Figure 3-3. MSRs, as the name suggests, are processor-specific registers that provide system software the ability to manipulate various hardware resources, such as enabling and disabling some processor features. They are often used for debugging and system monitoring.

The SYSENTER_EIP_MSR (176h) contains the address of the KiFastCallEntry function. But before this function is executed, the user-mode stack and the calling parameters have to be loaded into the kernel-mode stack, similar to the INT 2E calling process. The address of the kernel mode stack is taken from SYSENTER_ESP_MSR (175h). Once everything is set up and ready to go, the processor then executes the desired function in kernel mode.

> **LINGO**
> **SYSENTER/SYSCALL** is known as fast system call instructions. SYSENTER and SYSEXIT are for Intel processors. Its equivalent in AMD processors is SYSCALL and SYSRETURN. They function in a similar fashion.

MSR Name	Index	Usage
SYSENTER_CS_MSR	174h	Target Code Segment
SYSENTER_ESP_MSR	175h	Target Stack Pointer
SYSENTER_EIP_MSR	176h	Target Instruction Pointer

Figure 3-3 Model-specific registers (MSRs)

After successful execution, SYSEXIT is invoked to restore everything back to user mode. It is the same process as restoration from INT 2E: The code execution reverts back to user mode and the processor restores everything back to how it was before SYSENTER was invoked by the user-mode code. The original registers are restored, and the instruction pointer points to the instruction after the SYSENTER call.

Types of Rootkits

Now that there is basic understanding of the environment mechanics, let's go back to our discussion of rootkits. As previously discussed, there are basically two modes a code can execute in: the unrestricted kernel mode and the private, restricted user mode. Rootkits exist in both of these modes. So basically, there are two types of Windows rootkits. They are aptly called the following:

> **LINGO**
> **User-mode rootkits** and **kernel-mode rootkits** are also known as user-land rootkits and kernel-land rootkits, respectively.

- User-mode rootkits
- Kernel-mode rootkits

User-Mode Rootkits

User-mode rootkits are rootkits that operate in user mode or ring three. Their influence is limited to the user or process space of the affected application. Therefore, if it wants to affect other applications, the user-mode rootkit would need to do the same work in each of those applications' memory space.

User-mode rootkits operate mostly by hooking or hijacking system function calls made by an application. Since the execution flow follows a predetermined path, the rootkit can simply hijack different points along the path to point the execution flow to its code.

Kernel-Mode Rootkits

Kernel-mode rootkits are rootkits that operate in kernel mode or ring zero. They operate in kernel space. Their main modus operandi involves kernel modification and hooking in kernel space. This makes this rootkit much more powerful because it places itself in the lowest level possible. That means more control over the operating system and the underlying hardware.

Most kernel-mode rootkits take advantage of hooking execution paths that transition to kernel mode, as described in the previous section. They also utilize loadable kernel modules, such as a driver to "enhance" the kernel's functionalities with its rootkit code.

Ideally, a kernel-mode rootkit is what malware authors would like their creation to be, but since it requires familiarity with OS internals and hardware, this is not always the case because of the time needed to build these skills. This is important because a poorly written rootkit in kernel mode that has system-wide influence can crash the system.

Note

Windows rootkits do not really gain root-level access. This is contrary to what the true meaning of a rootkit is. For Windows rootkits to work, the user must grant them root privileges. Most of the time, this is achieved by fooling the user through social engineering techniques.

Rootkit Techniques

Our definition of a rootkit in the context of malware is a set of techniques coded into malware to gain root access and complete control of the operating system and its underlying hardware. Rootkits can use three techniques:

- Hooking
- DLL injection
- Direct kernel object manipulation

Hooking

Hooking is the most common technique used by rootkits. It involves hooking the application's execution flow. The rootkit redirects the normal path of execution to point to its code. It does this by intercepting API calls and system function calls.

The most common hooking techniques a rootkit employs are the following:

- IAT and EAT hooking
- Inline hooking
- SSDT hooking
- Kernel inline hooking
- IDT hooking
- INT 2E hooking
- Fast system call hooking

IAT and EAT Hooking

When a program is executed and loaded into memory, Windows checks whether it calls any APIs. If it does, Windows loads the DLLs exporting those APIs into memory, specifically in the program's address space. The APIs or functions needed by the program are listed in what is called an import address table (IAT). IAT is a table containing pointers to the APIs needed by the program. IAT is used because API addresses are not static. This is a way to allow for the API address to change with no impact to the program running in memory. The function pointers in the IAT are then populated by Windows as the needed DLLs are loaded. The address of the pointer that Windows uses to populate the IAT comes from the DLL's export address table (EAT). The EAT contains the pointers to the APIs exported by the DLL.

IAT hooking takes place when a malicious program overwrites a DLL's EAT with a pointer to its malicious code. For example, if the malware wants to hide registry keys it modified from an application that scans the registry, it can hook the API that the application uses to enumerate registry keys. Chances are this application uses RegEnumKey. If that's the case, the malware can hook the API RegEnumKey exported by ADVAPI32.DLL by modifying the pointer in the DLL's EAT to point to the malware code. The malware code can then manipulate what is enumerated by not showing the keys it modified. Since the execution control is now with the malware, it can do whatever it is written to do, such as infect the program importing the redirected API function.

Inline Hooking

Inline hooking is the process of modifying the API code itself that is imported by the DLL. In this hooking technique, the pointers are left alone, leaving the IAT and EAT unaltered. This beats rootkit detection that relies on address table modifications. In this scenario, the malware alters the first instruction of the code to jump to the malware code. This is the same technique used by parasitic computer viruses discussed in Chapter 2. To beat rootkit detectors that look for JMP instructions to an outside address, the malware can choose to put the JMP instruction to its malware code not in the first instruction but further down into the code.

Aside from inserting an unconditional JMP instruction into the API code to point to the malware code, it is also possible to overwrite the actual API function. But given the added complexity this brings, like size considerations among others, it is rarely done.

LINGO
Inline hooking is also known as hot patching.

SSDT Hooking

The SSDT contains pointers to or addresses of system call functions.

The main idea of SSDT hooking is to modify the pointers contained in this table to point to the malware code. As a result of this redirection the system call's function is altered to suit the malware's needs. And since all user programs access

this, the rootkit malware's reach becomes global or system wide. It is not locally confined to a single process space anymore as with IAT and EAT hooking.

Kernel Inline Hooking

This is the same concept as user-mode inline hooking discussed previously, but instead of modifying the API code pointed to by the IAT, the malware modifies the system service code pointed to by the SSDT.

IDT Hooking

The IDT contains pointers to or addresses of ISRs. As defined by Microsoft, an interrupt service routine is a software routine that hardware invokes in response to an interrupt. ISRs examine an interrupt and determine how to handle it.

The concept of IDT hooking is modifying the pointers contained in IDT to point to the malware code. Every time an interrupt is triggered, the malware code is executed instead of the ISR.

INT 2E Hooking

Hooking INT 2E falls under IDT hooking. The main concept here involves modifying the pointer to KiSystemService to point to the malware's code. As a result, all programs that utilize KiSystemService end up running the malware code.

Fast System Call Hooking

The concept of hooking the fast system call SYSENTER is to have SYSENTER_EIP_MSR (176h), which contains the address of KiFastCallEntry, point to the malware code. As a result, the malware code is able to filter all system calls without manipulating the SSDT. It can then control which system service it will act on and which it will let transfer to the real system service without running its malicious code. But since this hook is easy to detect, a malware can maintain the original pointer and have it point to the real KiFastCallEntry.

This is what Rustock.B is doing. It then overwrites the string "FATAL_UNHANDLED_HARD_ERROR" in the NTOSKRNL.EXE's virtual address in the resource section with a jump to its malicious code.

DLL Injection

DLL injection is a technique that loads a dynamic link library (DLL) into a running process's address space. There are legitimate uses for this, but in the case of malware, the injected DLL is a malicious DLL that exports malicious functions.

The most common DLL injection techniques a rootkit employs are the following:

- AppInit_DLL key
- Global Windows hooks
- Thread injection

AppInit_DLL Key

Executing a malicious DLL that can hook the IAT, perform hot patching, or modify other DLLs is as easy as modifying the registry key HKEY_LOCAL_MACHINE\Software\Microsoft\Windows NT\CurrentVersion\Windows\AppInit_DLLs.

This registry key is aptly known as the AppInit_DLL key. As defined by Microsoft, AppInit_DLLs is a mechanism that allows an arbitrary list of DLLs to be loaded into each user-mode process on the system. The DLLs are loaded as part of USER32.DLL's initialization. With this facility, a malicious DLL can be loaded easily. As a result, the malicious DLL is injected into processes that import from USER32.DLL.

Note
According to Microsoft, it modified the AppInit DLLs facility in Windows 7 and Windows Server 2008 R2 to add a new code-signing requirement. This will help improve the system reliability and performance, as well as improve visibility into the origin of software.

Since this is a registry modification, Windows has to be rebooted for the malicious DLL to be loaded. Also, this method limits the processes that can be infected by the malicious DLL to those that link to USER32.DLL only. This method is also not advisable if the malware directive is to stay low-key. Malware that wants to stay low-key usually injects itself into few and essential processes only, because malware that utilizes the AppInit_DLL key technique will have its malicious code loaded into every single application that links to USER32.DLL and this might trigger some behavior changes or performance sluggishness that might raise suspicion.

Global Windows Hooks

The use of the SetWindowsHookEx function makes it possible to inject a malicious DLL into a target process. SetWindowsHookEx, as defined by Microsoft, enables the installation of an application-defined hook procedure into a hook chain.

To accomplish the hook, the malware is deployed as a malicious DLL that hooks a certain event. For example, if the desired event is keystroke messages, the malicious DLL must have the capability to export KeyboardProc(). This is hookable via SetWindowsHookEx (WH_KEYBOARD, KeyboardProc). A DLL launcher can be made to register the malicious DLL. Once it is active, every time a keystroke message event takes place, KeyboardProc() will get called by the application, resulting in the malicious code running in the program's address space.

Thread Injection

The concept of thread injection is to be able to inject a malicious DLL into a target process and have it executed as a thread within that process address space. Three APIs play a major role in making this possible: GetProcAddress, LoadLibrary, and CreateRemoteThread. The main player of these three APIs is the CreateRemoteThread API. This API takes in two important parameters: LPTHREAD_START_ROUTINE lpStartAddress [in] and LPVOID lpParameter [in]. These parameters represent the starting address of the thread in the remote process and the pointer to a variable to be passed to the thread function, respectively. In the case of injecting a malicious DLL, the first argument is the loading address of the DLL and the second is the location of the malicious DLL in the system in the form of "C:\Malicious.DLL."

To get the starting address of the thread that will load the malicious DLL, LoadLibrary is used. This API can be used to load any DLL dynamically by any given process. Therefore, simply passing the address of LoadLibrary API that calls the malicious DLL to LPTHREAD_START_ROUTINE lpStartAddress [in] is sufficient to start the malicious DLL as a thread in the target process space. GetProcAddress helps in getting the address of the LoadLibrary API that is passed as an argument in CreateRemoteThread API.

Note
Jeffrey Richter introduced this concept in his article titled, "Load Your 32-bit DLL into Another Processes' Address Space Using INJLIB." It appeared in *MSJ* vol. 9, no. 5, May 1994.

Direct Kernel Object Manipulation

Direct kernel object manipulation is considered the most advanced rootkit technology utilized by malware. This technique concentrates on modifying kernel structures, bypassing the kernel's object manager to avoid access checks. Since the kernel itself is under siege and most of its data structures are modified to the malware's liking, hooking to gain control of the execution flow is not needed anymore.

Although this is the most effective method, it is also the most complicated. Manipulating kernel objects means understanding that object in detail. There are lots of things to be taken into account to ensure that the end result of manipulation will not break the system and will accomplish its malicious goal. This entails a lot of work, which is why some malware writers revert back to the old method of hooking.

Tackling Rootkits

To take on a malware rootkit challenge is to understand the rootkit technology being utilized by the malware. This holds the key in finding the presence of a rootkit malware. But then again, a system compromised with malware with rootkit capability can be a challenge to diagnose. This is because the information the OS is passing to the user or to an analysis or diagnosis tool cannot be trusted. This is especially true if the system is possessed by a kernel-mode rootkit.

The best way to detect the presence of a rootkit is to analyze the system with its operating system deactivated. This can be done by booting the system using a different boot media and then executing a forensics tool, or by removing the hard disk of the compromised system and analyzing it using a dedicated analysis box. The main goal of this is to not only identify the presence of the rootkit but also to identify the technique it is using to hide itself through malware analysis or even reverse engineering. The information that will be gathered can be used as a deployable solution that will detect and eventually remove the rootkit from the other infected machines. This is why some AV companies sometimes ask their customer to send them the hard disk of a compromised machine because it gives the AV researchers the chance to perform a deep-dive analysis and extract the malware for further study.

In Actual Practice

AV companies always instruct their customers to remove confidential and proprietary information from the hard drive before they are sent in for analysis.

Since the suggestion mentioned previously requires a certain level of malware expertise, it might not apply to some of the readers of this book. But all is not lost, as there are tools publicly available that can aid in the detection of rootkits. The following are some of the tools used by AV researchers to aid in the detection of the presence of a rootkit:

- Rootkit Revealer by Microsoft: http://technet.microsoft.com/en-us/sysinternals/bb897445
- GMER: www.gmer.net
- Memoryze by Mandiant: www.mandiant.com/products/free_software/memoryze/
- AV vendor-specific antirootkit technology

Rootkits have been there in the past, and they will still be there in the future. As long as they can be utilized to hide the presence of malware and to achieve total control of the compromised system, they will be an attractive technology for the attackers. The best way to tackle rootkits is by knowing how to use antirootkit tools, being aware of rootkit trends and technology, and the most important thing of all is being familiar with the environment (OS and hardware) that the rootkit operates in.

We've Covered

- What is a rootkit?
- The different privilege levels
  - Ring 0
  - Ring 3
- Mechanics of switching from user mode to kernel mode
  - INT 2E
  - SYSENTER/SYSCALL
- The types of rootkits
  - User-mode rootkits
  - Kernel-mode rootkits
- The common rootkit techniques
  - Hooking
  - DLL injection
  - Direct kernel object manipulation
- Popular tools that aid in the detection of rootkits

CHAPTER 4

Rise of the Botnets

We'll Cover

- What is a botnet?
- Main characteristics of a botnet
- Key components of a botnet
- What is command and control channel?
- Types of botnet C&C structures
- Usage of a botnet
- Protective mechanisms employed by a botnet
- Battlefronts against a botnet

This chapter demystifies botnets. It defines what a botnet is, its key components, the different methods it uses to communicate with the attacker, and the common evasion techniques botnets use to protect and preserve communication between the bots and the command and control (C&C) channel. The chapter also looks at how the botnet threat is being addressed, not just by researchers but also by the authorities.

What Is a Botnet?

First of all, a botnet, in the strictest sense of the word, is not malicious. Botnet is short for robot network. The term robot, or bot, is a generic term for automated programs that execute tasks without user intervention. The term is not limited to botnets alone. For example, in FPS (first person shooters) video games, soldiers that are not controlled by humans that are part of the game are called bots. These bots have a predefined directive, and that is to stay alive and kill opposing forces. An example of legitimate uses of bots appeared in Internet Relay Chat (IRC) channel administration. But since the term has been used to describe a new breed of threats, the term botnet throughout this book will be used to describe a malicious botnet.

Botnets are the most significant threat plaguing the Internet today. A botnet is a network of compromised machines that can be coordinated remotely by an attacker to fulfill a malicious directive. Coordination between infected machines is an important characteristic that distinguishes botnets from other malware. A simplistic view of a botnet

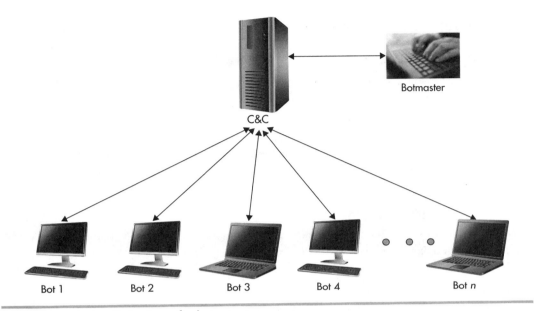

Figure 4-1   A simplistic view of a botnet

is seen in Figure 4-1. In a botnet, the compromised machines or infected hosts serve as the attacker's bots. Directed by the attacker's command, this network of compromised machines collectively function as intended by the attacker.

LINGO
Botnets have many alternate names. Among them are bot army, bot herd, zombie horde, and zombie network.

The attacker that has control over a botnet is known as the botmaster. The botmaster issues commands to the bots through the botnet's C&C, which serves as the botmaster's interface to the botnet. Without the C&C, a botnet degenerates into an uncoordinated group of independent malware-compromised machines. This is why the ability to be controlled is one of the major characteristics of a botnet. The other characteristics are discussed in the next section.

Main Characteristics

Based on our definition of a botnet, it has the following main characteristics:

- A network of compromised machines
- Can be coordinated remotely
- Used for malicious activity

A Network of Compromised Machines

A botnet is not just a massive infection of malware that results in a large number of compromised machines, but rather a network of compromised machines that can communicate with each other or to a central entity and act in a coordinated way based on a directive.

Can Be Coordinated Remotely

A botnet must have the ability to receive and execute commands sent by an attacker or the botmaster and act in a coordinated manner based on those commands. This is what sets a botnet apart from other malware infections, such as remote access Trojans.

Used for Malicious Activity

The main reason this threat exists is to carry out malicious activity. Its main purpose is to fulfill the attacker's directive.

Key Components

A botnet is made up of two major components:

- Host component
- Network component

Host Component

The bots are the compromised machines that the botmaster can control remotely. A malicious agent, active in the compromised machines, makes this possible. The malicious agent that enables a compromised machine to be remotely controlled by a botmaster is called a bot agent. This is the botnet's host component. A bot agent can be a stand-alone malware component in the form of an executable or a dynamic link library (DLL) file or a piece of code added to the malware code. The bot agent's main function is to establish communication with the botnet's network component. As a result of establishing communication, the bot agent is able to do the following, among other things:

LINGO
The botnet **host component** is also known as the malware component.

- Receive and interpret commands from the botmaster
- Execute attacks
- Send data back to the botmaster

Network Component

The botnet's network component is any online resource that a botnet utilizes to fulfill its directive. The most common uses a botnet has for its network component are the following:

- Command and control channel
- Malware distribution server
- Drop zone

Command and Control Channel   A command and control (C&C) is an online resource that changes or influences the behavior of the bots. It is the means by which a botnet is controlled. As previously mentioned, a C&C is the botmaster's interface to the botnet. The term command and control is actually a military term. According to the Department of Defense (DOD) Dictionary of Military Terms, command and control is the exercise of authority and direction by a properly designated commander over assigned and attached forces in the accomplishment of a mission. This definition aptly applies to botnets as well. The commander is the botmaster, and the assigned and attached forces are the compromised machines, aka the bots. This is where the botmaster exercises his authority and directs the bots to accomplish a malicious directive or mission.

The C&C is the most critical component of the botnet. This is what differentiates a botnet from other threats. The botmaster's ability to control the botnet lies in the C&C. Take down the C&C, and the botnet becomes useless. The botnet can live without the other network components, but it cannot live without the C&C. In other words, the C&C is required, the rest are just optional.

> **LINGO**
> What's the difference between a **C&C channel**, **server**, and **traffic**? The bots connect to a C&C channel to receive commands. The server hosting that C&C channel is called a C&C server, and the data flowing between the bots and the C&C channel is called the C&C traffic.

Malware Distribution Server   A malware distribution server is an online resource that hosts malware components, including the bot agents, other important files, and the updates that the botnet needs for its operation. Every time a malware component, or any malware-related files, needs to be updated, the botnet utilizes its malware server to update the malware components in the compromised machines. It is also used as the main source of the malware components being downloaded by malware installers during the infection phase. More about this in Part II of the book.

Drop Zone   A drop zone is an online resource that serves as the attacker's repository of stolen data. A drop zone is often utilized if the botnet is used as a harvester of information, including but not limited to financial credentials, proprietary data, and private information. More about this in Part II of the book.

C&C Structure

The structure of a botnet's C&C defines how commands and important information are disseminated to the bots. There are three types of C&C structures:

- Centralized
- Decentralized
- Hybrid

Centralized C&C Structure

The most common botnet C&C structure is centralized. In this structure the botnet is organized with a central C&C location. This means that all members of the botnet connect to a centralized node where commands are issued. This structure offers the botmaster a very effective and simple way of communicating with the bots. Plus, the centralized C&C can be easily managed by the botmaster.

Command Dissemination   The following are two types of how commands are disseminated in a centralized C&C structure [1]:

- Push style
- Pull style

In a *push style* centralized C&C structure, the botmaster pushes the command to the bot agents. In this scenario, the bots are actively connected to the C&C and simply wait for a command from the botmaster. As a result, the botmaster has real-time control over the bots. See Figure 4-2 for an example.

This is especially true for IRC-based C&C, where bots are logged in to a certain IRC channel waiting for a command from the botmaster. Once a command is issued, the bots take action and respond with the results if needed.

In a *pull style* centralized C&C structure, the bots pull information or updates from the C&C. In this scenario, the bots periodically establish connection to the C&C and check for the presence of a new command. The command is posted by the botmaster in the form of a file or information that the bots can interpret and have access to. Having the botmaster post the command and then having the bots pull it from the C&C does not give the botmaster

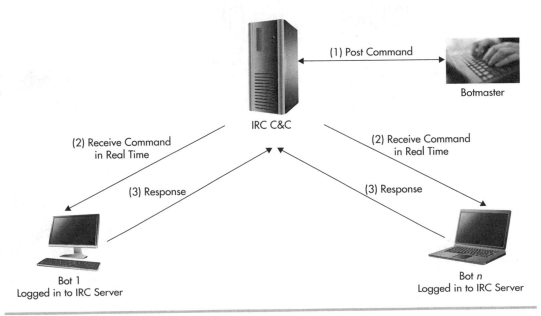

Figure 4-2 Push style centralized C&C structure

real-time control of the bots because of the delay from the time the botmaster posts the command and the bots connecting to the C&C to pull the command. See Figure 4-3 for an example.

This style is often seen in HTTP-based command and control. The botnets connect to the Hypertext Transfer Protocol (HTTP) server and receive the command via HTTP response.

Decentralized C&C Structure

Although the centralized C&C structure of a botnet offers several advantages, such as simplicity and manageability, it is also the botnet's biggest disadvantage. The centralized C&C is also the central point of failure for the botnet. Preventing access to the C&C or taking it down will render the botnet useless. The malware component of the botnet will still continue to function, but it will have no one to control it and feed it with new commands. The cybercriminals realize this and came up with a more resilient C&C structure, one that introduces redundancy through multiple C&C nodes. This is known as a decentralized C&C structure.

In a decentralized C&C structure, the nodes act as both C&C server and client. The nodes are the compromised machines themselves. This eliminates the central point of failure of the botnet. Taking down one C&C node does not kill the botnet. It does not even

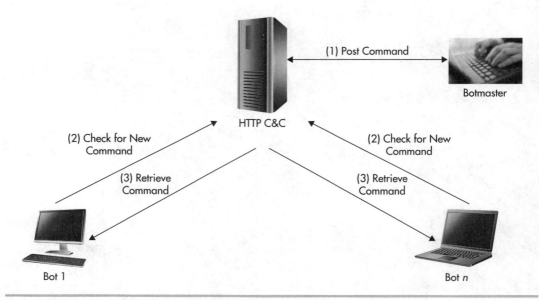

Figure 4-3 Pull style centralized C&C structure

cause significant disruption. The botmaster can control the botnet from another node. A decentralized C&C structure is also known as a peer-to-peer (P2P) botnet network. Its P2P nature makes it more resilient to countermeasures that work only for the centralized botnet C&C structure.

P2P Basics P2P file sharing enables a user to download files using a P2P client from other systems or peers with a compatible P2P client. A file index is used by a P2P client to locate the desired file. A peer queries for the desired file across the P2P network until the file is found or the query expires. The desired file can then be downloaded from the closest peers, or in segments from multiple peers, depending on the P2P protocol. Reassembling of the segments after download is taken care of by the P2P client.

Note
P2P has many other uses aside from file sharing. It is also used for voice and messaging.

Types of P2P Botnets A P2P botnet can be divided into the following types:

- Those that use the existing P2P network
- Those that build their own P2P network

P2P botnets that use existing P2P networks can be broken down further into what are called a parasite P2P botnet and a leeching P2P botnet [2]. In a parasite

P2P botnet, all the bots are hosts within an existing P2P network, while in a leeching P2P botnet, the bots can be any vulnerable hosts in the Internet and not just within an existing P2P network. In a parasite botnet, bootstrapping is not required since all the bots are already part of a P2P network, while in a leeching botnet, some bots that are not part of a P2P network will need to bootstrap to join the P2P network.

P2P botnets that build their own P2P network are also called bot-only P2P botnets. A bot-only P2P botnet [2] does not rely on existing P2P networks, although it can utilize them if needed. Instead, it builds its own network. This ensures that only bots are members of the P2P network.

Command Dissemination   The following are two types of how commands are disseminated in a decentralized C&C structure [2]:

- Push
- Pull

In a *push* style P2P C&C structure, the botmaster injects a command into a bot or group of bots, and then these bots forward it to their neighboring peers. Then the recipients forward it to each of their neighboring peers, and so on. The only drawback of this approach is that the flow of commands to other bots is slow because the number of neighboring peers might be low. This is a far cry from the real-time control a botmaster achieves in a push style centralized C&C structure. Plus, the flow of commands might even get disrupted, especially in parasite and leeching type P2P botnets that have legitimate peers as members of the network. To avoid the disruption and ensure that the commands are forwarded to bot members and not legitimate peers, a bot forwarding the command can have a predefined filename available that other bots in the network can query and search for. The bots that will appear in the search results for those files will then receive the command from the forwarding bot. If the receiving bot is part of the P2P network being utilized by the botnet, an in-band message is the way to go. The command is encoded into a query message that only the recipient bots can decipher. This method is easy to implement and hard to defend against because the traffic is similar to normal P2P traffic. Otherwise, an out-of-band message is sent, which risks getting detected by antivirus (AV) researchers.

In a *pull* style P2P C&C structure, the botmaster can simply insert records containing the botnet commands into the index and associate that with some predefined filenames or hash values. These predefined filenames or hash values are what the bots will regularly search for when they need to get new commands. In order for the bots to get or pull these commands, they will periodically initiate queries for the filenames and hashes associated with the record. The peers who have the corresponding records will then return query hits to the querying bots. From here, the querying bots can simply pull these records containing the commands that were published by the botmaster.

Hybrid C&C Structure

As expected, cybercriminals will always leverage anything that they can to achieve their malicious goals. They recognized the advantages and disadvantages of a centralized and decentralized botnet C&C structure. They also understood that under certain conditions, one C&C structure might be better than the other. So to increase the chances of success of a botnet, the attackers implemented a hybrid C&C structure that uses both centralized and decentralized C&C. One example that utilizes a hybrid C&C is the ZeusP2P/Murofet combo.

This botnet uses P2P as its primary C&C and when connection to its peers fails, it goes to its backup C&C, which uses a centralized C&C structure. But there's a kicker. Instead of connecting directly to its C&C using a predefined set of domains, it uses a set of an almost infinite number of domains produced by a domain generation algorithm (DGA) that is coded into the malware. What's a DGA? This will be explained further in the upcoming sections.

Botnet Usage

Now that we have a basic understanding of what a botnet is, it is clear that the attacker is able to accomplish a lot more with botnets compared to conventional malware infections. A botnet's strength is in its massive numbers. The more there are, the more powerful they become. Botnets are like ants. A single ant is nothing more than a nuisance, but an attack from the whole colony can bring down an animal that is a hundred times bigger. This is because aside from their large number that overwhelms the victim, the ants function collectively with a single purpose. The same is true for the botnet.

Note
Attackers who specialize in targeted attacks prefer smaller-size botnets to stay under the radar and avoid being detected.

With this amount of computing power available, the attacker is able to perform tasks that were not possible before. Plus, it's like having a computing cloud infrastructure. The power to control the botnet made it possible to perform tasks that are only effective using a massive collection of bots. Some of these are the following:

- Distributed denial of service attack
- Click fraud
- Spam relay
- Pay-per-install agent
- Large-scale information harvesting
- Information processing

Distributed Denial of Service Attack

The more participants there are, the more effective a distributed denial of service (DDoS) attack is. An army of bots aimed at a single target can cripple that target quickly. The relationship between the number of participants and the time it takes to take down a target is inversely proportional.

There are actually two victims in this attack, as seen in Figure 4-4:

- The compromised machines from which the DDoS attack is being launched from
- The systems that are being attacked

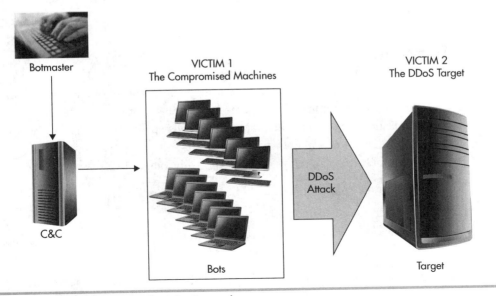

Figure 4-4   The two victims of a DDoS attack

Click Fraud

Instead of directing the thousands of bots to launch an attack, why not direct them to click ads to generate income for the attacker? This is called click fraud. This is the fastest money-making scam for the cybercriminals. And the biggest losers are the online advertisers.

Online advertisers pay for each click of the ads they have on websites and search results. If the ad was clicked because it showed up during a keyword search, the website search gets all the money. But if the ad is clicked on a website, the website owner gets paid. Payment is usually routed through an ad affiliation program. The website owner does not get 100 percent of the payment. Instead, the program provider keeps a small percentage of the income and then the rest goes to the website owner.

Let's say an online advertiser is willing to pay 10 cents per ad click. So, if an online ad posted in website X generates 100,000 clicks, the online advertiser will pay the owner of website X $10,000 minus the ad affiliation program's commission. And since the money is usually coursed through the program provider, it is already a form of money laundering because on the surface it appears to be a legitimate income generated by the ads found in the owner's website.

Let's take a look at how a click fraud is executed. First, the attackers put up a website that contains nothing but ads. They then sign up with one or more ad affiliation programs such as Google adSense and Yahoo! Affiliates. Once everything is set, they instruct the botnets under their control to click the ads found on their website. This will then trigger payments from online advertisers. And since they are affiliates, the payment will be coursed through either Google or Yahoo!. This, as previously mentioned, is already an effective way to launder money.

Spam Relay

Botnets generate massive volumes of spam every day. These spam-generating bots are called spambots. Before, spam was sent using a single or a handful of machines owned or under the control of a spammer. This method of sending spam is not efficient, plus the source can easily be discovered and taken down. The spammers need a new way of sending out spam. This is where botnets come in.

The use of botnets as spam relays offers several advantages [4]:

- The identities of the spammers can be hidden.

- The source of the spam is almost impossible to trace.

- The high availability of computing power and bandwidth allows for large amounts of spam to be transmitted instantly.

- The spamming process can be carried out in collaboration between bots performing different tasks.

Each spam campaign has at least three elements that enable the attacker to generate dynamic spam messages, making it a challenge for antispam solutions to detect an e-mail spam using pattern matching. These elements are: [4]

- Senders list
- Receivers list
- Message template

As seen in Figure 4-5, the spammer initiates the spamming via the botnet's C&C. The command and other configuration files containing the spam campaign elements are either pushed to or pulled by the spambots from the C&C. After which, the spambots generate the dynamic e-mail spams using the spam campaign elements. And then the spamming begins.

One of the most notorious spamming botnet is the Rustock botnet. According to Microsoft's Security Intelligence Report [5], the Rustock botnet was estimated to have had

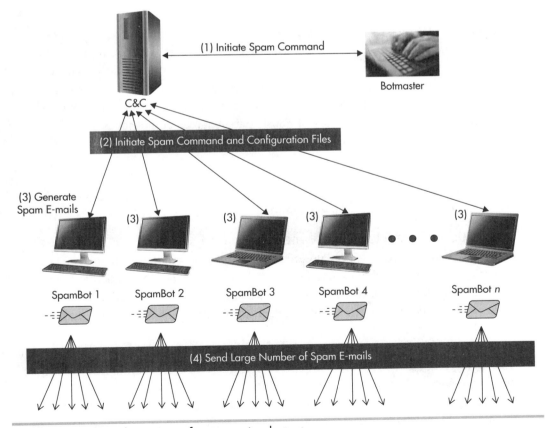

Figure 4-5   A simplistic view of a spamming botnet

approximately a million compromised machines serving as spambots capable of sending billions of spam e-mail messages a day.

Pay-Per-Install Agent

The main idea here is profiting from installing software to a compromised system. There are two ways a botmaster can profit from this:

- Installation of legitimate software
- Installation of malicious software

A very good paper on pay-per-install (PPI) was presented in USENIX Security 2011. The paper is titled "Measuring Pay-per-Install: The Commoditization of Malware Distribution," and is written by Juan Caballero, Chris Grier, Christian Kreibich, and Vern Paxson. It can be downloaded from www.usenix.org/events/sec11/tech/full_papers/Caballero.pdf.

Installation of Legitimate Software

Imagine someone who owns a website that hosts different software. The owner of that website gets paid by the software manufacturer every time software is downloaded and installed. Now, if the owner of that website contracted a botmaster to direct the hundreds of thousands of bots to the website and then download and install software to the compromised machines that will translate to hundreds of thousands of software installations, resulting in a fat commission for the website owner.

Tip
One indicator of a possible infection is seeing the amount of software suddenly installed in a system that was not installed there by any user.

Installation of Malicious Software

In this scenario, instead of legitimate software, malware is installed in the system. This is usually an underground transaction wherein the botmaster becomes a deployment provider. A deployment provider is someone who provides service that delivers malware to the attacker's desired target. There will be more discussion about deployment providers in Part II of the book.

Someone who wants to have malware deployed or installed approaches the botmaster to have his creation installed on thousands of machines. The price for this service differs for every country where the malware will be deployed and whether the installation will be in an enterprise system or a home PC. The botmaster can simply instruct his bots to download and install the malware from a specific location, usually a malware server, to the victim PC. Another method is utilizing the botnet's spam relay capability to spam the malware as an attachment or a link to a drive-by download site.

Large-Scale Information Harvesting

A compromised machine can be a gold mine of data for cybercriminals. This is why information stealers came to be. The directive of this type of malware is to basically steal information. It can be passwords, documents, or any other information that the attacker can monetize. Usually the collection is done in a very small setup. But with the advent of botnets, the potential to steal information from hundreds of thousands to even millions of machines became a possibility. And since there is coordination, the stolen information can be funneled out to a handful of information drop zones that the cybercriminals control.

This is usually done by installing an information stealer component to all the compromised machines that are part of a botnet. The installation can be in the form of an update or through a PPI agent. Once the information stealer component is installed and activated, it will start stealing information from the hundreds of thousands of compromised machines, exfiltrate the stolen data to a designated network location controlled by the attackers, and start collecting data again. The cycle goes on and on until the botnet is killed or the malware component has been removed from the compromised machines. But this is easier said than done.

Imagine the amount of stolen data within reach for the attackers. The potential for financial gain is high.

Information Processing

A botnet is an attacker's malicious cloud. It's like having massive amounts of computing power in the control of the attacker. This computing power becomes handy especially if an attack calls for data crunching. One example is cracking passwords. Having this much computing power cuts down the time it takes to figure out a password through brute force.

Botnet Protective Mechanisms

The botnet's biggest strength, its C&C, is also its weakest link. The C&C infrastructure and the means to access it must be protected if the botnet is to thrive. Therefore, it is imperative to protect the botnet's C&C channel. This is done through the following:

- Bulletproof hosting
- Dynamic DNS
- Fast fluxing
- Domain fluxing

The other network components of a botnet also need protection but not as much as its C&C, because if any of these other network components become unavailable, the botmaster can simply reconfigure the bots to use a different network resource. This is possible because the botmaster can still communicate with the bots through its C&C, but if the C&C is down there's no way for the attacker to communicate to the botnet anymore.

Bulletproof Hosting

Bulletproof hosting is a service provided by unscrupulous webhosting companies. Ordinarily, hosting companies are governed with and have terms of service that prohibit an account user from uploading certain materials, such as malware and copyrighted content, and using the service for malicious or criminal purposes. If an account user is found to be in violation of these terms, the account is suspended and the user is held criminally liable. Bulletproof hosting is the opposite. Although it has a terms of service, it is only for show—the account users can do virtually anything they want as long as the bulletproof hosting provider gets paid. Plus, bulletproof hosting providers are less likely to cooperate with or even respond to law enforcement. This makes bulletproof hosting very attractive to criminals.

One of the most notorious and now-defunct bulletproof hosting providers was the Russian Business Network (RBN) based in St. Petersburg, Russia. RBN was known for hosting malware server sites, phishing sites, spam hosts, and pornography. It quickly became a haven for cybercriminals and became the springboard for launching attacks.

Most bulletproof hosting is based overseas where our laws do not apply. Even if there are local laws in those countries governing hosting abuses and fair Internet usage, account users are still allowed or given lots of leeway to do as they please. So it might be hard to believe that another infamous and also now-defunct bulletproof hosting provider is based in the United States.

McColo was a bulletproof hosting provider out of San Jose, California, founded by a teenage Russian hacker and student known as Kolya McColo. Aside from hosting botnet network resources, the company was believed to be responsible for almost 70 percent of the world's spam e-mail.

Dynamic DNS

Dynamic domain name service (DDNS) is a service that links a domain name to a dynamically changing IP address. This means that a domain name will keep on pointing to the same host, regardless of its constantly changing IP address. This makes this solution ideal for people operating home systems or servers, such as those configured as a web server, a game server, a File Transfer Protocol (FTP) server, or a mail server with a dynamic IP address assigned by an Internet service provider (ISP). The solution is also useful for corporate users who need to remotely connect to a system inside the organization with a Dynamic Host Configuration Protocol (DHCP)–assigned IP address.

Setting Up DDNS

Utilizing a DDNS service takes only two steps:

- Register with a DDNS provider
- Install DDNS software in the host

But as with other technologies, cybercriminals always find a way to take advantage of DDNS and abuse it for their own malicious purpose. Most DDNS providers offer free service without requiring the registrant to divulge too much information. An e-mail address and a fake identity is enough to get free DDNS service. This makes the service attractive to cybercriminals.

Disadvantages of DDNS

Although DDNS gives the attacker the advantage of using different Internet Protocol (IP) addresses to have the malicious domains resolve to, thus giving him the flexibility to use any host as a malware resource, this service is far from perfect when it comes to cybercrime because it has the following disadvantages:

- The free service only offers fixed (second level domains) 2LD domains (e.g., No-IP's zapto.org and hopto.org), which results in easy detection.
- DDNS providers are responsive to abuse reports.
- DDNS requires software to be installed in the host, which is another point of failure. If the software fails, the bots will not be able to communicate to the C&C.

Fast Fluxing

Flux, as defined by *Merriam-Webster*, is a continuous moving on or passing by. Fast fluxing, therefore, is a fast, continuous

LINGO
Fast flux is also known as IP flux.

moving on or passing by of an object. In this case, the object is an IP address. Fast fluxing refers to having a single domain name resolve to a frequently changing IP address. The result is multiple IP addresses assigned to a single domain name.

One way of achieving fast fluxing is through round-robin DNS with each DNS resource record (RR) having a short time-to-live (TTL) value. So instead of responding to DNS requests with only one IP address, a list of IP addresses is returned.

Note

Round-robin DNS is primarily used for load balancing and fault tolerance.

There are two types of fast flux networks [3]:

- Single flux
- Double flux

Single Flux

A single flux network uses compromised machines as redirectors. The different IP addresses in the flux network are IP addresses of the compromised machines. They take the role of redirectors, aka flux-agents. These flux-agents redirect requests and data to another backend server known as the fast-flux mothership. Fast-flux motherships are the backbone of fast-flux service networks. They provide both DNS and HTTP services; therefore, the motherships host the data and serve the content. In a single flux network, the mothership does not provide DNS service.

Flux-agents are designed to protect the mothership from discovery. In effect, the domains deployed by the attackers do not

LINGO
Flux-agents are also called flux-bots.

resolve to the IP of the mothership or the actual server hosting the malicious content, but instead resolve to any of the flux-agents, which forward all requests to the mothership and serve whatever content the mothership sends to the flux-agent to the target.

Aside from shielding the mothership from being discovered by researchers, the use of flux-agents also provides resiliency. Since single flux networks change the DNS records constantly in short periods of time, a new one will quickly replace a flux-agent that is down or unavailable.

Figure 4-6 shows how a single flux lookup works. In this example, the client wants to resolve the domain flux.example.com. Let's assume in this example that the preferred DNS server does not have a matched answer either from its cache or zone information. Therefore, the client will trigger the preferred DNS server to use recursion to resolve the domain. This goes on until example.com returns the IP addresses of flux.address.com. Take note here that example.com is under the control of cybercriminals and is protected via bulletproof hosting. The client then initiates connection to flux.example.com using one of the returned IP addresses in Step 9. Notice that flux.example.com is fluxed; therefore, its IP address changes constantly. In Steps 10 and 11, the flux-agent redirects the query to the mothership and the mothership replies with the appropriate content. It can be web content, especially if it is hosting phishing sites or drive-by download sites. The content is then served to the client.

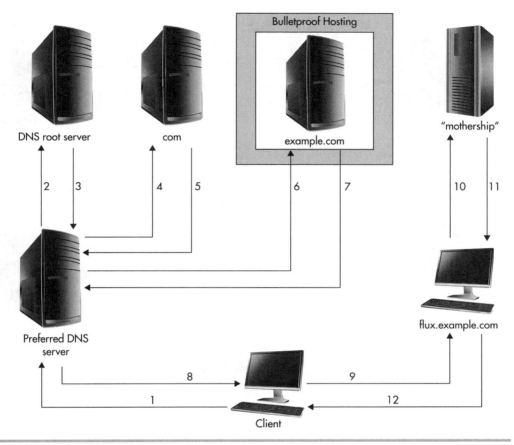

Figure 4-6   Single flux network lookup process

Double Flux

In a double flux network, it is not only the DNS A record that is changed constantly, but also the glue records for the malicious domain. A glue record is the IP address of a name server in the domain name registry. Compromised machines play the role of the authoritative DNS, and their IP address changes frequently, as it is also being fluxed. In this scenario, the mothership not only serves HTTP but also DNS. Figure 4-7 shows how a double flux lookup works. In this example, the client wants to resolve the domain flux .example.com, similar to the single flux network example, but this time there is additional fluxing going on. Instead of having a bulletproof hosted example.com name server, it has flux-agents that redirect DNS requests (Step 7) to the mothership and then the mothership replies (Step 8) with the IP addresses of flux.example.com. This information is then

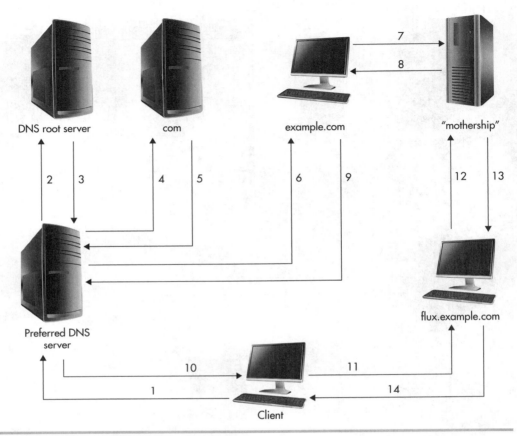

Figure 4-7 Double flux network lookup process

relayed (Step 9) by the flux-agent to the preferred DNS server. The client then initiates connection to flux.example.com in similar fashion as explained in the single flux example in the previous section.

Domain Fluxing

As we have seen in previous sections, botnets rely on domains that are distributed with the bot agent. These domains are either hard-coded in the bot agent or come in configuration files deployed with the malware package. The only time these domains are updated is by the attacker pushing a new one to the bot agent or by the bot agent pulling information or a configuration file from a C&C.

Since the C&C enables the botmaster to control the bots, their efforts are more focused on protecting the C&C, which results in the botnet's resiliency. But attackers soon realized that simply blocking the domains pointing to the C&C prevents the bot agent from communicating to the C&C. It does not matter how sophisticated the techniques used to hide the C&C are. If the bot agents have no way to connect to the C&C, it becomes useless and free from the botmaster's control.

Note

Some bot agents use hard-coded IP addresses to connect directly to the C&C. This is very easy to detect and block.

Since cutting communication to the C&C results in the bot agent not having the ability to get updated commands, it will continue trying to connect to the C&C using its outdated and already blocked domains or IP addresses. No matter how hard the bot agent tries, however, it will not be able to communicate back to its C&C. This situation also renders the botmaster helpless because there is no way for him to send updated commands or fresh domains to the bot agent. He can simply chalk this one host up to the ones that got away.

But what if the bot agent has the capability to come up with its own set of domains without relying on configuration files or updated commands from the botmaster? This would enable the malware to actively look for a live C&C instead of waiting for the attacker, which is futile anyway given that the communication lines have already been blocked. This ability of the bots to generate unique domain names on regular time intervals is called domain fluxing. The thing that makes this possible is a DGA, short for domain generation algorithm.

It's like two criminals who buried stolen jewelry and money in an undisclosed location and agreed to part ways while the situation cools down. Criminal A and Criminal B split the map and the combination to open the chest lock. The agreement is for Criminal A to contact Criminal B in a couple of years using a list of phone numbers. But just in case these numbers no longer work, probably because the authorities found out about them, Criminal A is instructed to do the following. Try using different area codes allocated to the state where the stolen loot is buried, use the numbers between 800 and 900 for the first three digits of the phone number, and use the same last four digits Criminal B always uses to complete the phone number. So basically the format for the phone number is [Available Area Codes] – [Number between 800 and 900] – [Constant Last Digits, e.g., 5611]. With this instruction, Criminal A will know how to come up with a new number to reach Criminal B in case the numbers he has in his possession right now are no longer valid. Criminal B will also know what number to register if his current number needs to be disconnected. For example, if the loot is buried in Georgia, Criminal A can come up with 909 phone numbers. This is from the nine area codes allocated to Georgia multiplied by 101 possible first three digits and multiplied by one, since the last four digits are constant.

Criminal A might dial a nonexistent number or a wrong number until finally he reaches Criminal B. And they will know it's each other once they exchange the secret passphrase they talked about before they parted ways.

The botmaster wants the bot agent to do the same thing as Criminal A. If its connection to the C&C fails, it must be able to come up with new domain names based on a specific instruction and then use those domains to try connecting to its C&C. This instruction is known as a DGA.

A DGA is a code embedded in the malware or bot agent that is deployed by the botmaster. The main purpose of this code is to generate domains that the bot agent can use to connect to its C&C. Typically, a DGA produces a different set of domains per day. For example, Conficker.A and Conficker.B DGA produces 250 domains per day, while Conficker.C produces 50,000 domains per day, but out of those domains, only 500 are used by Conficker.C.

Note

Domains generated by a DGA are not random, although they might appear that way. They are a product of a set of instructions that includes mathematical and string operations.

Advantages of Domain Fluxing

Using a DGA offers several advantages, some of them are:

- It evades blacklisting. Collecting all the domains generated and adding them into a blacklist does not scale (e.g., the three variants of Conficker generate more than 18 million domains a year).

- It enables the attackers to take control of the botnet by registering a domain to be generated in the future and then pointing it to a new C&C.

- Generated domains are expendable and used only for a short period of time; therefore, domain reputation systems will be useless against them.

Disadvantages of Domain Fluxing

DGA is not perfect. As with Criminal A experiencing a nonexistent number and a wrong number, a DGA is subject to the same results, especially if it is producing massive amounts of domains per day. A DGA will generate a massive amount of NXDomains, and once in a while, it might generate domains that are used by legitimate entities.

Also, since the DGA is a code embedded in the bot agent, capturing a sample gives AV researchers the chance to reverse it and understand the inner

LINGO
NXDomain means nonexistent domain.

workings of the DGA code. As a result, the AV researchers will be able to predict the domains on a given day. This gives the researchers a chance to take control of a botnet by registering those domains and having it point to their own server for further analysis. This process is known as sinkholing and will be discussed further in the latter part of this chapter.

A DGA also has several disadvantages:

- The amount of NXDomains a DGA produces causes a lot of noise, which can be leveraged to detect the presence of a DGA-capable malware.
- Reversing the malware's DGA component will enable the researchers to take control of the botnet by registering a domain to be generated in the future and then pointing it to a sinkhole.

The Fight Against Botnets

A botnet is a complicated monster. It is a complex problem that requires a complex solution. It is unlike any other malware threat wherein eliminating the malware in the host eliminates the threat. A botnet is made up of components that are beyond the host; thus, eliminating the malware and fixing the compromised machine does not kill the botnet. The process simply removes that host from the botnet. The botnet itself is still alive and kicking. I doubt that the botnet will miss that one asset. One might argue that deploying a detection signature to all compromised machines will eradicate all the malware that enables the control of compromised machines and will therefore kill the botnet. That, of course, will work only if the botnet utilizes only one malware family with no protective mechanisms. But that is not the case. Aside from utilizing malware technology to avoid detection, there is no one-is-to-one correspondence between malware families and botnets. A botnet can have multiple malware families, and multiple malware families can be a member of different botnets. The challenge in the host is already great, given how complicated malware has become. And this is just one component of a botnet. The network infrastructure supporting the botnet must also be thwarted to completely take down a botnet.

But the technology components alone do not define the botnet. It is just a malicious tool under the control of cybercriminals. Taking down one botnet will not stop the cybercriminals from deploying a new one. Therefore, to effectively wage battle against a botnet, the criminals behind them must also be addressed. This is why the fight against botnets is battled on two fronts:

- The technical front
- The legal front

The Technical Front

The technical front focuses the battle on the two major components of the botnet: the host and the network.

Host Component

As previously stated, the botnet's host component is a malware with the capability to communicate with a botmaster. Therefore, removing a botnet's host component is the same as dealing with a malware infection. The same tools and methodologies are used to detect, extract, analyze, and remove the botnet's host component.

Network Component

The difference a botnet has with traditional malware is that it has a network component. Therefore, it is not enough to deal with just the host infection to eliminate a botnet. The network component must also be addressed. The network component includes the C&C, the malware server, drop zones, and any other network resource the botnet needs to operate effectively. The traditional approach taken before to address this was blacklisting and blocking the connection. Unfortunately, this does not address the root cause of the problem. It's like having a bulletproof vest against a gunman. The gunman will keep on shooting unless the gun is taken away from him. To get to the root cause of the problem, the network service supporting the malware must be taken down. Without the network service supporting the botnet's network component, the botnet becomes useless.

The first step in dealing with the botnet's network component is to understand and identify what it is. This information will then be used to take it down. To achieve this, the following actions are taken:

- Sinkhole
- Takedown

Sinkhole   Taking control of a botnet's network resource leads the researchers to understand the botnet's communication and network behavior. This is achieved through sinkholing.

Sinkholing is the process of taking ownership of a botnet's network resource, particularly its C&C, by hijacking the domains being utilized by the botnet to connect to its C&C. These domains are registered so the researchers can receive botnet communication intended for that network resource. In other words, the researchers take over the botnet's operation. This gives them the power to receive information from the botnet and issue commands to control the botnet. The only difference between the two is the malicious intent. Instead, it is replaced by that of curiosity and with a mindset of identifying the appropriate solution on how to stop the botnet.

Through sinkholing, researchers gain knowledge on the following:

- Size of the botnet
- Location of compromised systems
- What information is being sent by the bots

The last item carries with it some controversy, given that the researchers gain access to the stolen information being sent by the bots. It is possible that these are all private information and, therefore, might lead to possible ethical and privacy violations.

Takedown   Sinkholing aids in analyzing and understanding the botnet's network communication. It also aids, in combination with host component analysis result, in identifying the network infrastructure behind the botnet. And once the network resources have been identified, the next step is to take them down.

A botnet takedown refers to taking down or making unavailable the network service account or infrastructure that supports or provides the botnet's network resource. Taking down a network resource can be very easy or very hard, depending on what type of network resource it is. For example, a botnet that uses a Facebook account as its infection vector can be easily taken down just by reporting the offending account to Facebook. A Twitter account that is used to control a botnet is also very easy to take down. While these are very easy takedowns, botnets that use network resources hosted by bulletproof hosting providers are very hard to take down.

A takedown is often achieved through collaboration with law enforcement, network service providers, industry and academic experts, and other government agencies worldwide. For example, the takedown of the Rustock botnet was spearheaded by Microsoft Digital Crimes Unit with the help of the aforementioned.

The Legal Front

Another battle being waged against the botnet is on the legal front. Taking down the technical components obviously is not enough. The people behind the botnet can easily create a new botnet and profit again without even caring for the previously taken-down botnet.

The fight against botnets in the legal front can take the following forms:

- Exhaust all legal remedies available.
- Assist law enforcement officers.
- Introduce anti-botnet or anti-cybercrime legislation.

Legal Remedies

The people behind a botnet must be held responsible for their actions so they will be prevented from doing it again and serve as examples to other cybercriminals still at large. The legal remedy a party can take is to file a criminal lawsuit against the cybercriminals, as Microsoft did against the Rustock operators, shown in Figure 4-8.

Taking advantage of the criminal system to go after the people behind the botnet is a good first step in apprehending these cybercriminals.

Assist Law Enforcement Officers

The research community holds vital information about a botnet from the results of analysis and technical investigation. Providing this information to law enforcement officers will help in tracking down and leading to the arrests of these cybercriminals. Plus, this same information can be used as evidence against the cybercriminals.

Anti-Cybercrime Legislation

Sometimes, most digital crimes are not covered by any penal code, and if they are, have loopholes in them. This limits the law enforcement officer's abilities to investigate, capture, and prosecute an already identified cybercriminal. This is why introducing new

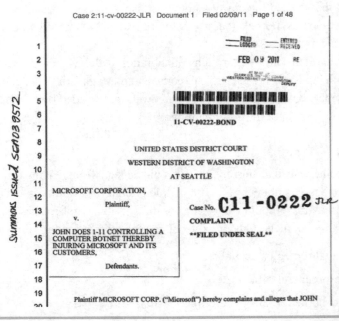

Figure 4-8 First page of Microsoft's lawsuit filed against Rustock botnet operators

legislation that addresses cybercrime is a major key in empowering law enforcement officers in apprehending cybercriminals that result in not only disrupting a botnet business model but completely eradicating it. At least for now…

We've Covered

- What is a botnet?
    - A network of compromised machines
    - Can be coordinated remotely
    - Used for malicious activity
- Main characteristics of a botnet
    - A network of compromised machines
    - Can be remotely controlled
    - Used for malicious activity
- Key components of a botnet
    - Host component
    - Network component
- What is command and control?
    - The means by which a botnet is controlled
    - The botmaster's interface to the botnet
- Types of botnet C&C structure
    - Centralized
    - Decentralized
    - Hybrid
- Malicious usage of a botnet
    - DDoS attack
    - Click fraud
    - Spam relay
    - Pay-per-install agent
    - Large-scale information harvesting
    - Information processing

- Protective mechanisms employed by a botnet
  - Bulletproof hosting
  - Dynamic DNS
  - Fast fluxing
  - Domain fluxing
- Battlefronts against a botnet
  - The technical front
  - The legal front

References

1. Guofei Gu, Junjie Zhang, Wenke Lee. BotSniffer: Detecting Botnet Command and Control Channels in Network Traffic: http://users.csc.tntech.edu/~weberle/.../17_botsniffer_detecting_botnet.pdf.

2. Ping Wang, Lei Wu, Baber Aslam, Cliff C. Zou. A Systematic Study on Peer-to-Peer Botnets: http://citeseerx.ist.psu.edu/viewdoc/download?doi=10.1.1.153.8296&rep=rep1&type=.pdf.

3. William Salusky, Robert Danford. How Fast-Flux Service Networks Work: http://www.honeynet.org/node/132. Accessed July 2, 2012.

4. Areej Al-Bataineh, Gregory White. Detection and Prevention Methods of Botnet-generated Spam: http://projects.csail.mit.edu/spamconf/SC2009/Areej_Al-Bataineh/Bataineh_Spambot.pdf. Accessed July 2, 2012

5. www.microsoft.com/security/sir/story/default.aspx#!rustock. Accessed July 2, 2012.

PART II

Welcome to the Jungle

CHAPTER 5

The Threat Ecosystem

We'll Cover

● The technical elements that make up a threat ecosystem

● The different roles of the people behind a cybercrime organization

● The nature of advanced persistent threats

● The four stages of an attack

● Common attack types

● The underground malware economy

Chapter 4 showed us the capabilities of botnets, how they brought the malware problem to a whole new level, and how interactive a compromised system became. Botnets opened up many opportunities for the attackers, giving them the ability to wage a much more effective attack on a target, with better control of and interaction with compromised systems compared to the old method of "infect and forget."

In this chapter, I will discuss how the new capabilities offered by a botnet redefined the threat ecosystem to a more active and robust interdependency of people and technologies, and how cybercriminals harnessed them against a specific target.

The Threat Ecosystem

A threat ecosystem is an interdependency of different technologies and the people behind them that are vital to the success of an attack. As with a natural ecosystem, both living and nonliving things must be in harmony with each other to ensure the continuous survival of the community of living organisms that depend on it. While a natural ecosystem is composed of biotic (living) and abiotic (nonliving) elements, a threat ecosystem is composed also of two major elements: the technical (abiotic) element and the human (biotic) element. These two major elements must work together in harmony to ensure the success of an attack.

The Technical Element

The technical elements of a threat ecosystem are the different technologies that support the attack (see Figure 5-1). These technologies have different roles to play that complement each other. These technologies can be categorized into the following:

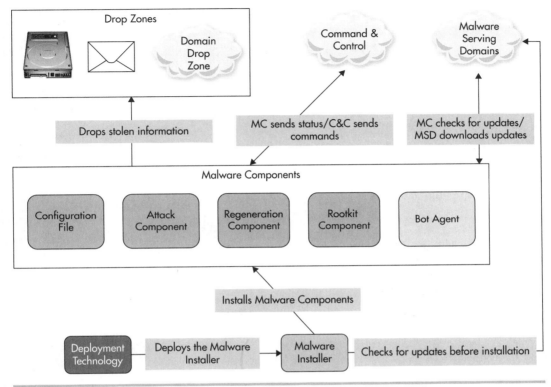

Figure 5-1   The technical element of the threat ecosystem

- Deployment technology
- Malware installer
- Malware-serving domains
- Command and control (C&C)
- Drop zone
- Malware components

Deployment Technology

The deployment technology is what's behind the spread of malware. It distributes the malware installer or the malware itself to the intended target using a single infection vector or a combination of different infection vectors that includes but is not limited to the following:

- Physical media
- E-mails
- Instant messaging and chat
- Social networking
- Universal Resource Locator (URL) links
- File shares
- Software vulnerabilities

Note

Chapter 7 will discuss this topic in more detail.

Malware Installer

The malware installer is deployed by the chosen deployment technology and is responsible for installing the malware and all its components in a target system. There are three types:

- Dropper
- Downloader
- Hybrid

Malware installers are considered a commodity. For them to be effective in future missions, they must remain hidden. They are like choppers used to carry soldiers into the battlefield. They usually fly in and then immediately fly out of the hot zone after transporting the soldiers to avoid the risk of being shot down and then studied by the opposing forces. The chopper then comes back again to extract the soldiers once the mission is complete. A malware installer's purpose is almost the same, except for the part that involves extracting the soldiers out of the hot zone once the mission is finished. Its main mission is to penetrate the system, install the malware, and then "fly out" or vanish. The vanishing act is achieved by the malware installer "killing" itself. That is, after passing control to the newly installed malware, the malware installer unloads itself from memory and then deletes itself from the file system. This is usually done by the aid of a script that the malware installer placed on the system during installation. This vanishing act helps ensure that the antivirus (AV) researchers don't get their hands on the malware installer easily.

Note

Some droppers and downloaders require some level of user-interaction to gain root access to successfully install the malware it is deploying. With a sprinkle of social engineering and the malware installer's ability to not trigger any traditional AV solutions, the normal user will be more inclined to run it and grant it root permission to execute and install what it needs to on the system. Once the downloader gets this explicit permission, it can now successfully install and execute the malware on the same root context.

Dropper   A dropper (see Figure 5-2) is a malware installer that contains all the malware and all its components. It is like a typical software installer. Upon execution it installs the malware and all its components, aka the malware package, to the appropriate location in the system. Control of execution is then passed to the newly installed malware and the dropper exits, after which, the newly installed malware becomes active and ready to execute its directives.

Downloader   A downloader (see Figure 5-3), on the other hand, does not contain the malware package. Instead it downloads the package to be installed from the malware-serving domains. A downloader is similar to a download manager used by some software vendors wherein the user downloads a small executable, which upon execution, checks the system for compatibility and then downloads and installs the appropriate software package. The same thing is done by a malware downloader, except for the fact that it downloads and installs malware instead of legitimate software.

Tip

It is easy to determine whether a malware installer is a dropper or a downloader. The dropper's file size is significantly larger than that of a downloader because it carries with it the malware package it is tasked to install.

One major difference between a malware downloader and a malware dropper is that a downloader relies heavily on the target system having an Internet connection. If there is no connection, the malware downloader will continue to check until an Internet connection

Dropper — Installs Malware Package →

Figure 5-2 Malware dropper

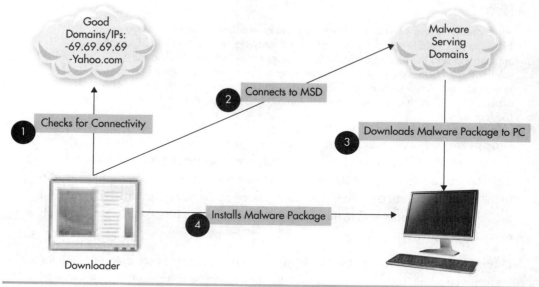

Figure 5-3 Malware downloader

is detected. Depending on how the downloader is designed or written, it can check for an Internet connection in a specific time frame, or it can check infinitely and stop only if an Internet connection is detected. The frequency of the checks can also vary depending on how stealthy the downloader wants to be. The less frequent the checks are made, the fewer network connection footprints it leaves. The more frequent the checks are, the noisier the downloader becomes, thus, increasing the risk of it being detected. If an Internet connection is finally detected, the downloader proceeds in downloading and installing the malware package.

But an Internet connection is not the only thing a downloader depends on. It also relies on the malware-serving domain being available or live online and the malware package being there. If one of these conditions is not satisfied, no malware is installed on the system.

To summarize, a downloader relies on the following to be able to install the malware:

- Internet connection
- Malware-serving domain availability
- Presence of the malware package in the malware-serving domain

The reliance of a downloader on these three things might be viewed by some as a disadvantage, but in fact it is more advantageous to the attacker because it decouples the main malware from the malware installer. This is in line with the principle that the more decoupled the technical elements are, the easier they can be disassociated with one another; thus, the discovery of one does not lead to the discovery of the rest.

Some advantages the downloader offers over a dropper or any malware installer that carries the actual malware with it are the following:

- The spread of malware is controlled. If the downloader finds itself in a system that is not intended to be infected—let's say the location is not in the target country—the downloader ceases operation and kills itself without revealing anything about the malware.

- The malware components are protected. The downloader does not carry with it the malware it is spreading. If AV researchers capture a downloader, the attackers can simply block access to the malware-serving domains, thus, rendering the downloader useless because it cannot be used to capture the malware it is spreading.

Note

Most downloaders are deployed using technologies that work only when the target system is online, for example, a URL link infection vector that serves as a fake antivirus scanner. The very nature of the infection vector establishes that the target system already has an Internet connection so there is no need for the malware installer to check for one.

When deployment is successful, a downloader is the one that first touches the target system. Aside from it being small in size, making it easy to deploy, it also does not contain the usual malware code that will trigger any security solution such as an AV scanner. It contains mostly codes similar to a typical software download manager.

Hybrid   As stated previously, downloaders rely on a target system having an Internet connection, the malware-serving domain being live, and the malware being present in the malware-serving domain. These three conditions have to be met to successfully install the malware. But in situations wherein the attacker does not want to be hampered by these limitations, even with the advantages the downloader offers, and just wants the target system infected the moment the malware installer reaches it, the attacker relies on a hybrid form of malware installer.

A hybrid malware installer functions as a downloader first to ensure that the

LINGO
A **hybrid malware installer** is also referred to as an online dropper. The word "online" is attached to convey the idea that the dropper has the ability to check for the presence of an updated malware package from the malware-serving domain similar to that of a downloader.

updated version of the malware is installed in the system. But instead of terminating execution when there is no Internet connection or when the malware is not located in the malware-serving domain, either because the malware is not there or the malware-serving domain is down, the hybrid malware installer proceeds with the malware installation process similar to that of a dropper by installing the malware package it is carrying. The newly installed malware then takes care of fetching the updates once the compromised system goes online.

Malware-Serving Domains

Malware components, configuration files, and updates to these files are hosted in a network resource called a malware-serving domain.

A malware-serving domain, or a serve malware site, is not limited to hacked legitimate sites or to specialized domains created for the sole purpose of serving malware. It can also be a legitimate site that is abused by the attacker to serve malware. Some of these often-abused legitimate sites used as malware-serving domains are online dropboxes, free web hosting sites, free cloud drives, or any site that users can upload to and download files from.

Using legitimate sites for the purpose of serving malware has its pros and cons. The main advantage is that it usually escapes URL blacklists. And the only way to find out the exact location of the malware being hosted in the legitimate site is through analysis of a captured malware sample. The main disadvantage is that some of the owners of the legitimate websites are quick to respond to reports of abuse, which results in the malware server being taken down easily. But unfortunately, not all are as quick to respond as others. There are still instances wherein response time takes almost a week even if there are abuse reports coming from reliable sources.

Command and Control

The C&C is where the malware or the bot agent gets its directives. The directives can be in a form of a command sent through the wire, a configuration file, or information posted on the C&C domain. C&C is the main communication point between the compromised machines and the attackers. Without the C&C, the malware inhabiting a compromised machine becomes blind. The malware will still continue to function, and even use the last directive it received as its guiding point, but without any new directives and the old ones becoming stale, it becomes useless.

As with malware-serving domains, benign network services can be abused and used as C&C. The most often abused sites that are used as C&C are Web 2.0 sites.

Drop Zone

A successful attack, especially one that involves stealing information, is always about two things: getting in undetected and getting out with the loot. Getting in and compromising a machine is just one aspect; the other is getting the stolen information into the hands of the attacker. This is done by using a drop zone. A drop zone is where stolen information is dumped by the malware. It can be any of the following:

- Local storage
- E-mail address
- Instant messaging (IM) account
- Domain

Local Storage   Dumping stolen information in a local storage or a specified location in the compromised machine was the usual practice by early information-stealing malware. The dumped information was usually encrypted and hidden somewhere in the hard disk, waiting for the attacker to grab it. This method became popular with attackers spying on other people who used systems that the attacker had access to or that were under his control. Early keyloggers and spywares were known to use this method of dumping stolen information, especially those that were offered for sale as monitoring software.

Note

Since most software vendors offer so-called monitoring software and have it in their end-user license agreement (EULA) that the software is to be used on machines the purchaser owns for the purpose of "monitoring" it, detection of these became a grey area in the antivirus industry. So the terms **greyware** and **riskware** came to be.

The availability of off-the-shelf information-stealing software that has keylogging capabilities made this method of collecting stolen information very popular, with people spying on their spouses and/or children, and also with people running Internet cafés that put this software, unknown to the users, in the personal computers that were rented out. And since they have access to and have control over the physical machines, collecting information from the system's local storage is as easy as turning on the system.

Tip

When using systems in Internet cafés, airport lounges, hotel business centers, and other places where PCs are available for public use, please refrain from visiting sites wherein you need to provide your credentials such as online banking and e-mails because there is no assurance that the PC is not rigged to collect this information. It is also advisable to run a free online virus scanner like those offered by Trend Micro and F-Secure to check for the presence of any information-stealing malware. But given the AV evasion technologies employed by malware, as discussed in Chapter 6, there is a big chance that most keyloggers or information-stealing malware will not be detected, especially those that are newly deployed by the attackers.

E-mail Address Accessing and moving stolen information dropped in the compromised system's local storage requires that the attacker have physical or backdoor access to the compromised machine. This method of collecting stolen information is not feasible for attacks that are aimed at thousands of target systems. Using backdoor access to actively collect the stolen information from the compromised machines is very risky because this means that the attacker has to do this for every machine that is compromised. This activity leaves traces, plus there's no telling which of these systems are already being watched.

So instead of the attacker going to the machine to collect the stolen information, why not let the stolen information go to the attacker? Sending stolen information back to the attacker via e-mail made this possible. It does not matter how many machines are compromised; the attacker simply waits for the stolen information to be e-mailed to him. He does not need to concern himself with accessing the compromised machines.

Instant Messaging Account Some attackers are fastidious. They want to get their hands immediately on the stolen data as soon as it is collected in a way that is faster than e-mail and with a minimal footprint.

E-mail revolutionized the way we communicate. Written messages can now be delivered and read faster compared to traditional snail mail. But it wasn't fast enough. People wanted to exchange messages in an instant, so instant messaging was born. Instant messaging became very popular very quickly. The exchange of messages is as quick as pressing the RETURN key. Plus, as with e-mail, instant messaging is not confined to text messages alone. Files can be sent using instant messaging protocols. Because of this, information dissemination became instant. This capability of fast information dissemination and the challenge of securing IM communications within an enterprise made the use of instant messaging an attractive way to deliver stolen information to the attacker. No matter where he is in the world, as long as his receiving instant messaging account is online, he will be able to get his hands on the stolen information in an instant. For this to work, however, the malware has to have the right instant messaging module, either built in or as a separate component.

Although the movement of stolen information is considered faster when using instant messaging, one disadvantage of this is that the receiving instant messaging account has to be online all the time. If this becomes unavailable, the stolen information has nowhere to go and is often dropped, unlike with other drop zones wherein the stolen information sits there archived waiting for the attacker to access it.

In Actual Practice

Some malware implementations do not settle on one drop zone alone. Some use a combination of different drop zones.

Domain Drop Zones   In most cases, instant access to stolen information is not needed but still the attacker wants to keep the transfer of stolen information as quiet as possible. Using domains as a stolen information drop zone makes the transfer much more under the radar. Information can be transferred in small chunks to the drop zone domain without triggering any defenses. Plus, the stolen information that is dropped in a domain is easily organized, compared to retrieving it one piece at a time from an e-mail drop zone or from a system hosting the attacker's receiving instant messaging account.

Although the use of online drop zones has become popular, some information stealers have not totally abandoned the use of local storage to tuck away stolen information. They often use it as a buffer store in case there is a connection interruption or the online drop zone is not available.

In Actual Practice

Domains or network resources used by the attackers are repurposed all the time. A domain that was used for C&C today can be repurposed by the attacker to be used as a domain drop zone the next day. Also in some cases, a single domain is used as a C&C, malware server, and drop zone at the same time.

Malware Components

The malware components or package consists of the malware itself plus component files that have specialized purposes. The following are the malware components that are often involved in an attack:

- The malware bot agent
- The rootkit component
- The regeneration component

- The attack component
- The configuration file

The Malware Bot Agent   The malware bot agent is the one responsible for communicating to the C&C. It sends status updates to the attacker and directs the components to do their purpose based on the commands it receives from the attacker. This is considered the main malware that ties everything together. It is also responsible for checking for available updates of the malware components from the malware serving domain.

The Rootkit Component   As discussed in Chapter 3, the rootkit component makes sure all the malware components are hidden. It protects the malware components from memory and file system enumeration tools and techniques. As long as the rootkit is active, the cloak over the malware components will remain.

The Regeneration Component   The regeneration component rebuilds malware. It periodically checks whether the malware still exists or not. If the malware does not exist anymore, probably due to a cleanup operation, the regeneration component rebuilds the malware from an encrypted backup source found in the compromised system or downloads it directly from a malware-serving domain.

LINGO
In some conversations and presentations I had, I fondly call the regeneration component as the **horcrux** of malware. The name horcrux came from J.K. Rowling's *Harry Potter* series. These are objects where Voldemort hid a piece of his soul to make himself immortal. As with malware, the horcrux component ensures that the malware regenerates every time it is removed or cleaned from the system.

The Attack Component   The attack component is the one responsible for, and that contains, the features that satisfy the main purpose of the attack. If the attack's main purpose is to gather information, the attack component can be a keylogger, a random access memory (RAM) scraper, or spyware. If the attack is designed to take down the compromised machine, the attack component might include Trojans that totally trash a compromised system. If the attack is designed to take down another machine, the attack component might include DDOS functionalities.

The Configuration File   The configuration file is the component that contains vital information for the other malware components. The information can include targets, special instructions, and all the network resources that the malware components need, such as malware-serving domain, command and control, and domain drop sites. Not all malware components come with a configuration file. Instead of getting information from configuration files, which are updated by the attackers from time to time, the malware components get their directive on the fly from the C&C.

Note

Malware components can be separate files or a single malware file that contains all the functionalities of the components. For malware components that are separate, some of them can be in the form of dynamic link libraries (DLLs) or DAT files that the main malware bot agent uses.

The Human Element

The group of people behind the threat ecosystem is commonly known as a cybercrime organization. A cybercrime family is a collection of opportunistic, business-minded, and highly skilled individuals banded together by a single purpose of reaping financial gain through the misuse of technology. A cybercrime family does not have to be collocated or even know each other in person in order to function. This maintains a level of protection between the people involved. As long as the practicalities, like communication and payment methods, are defined and understood between all the parties, the group will function. They can even be an exclusive or nonexclusive virtual group, exclusive meaning they only work with each other and no one else.

LINGO
Cybercrime organizations are also called cybermafia.

A cybercrime organization can be divided into different entities:

- The sponsor
- The technology providers
- The cybercrime boss
- The money mules

Note

All of these entities or roles can be one and the same entity. For example, a single attacker can be the sponsor, the cybercrime boss, and the technology provider. That individual has the funds, motivation, and knowledge of the target (sponsor), runs the show (cybercrime boss) since he only manages himself, and controls the technologies needed for the attack (technology provider).

The Sponsor

This is the entity that finances and directs the attack. A sponsor can be any of the following:

- Government
- Commercial organization
- Noncommercial organization

- Activist groups
- Terrorist organization
- Individual
- The cybercrime group itself

Although some sponsors are usually considered a third party or client of the cybercrime organization, their active involvement in the attack and reaping its rewards, plus the money they spend every time they employ these criminal organizations, make them part of what fuels the threat ecosystem.

A sponsor can be an active participant in the attack, like taking the role of a bot operator. But most sponsors, especially those that are involved with government and corporate espionage, always stay at the background with minimal contact with the cybermafia.

The Technology Providers

The technology providers are the highly skilled individuals behind the technologies of the threat ecosystem. They are the ones who research and develop the technologies, both malicious and benign, for use in an attack. They are known as

- Deployment providers
- Malware writers
- Botnet masters
- Resilience providers

Deployment Providers   Deployment providers supply the deployment technologies used in spreading the malware. They provide the latest infection vectors that are specifically tailored for the target. They also specialize in social engineering tactics needed to entice would-be victims. Aside from the deployment technologies they provide, they also own the platform from which these are all deployed, like e-mail spamming botnets and exploit hosting domains.

Note
Chapter 7 will discuss this topic in more detail.

Malware Writers   The malware writers are the ones with the real technical skills that create the malware. They are the brains behind the most sophisticated malware ever seen. They research a target system and find ways of circumventing it. This knowledge is then applied to their malware creation.

Since the cybermafia is an unholy alliance glued together by greed, everyone has to take steps to protect themselves, especially the malware writers. Some protect themselves by commoditizing their skills. Instead of having direct contact with the buyer, the malware writers create kits in favor of writing a customized malware. They pour their malware technology know-how into a kit, and anyone who wants malware for themselves does not need to conduct business directly with the malware author but instead only needs to buy the do-it-yourself (DIY) kit. The malware writers also provide the malware DIY kits that generate unique malware samples in bulk and armoring tools that enable the created malware samples to evade AV detection technologies.

Botnet Masters   The botnet master, or bot master for short, is the one who owns and maintains the botnet. The bot master has control over the compromised systems and owns the C&C the botnet communicates with. They tend to this collection of computer sheep that follow their whim; hence, they are also called bot herders.

> **LINGO**
> The terms **botnet master** and **botnet operator** are always thrown together, which causes a lot of confusion. A botnet master owns the whole botnet, while a botnet operator is someone who pays to get a slice of the botnet pie. For a price, the operator is granted access to operate part of the bot master's botnet. All bot masters are botnet operators, but not all botnet operators are bot masters.

Resilience Providers   Resilience providers own the network where the malware-serving domains, C&C, and other network resources needed for the attack are hosted. They provide bullet-proof domain hosting, fast-flux DNS services, and any applicable anti-takedown technologies that help keep communication between the compromised systems and the attackers alive.

The Cybercrime Boss

The cybercrime boss runs the show. This is the entity, individual, or group that organizes the technology providers and manages the technology they produce. This entity serves as the business manager of the organization and the middle man between the sponsors and the technology providers. This entity has close ties with the underground hacking scene and also with sponsors that want to operate in secrecy.

The Money Mules

Like mules transporting or moving cargo in a treacherous terrain that no vehicle can handle, money mules move money for the cybermafia. The money being moved is usually from buyers of stolen data, sponsors of an attack, or payment to technology providers. These are people who are unwitting participants in the malware business. As far as they are concerned, they are working as financial managers that process payments and they get a percentage cut for every payment they process. To qualify for this position, all they need is to have a bank account that can accept online transfers and knowledge of computers. The hours are flexible, plus they get to earn a lot of money without leaving their home. These people are recruited usually through e-mails or online ads, a sample of which is shown in Figure 5-4.

The process of moving money typically starts when a money mule receives a money transfer to his bank. He then transfers this to an untraceable bank account in a country with no money laundering laws. Or if the receiver of the funds elects to receive the money locally and fast, the money mule simply cashes out the money transfer and then goes to a brick-and-mortar money sending agency and sends it to a person—with a fake identity, of course—to a different city or state. Whatever method is used to move the money, there is always the element of untraceability, plus the money mule gets a cut just large enough to motivate him to continue with the job.

Sometimes money is not the only thing that is moved. In some instances, money mules receive parcels in the mail. Then they are tasked to mail it again, with no tracking and no return address, to a PO Box. Again there is the element of untraceability in this scenario. This is usually done when attackers use stolen credit cards to buy merchandise from the Internet.

FINANCIAL AGENT
This vacancy is valid for American, Australian, Bulgarian, Danish and Indian citizens ONLY at the moment.
AVAILABLE

Location: Australia, USA
Status: Opened
Employee Type: Part-Time Employee

The major duty of the incumbent is to promptly receive and process stockbrokers' payments to further transfer them applying specified method. Please enquire for detailed work scheme.

Requirements:

- Expert skill in managing payments and transfers between our company and clients.
- Knowledge of basic payment systems.
- Ability to schedule working hours effectively.
- Availability of spare time (3-4 hours per day).
- Advanced user ability to operate computer and to use Internet and e-mail.
- Legal age.

Payment basis: During the trial period you will be paid 1500 USD per month. You will also be keeping 8% commission from every payment received from a client. With the current volume of clients on average your overall income will add up to 3000 USD per month. After the trial period your base salary will go up to 2000 USD per month, plus 8% commission (**11% for financial agents with corporate bank account**).

Figure 5-4 A sample ad for recruiting money mules

The money mules think they have a legitimate job. They earn money and probably file taxes reflecting this work-from-home income. They always realize later that they were duped and used as pawns by the attackers when law enforcement agents come knocking on their door because their bank account was tagged as a possible conduit for money laundering, and credit card companies start contacting them on fraudulent purchases delivered to their address.

The Evolution of the Threat Ecosystem

The rise of the botnets redefined the threat ecosystem. Before, an attack was simply conducted and the attackers waited for the result. There was no control. They let something nasty go into the digital world, hoping that it will fulfill its purpose. If nothing happened for a period of time, the attacker assumed that the attack failed and the malware was eliminated or captured.

This is similar to a king deploying knights on a mission during medieval times. The knights were armed with the weapons they needed and briefed on their mission. But given the technology back then, instant communication to and from the kingdom was impossible. The king might discover new intelligence that needs to be acted upon immediately to ensure the success of the mission, but without any way to instantly communicate with the knights, he will not be able to direct them on the path to successfully fulfill their mission. The king simply hopes and waits for any indication of success, or sends out another party to find out the status of the mission and to communicate new information to the knights. As time goes by and nothing is heard, the knights are either presumed dead or captured by the enemy.

Now, with the introduction of new technical elements derived from botnets to the threat ecosystem, the attack has become more interactive. There is now control. Real-time status updates and instant communication between the attacker and the thousands of pieces of malware that sit on compromised systems is now possible. This is like the army of today. Armed with state-of-the-art communications, HQ can instantly communicate to the soldiers on the field, getting status updates and issuing commands.

The infusion of botnet technologies, coupled with advances in malware technologies, changed the threat ecosystem. Its evolution gave the attackers more control in directing an attack, making it more agile and able to react to the changing conditions of the target. This made the attack more successful, stealthier, and more dangerous because of the active participation of the attacker.

With better control and agility, the attackers are able to wage a campaign of silent and persistent attacks against specific targets, which earned this threat a new name: the advanced persistent threat.

Advanced Persistent Threat

First off, an advanced persistent threat (APT) is not any of the following:

- A new type of highly sophisticated malware
- A new method of attack
- An attention-grabbing attack
- An attack comprising a multitude of infections

But instead, it is:

- A targeted attack
- A well-thought-out attack
- An effective utilization of the threat ecosystem

LINGO
Advanced persistent threat originally was a military term.

There are lots of definitions of APT out there, but I always define it as:

- **Advanced** (adjective)   It is an advance attack because it is made up of a broad spectrum of infection vectors and malware technologies that are available to the attacker, blended together to result in a successful compromise of a system. What combination the attackers use is dictated by the result of the threat modeling they conducted.

- **Persistent** (adjective)   It is persistent because the threat of being compromised is always there. There is an active and conscious effort from the attackers to continuously attempt to attack a target system, resulting in a wave of a continuous campaign of attacks.

- **Threat** (noun)   This is not a typical, run-of-the-mill system compromise. This attack poses a real threat to the target not only because it is backed by highly organized, well-funded, and motivated criminal elements but also because if the attack is successful, it can have dire consequences for the target way beyond a normal system cleanup.

The Attack Method

This attack method is nothing new. It has been around for a long time. It was previously called "targeted attacks." But when the attacks on high-profile companies such as Google and Adobe became public, a new term, which is sexier, was introduced: the advanced persistent threat.

Unlike other attacks that are noisy and often garner lots of attention, APTs are more subtle and silent. Their motivation is to maintain a foothold on compromised systems while staying under the radar. The more they linger in a system, the more that system becomes their cash cow. It can be a source of a continuous flow of stolen data, or a system that becomes part of the attacker's botnet-for-rent business. In some instances, a successful attack can last undetected for years. To achieve this takes lots of work and patience from the attackers. They are willing to invest the time because they know that the payout is huge.

The attack can be divided into four stages:

- Identify the type of attack
- Gather information
- Compromise the system
- Execute the directive

Identify the Type of Attack

Depending on the sponsor's direction, an attack can result in any of these things or a combination of the following:

- Access to stolen information
- System takedown of a competing organization
- Sabotage of a competing organization

Access to stolen information is the most common attack type the APT is used for. The stealthy and low-key nature of the advanced persistent threat makes it a perfect method of attack for stealing information. The most common areas of targeted information are:

- Personally identifiable information (anything unique to an individual)
  - Social Security number
  - Health records
- Private information
  - Company log-in credentials
  - E-mail passwords
  - Social network passwords
- Financial information (anything that will grant access to an individual's or a company's money)
  - Online banking credentials
  - Credit card information

- Proprietary information (any important information that an individual or a company owns that is not for public consumption)
  - Source code
  - Trade secrets
  - E-mail and chat correspondence

System takedown of a competing institution is usually done in two ways: system destruction via Trojan functionalities or through DDOS attacks. For system takedown via a Trojan, a destructive payload is released once the malware is in, resulting in the system's destruction. For DDOS, takedown is more about crippling an organization's service and not total destruction of its system. There are actually two victims in this type of attack: the compromised machines used to launch the DDOS attack and the target institution bearing the brunt of the attack.

Sabotage of a competing institution can be in the form of planting false data once the systems have been compromised or the defacement of public-facing assets, such as the institution's webpage.

Gather Information

When plotting their attack, the attackers take into consideration different factors such as systems information, software installation, external and internal defense systems, and public-facing digital assets, among other things. The approach they take is similar to information security's threat modeling, but with the purpose of conducting a successful attack instead of defending against a possible attack.

Once a target is selected, information gathering begins. Information gathering is very important because the technologies that will be chosen to support the APT are dependent on the result of these findings. Information about the target is gathered from

- Public information
- Insider information
- System reconnaissance

Public information gathering is always the first step, and sometimes reveals enough information that there is no need to gather further information. Career ads, forums, and social networking sites are a good place to start. A very useful career ad posting is usually one that looks for technical positions to be filled, such as a system administrator. The applicant qualification for a system administration usually contains the skills to manage a certain server, skills about an OS, or skills about a security solution that is deployed in the company. From this information alone, the attackers are able to determine the server, the OS running in the server, and the security solutions deployed within the company. Another thing that is usually trolled by attackers is support forums where people ask for help on technical problems that they face inside their company. Forums are a gold mine for information, especially if the one posting the question uses his company e-mail address. Some even go to the extent of describing in detail the systems they are having problems with so the other posters in the forum can help them better.

Social networking sites are also a good source of information, especially those that are used in social engineering tactics. Take, for example, an executive posting that he had a good time attending a seminar in an exciting city in a boring state. This information just gave the attackers a good whale phishing topic headed to that executive's inbox.

> **LINGO**
> **Whale phishing** is a phishing attack against people holding executive and senior management position in an organization.

Insider information is always valuable, but not all attacks are afforded this convenience unless someone from within the company is willing to sell information, or in some cases, the sponsor is a disgruntled employee.

System reconnaissance work yields the best result, but it is more risky. This is where the cybercrime organization's hacking skills are put to the test.

After all the needed information is collected, the threat modeling begins. The attackers look for cracks that they can use to compromise the target systems. This includes holes or weaknesses in the following:

- Hardware (servers, workstations, routers, security appliances)
- Software (OS, security solutions)
- Human (executives, staff)

Once this activity is concluded, the technology to support the attack is chosen and the process of system compromise begins.

Compromise the System

When the technical components that support the APT are in place, execution of the attack commences, with the aim of full system compromise. Successful system compromise is achieved through careful selection of infection vectors, malware installers, and malware components. Once a system is compromised, the malware bot agent reports back to the attackers with a status stating that compromise was successful.

Note
Chapter 8 discusses this in detail.

Execute the Directive

After a successful system compromise, the malware bot agent waits for further commands from the attacker on what the next move or set of moves will be. The command is often inline with the attack directive requested by the sponsor. The directive can be communicated through the C&C channels once the malware reports back successful compromise, or it may be included already in the configuration file that came with the malware during installation.

The Attack Profitability

The attack must bear fruit. The sponsors expect a return on their investment (ROI) from the attack conducted. The ROI can be in the form of a successful takedown or sabotage of an opposing institution, or it can be in the form of stolen data.

Of all these, the most profitable in terms of liquidity is the one that gives access to stolen information. It usually has the best return on investment. The profitability of stolen information is what gave rise to a new breed of information-stealing malware, as discussed in Chapter 2, and was also the main driver that led to the evolution of malware from a nuisance to a real threat.

Some sponsors keep the information for themselves or release it freely to the public, while others sell it. Depending on the nature of the stolen information, it is usually sold to a competing business, another government, or to the public. Almost all the information can be sold to the public, but the most common information offered to the public is financial information such as credit card numbers and online banking credentials. See Figure 5-5 for an example ad posted in Pastebin.com.

The ad also includes the seller's contact information. Some sellers even offer trials wherein they will send the buyer a couple of credit card numbers to try out to seal the deal. Some hacker forums even offer reputation ratings for the sellers, similar to what Amazon and eBay have. Once a transaction is finalized and payment is ready to be made, the purveyor of stolen information uses several payment methods all designed to leave no trail pointing to the seller. The payment method of choice depends on the amount of money being moved and how risky a transaction is. It can be as simple as accepting prepaid credit or debit cards or a more robust payment processing method that involves finance managers and payment agents, also known as money mules.

Figure 5-5   A sample ad in Pastebin.Com selling stolen credit and debit card information

The willingness of sponsors to pay for an attack, plus the profitability and high return on investment of stolen information, made malware a thriving business. As long as the money keeps coming in, the cybercrime organization and independent technology providers will continue to provide service to whoever is willing to pay for it. This profitable underground trade became a bustling economy of its own.

Malware Economy

Economy, as defined by *Merriam-Webster*, is the process or system by which goods and services are produced, sold, and bought in a country or region. This definition also holds true in a malware economy. The only difference is that it is not bound by any country or region. As in a typical economy, money has to flow to keep the economy going. In a malware economy, money flows as shown in Figure 5-6.

Once an attack is conducted and the directive fulfilled, the sponsor pays the cybercrime boss. The cybercrime boss then takes his cut and pays the technology providers their share. If the attack type is data theft, the stolen information is liquidated, earning the sponsor a hefty sum. He then reinvests some of this money again to conduct another information stealing expedition, and the cycle continues.

Technology providers usually have their own independent ventures on the side, especially if their relationship to the cybercrime family is not exclusive. They offer their wares and services to whoever is interested. Figure 5-7 shows a typical ad commonly found in hacker forums.

The most profitable side business for technology providers, aside from renting out botnets, is the malware kit business. The latest malware DIY kit can fetch sums up to a thousand dollars. Competition in this space is stiff, causing one kit to remove the presence of a competing kit and its creations. Figure 5-8 shows an ad for a DIY kit.

Malware Outsourcing

As the malware economy grows, jobs are created. The bad guys realized that they couldn't do this alone, so some activities got outsourced to the public, which led to the introduction of a new malware affiliate program known as a pay-per-install scheme.

The scheme starts with attackers signing up and submitting to the pay-per-install (PPI) provider the malware samples they want deployed. The cost per installation depends on the conditions of the installation. A malware installed in a corporate system, for example,

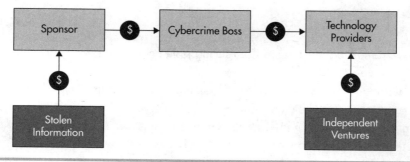

Figure 5-6   The flow of money in a malware economy

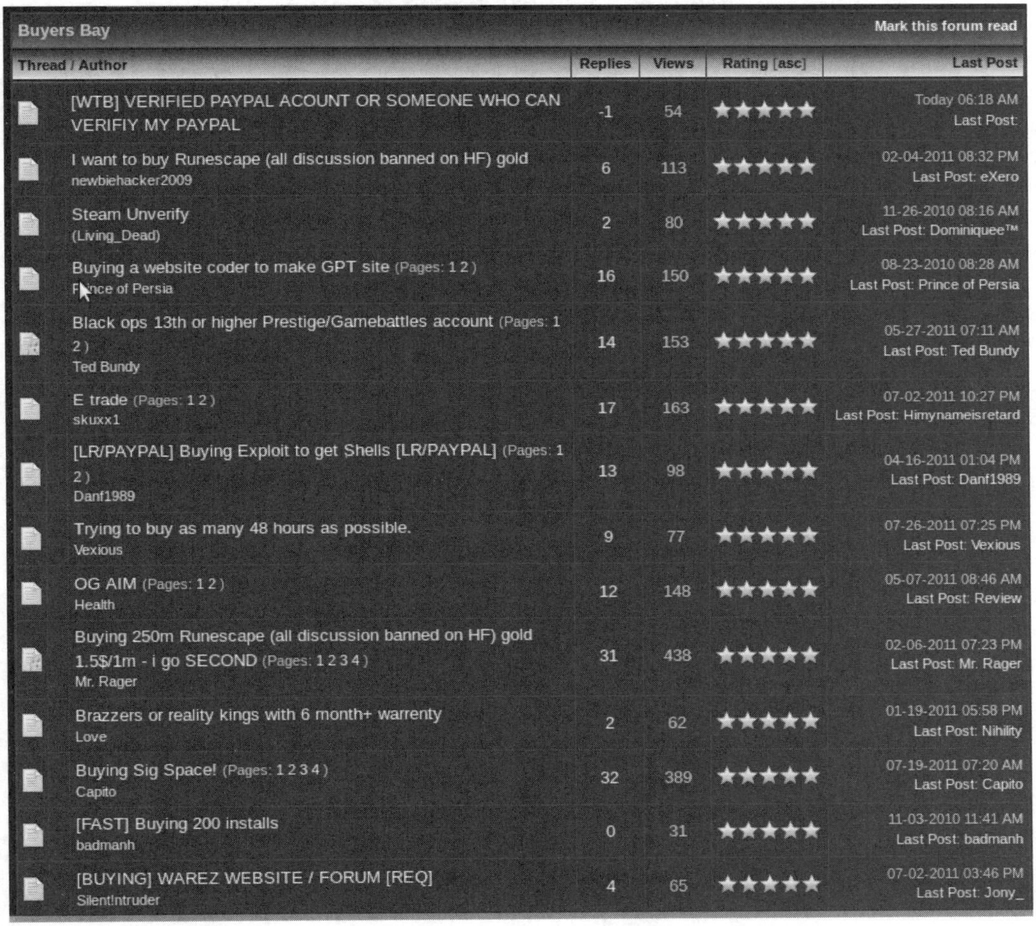

Buyers Bay — Mark this forum read

Thread / Author	Replies	Views	Rating [asc]	Last Post
[WTB] VERIFIED PAYPAL ACOUNT OR SOMEONE WHO CAN VERIFIY MY PAYPAL	-1	54	★★★★★	Today 06:18 AM Last Post:
I want to buy Runescape (all discussion banned on HF) gold newbiehacker2009	6	113	★★★★★	02-04-2011 08:32 PM Last Post: eXero
Steam Unverify (Living_Dead)	2	80	★★★★★	11-26-2010 08:16 AM Last Post: Dominiquee™
Buying a website coder to make GPT site (Pages: 1 2) Prince of Persia	16	150	★★★★★	08-23-2010 08:28 AM Last Post: Prince of Persia
Black ops 13th or higher Prestige/Gamebattles account (Pages: 1 2) Ted Bundy	14	153	★★★★★	05-27-2011 07:11 AM Last Post: Ted Bundy
E trade (Pages: 1 2) skuxx1	17	163	★★★★★	07-02-2011 10:27 PM Last Post: Himynameisretard
[LR/PAYPAL] Buying Exploit to get Shells [LR/PAYPAL] (Pages: 1 2) Danf1989	13	98	★★★★★	04-16-2011 01:04 PM Last Post: Danf1989
Trying to buy as many 48 hours as possible. Vexious	9	77	★★★★★	07-26-2011 07:25 PM Last Post: Vexious
OG AIM (Pages: 1 2) Health	12	148	★★★★★	05-07-2011 08:46 AM Last Post: Review
Buying 250m Runescape (all discussion banned on HF) gold 1.5$/1m - i go SECOND (Pages: 1 2 3 4) Mr. Rager	31	438	★★★★★	02-06-2011 07:23 PM Last Post: Mr. Rager
Brazzers or reality kings with 6 month+ warrenty Love	2	62	★★★★★	01-19-2011 05:58 PM Last Post: Nihility
Buying Sig Space! (Pages: 1 2 3 4) Capito	32	389	★★★★★	07-19-2011 07:20 AM Last Post: Capito
[FAST] Buying 200 installs badmanh	0	31	★★★★★	11-03-2010 11:41 AM Last Post: badmanh
[BUYING] WAREZ WEBSITE / FORUM [REQ] Silent!ntruder	4	65	★★★★★	07-02-2011 03:46 PM Last Post: Jony_

Figure 5-7 An ad showing buying and selling of malware commodities and services

will fetch a higher amount compared to one installed in a home user system. An infected machine located in the United States costs more than one installed in a third-world country. Depending on the agreed-upon conditions, the cost ranges from a couple of dollars to hundreds of dollars.

The PPI provider then advertises its need for affiliates in several websites and hacker forums. The affiliates are offered money, depending on the number of successful installations they are able to accomplish. The affiliates can be as creative as they want. They can resort to spamming all their friends, posting a link to their social networking sites, sharing the installers on file hosting sites, hacking to gain access to systems that they can infect, or even using the machines under their own control to install the malware.

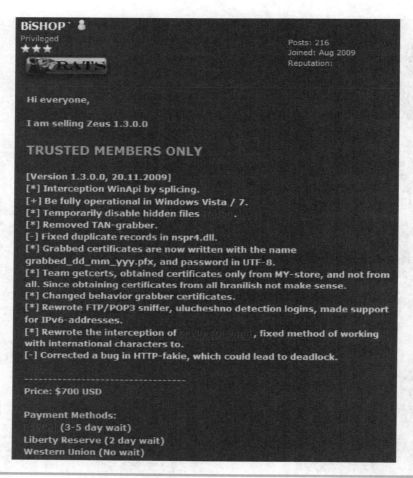

Figure 5-8   An ad showing the Zeus DiY Kit for sale

Unlike money mules, these affiliates know that they are in bed with the wrong crowd. Some of them are budding hackers or people who just want a piece of the action. This gig has become so profitable that some affiliates try to hack other affiliate accounts so they will get credited for installations made under those accounts.

Note
PPI is considered a deployment service; hence, it falls under the ownership of deployment providers.

We've Covered

- The technical elements that make up a threat ecosystem
  - Deployment technology
    - Physical media
    - E-mails
    - Instant messaging and chat
    - Social networking
    - URL links
    - File shares
    - Software vulnerabilities
  - Malware installer
    - Dropper
    - Downloader
    - Hybrid
  - Malware serving domains
  - Command and control
  - Drop zone
    - Local storage
    - E-mail address
    - Instant messaging account
    - Domain drop zones
  - Malware components
    - The malware bot agent
    - The rootkit component
    - The regeneration component
    - The attack component
    - The configuration file
- The different roles of the people behind a cybercrime organization
  - The sponsor
    - Terrorist organizations

- Governments
- Commercial or noncommercial organizations
- Activist groups
- An individual
- The actual cybercrime organization
- The technology providers
  - Deployment providers
  - Malware writers
  - Botnet masters
  - Resilience providers
- The cybercrime boss
- The money mules
- The nature of advanced persistent threats
  - It is a targeted attack
  - It is a well-thought-out attack
  - It is an example of effective utilization of the threat ecosystem
- The four stages of an attack
  - Identify the type of attack
  - Gather information
  - Compromise the system
  - Execute the directive
- Common attack types
  - Stealing information
  - Taking down a competing organization
  - Sabotaging a competing organization
- The underground malware economy
  - The flow of money in a malware economy
  - Hacker forums as a form of marketplace for sellers and buyers of malicious wares and services

CHAPTER 6

The Malware Factory

We'll Cover

- The malware incident handling process

- The basic antivirus product functions and features

- The different malware technologies for evading malware analysis and antivirus detection

- The different tools for evading malware analysis and antivirus detection

- The assembly line approach to building an army of malware

Chapter 5 introduced us to the different elements that make up a threat ecosystem, the individual or groups of individuals behind each element, and how these groups organized themselves to form a cybercrime organization. From this organization a new level of harmony between human and technical elements emerged that made attacks much more advance and persistent. The elements of the threat ecosystem have evolved to become a new support ecosystem for advance persistent threats, with each element having its own role to play that is vital to the success of the attack. But none is more important than the chosen malware.

No matter how successful the other elements of the threat ecosystem are, an attack is only as successful as the chosen malware. For the attackers, malware is an indispensable tool. Malware is the means by which they steal information from, take control of, or launch an attack using the targeted system. The more effective the malware is, the higher the chance it has in compromising a targeted system, and the more successful a malware is in compromising a targeted system, the more persistent the attack becomes.

For malware to be successful, it must take on and beat its long time arch-nemesis, the antivirus (AV) product. The AV product's main purpose is to detect the presence of malware in a system. To beat it, the malware must be able to evade AV detection. This need led to the development of multiple AV evasion techniques in malware.

But even with advances in AV evasion techniques, the attackers are still wary that one malware is not enough. History has taught them that a single malware is likely to fail. Once AV researchers catch it and a solution comes out, the attack is neutralized and the persistency of the threat is eliminated. No matter how many instances of this malware are out there, since they are all exact copies of the same malware, a single AV signature is enough to stop the threat. The attacker has to go back to the start of the infection process, wasting whatever success they had with the other elements of the advanced persistent threat (APT) on the way to compromising the system. The need to address this problem led to the use of multiple malware, better known as an army of malware in antivirus parlance. If one gets caught, the others pick up the slack and the system remains compromised. This is what makes the threat persistent.

In this chapter, I will discuss how the advances in malware technology enabled the attacker to create an army of malware that is able to evade AV detection and analysis, and how this process evolved from manual to the automated process we know today that is the malware factory.

The Need to Evade Antivirus

For malware to be successful, it must have the capability to evade AV detection. The attacker knows that every time malware is deployed, it carries with it the risk of being captured and scrutinized for the purpose of eradicating its existence. In previous chapters, I have discussed how malware hides or even destroys itself to avoid being captured. But what if the malware is captured? What safeguards must it possess to avoid being analyzed by AV researchers that ultimately leads to its detection and eradication by AV products?

Think of malware as a soldier. If the soldier is captured alive, the first thing that happens is that he gets interrogated. It can be a simple interrogation process initially that progresses into an enhanced interrogation process. Depending on the soldier's physical and mental toughness, he might spill the beans immediately or be stubborn enough that it takes forever to extract information from him. And if ever information is extracted, the question remains whether that information is reliable or not.

Similarly when malware is captured, it undergoes analysis (interrogation). It can be a simple malware analysis (simple interrogation) session initially that progresses into a full-blown malware reversing session (enhanced interrogation). Analysis is important because it is the first step in stopping the malware. Malware analysis not only reveals the malware's functions and capabilities, but also gives the AV researcher access to its most important asset, its code. Access to the malware's code strips the malware of all of its secrets and it enables the creation of an effective signature to detect and eradicate the malware.

As the soldier is able to resist interrogation, or at least prolong it by having the physical and mental toughness to do so, the malware writers want their malware to hide as much information as it can during analysis. The soldier develops these traits through years of hard work and training. But for malware to possess this capability, it has to be coded in. The malware writers must figure out what needs to be coded. They need to know the right ingredients to make this happen. They must know exactly what they are up against and then try to defeat it. They must understand how AV is stopping their creation.

They need to understand the following:

- How malware is handled by AV researchers
- How malware is detected by AV products

Having this knowledge will be the key to circumventing the antivirus product.

Malware Incident Handling Process

In the antivirus profession, every malware infection is considered an incident. AV companies have their own team of AV experts that respond to malware infection reports from all over the world. These are the good guys that are responsible for analyzing and creating signatures to detect and eliminate the malware infection. This process is called the malware incident handling process (MIHP). It is a straightforward process. When malware is captured or collected, it undergoes several stages of processing:

- Malware analysis
  - Static analysis
  - Dynamic analysis
- Reverse engineering

The first stage is malware analysis, which is divided into two smaller stages: static analysis and dynamic analysis. If the extracted information from static analysis is not enough, the malware undergoes dynamic analysis. If this still does not yield the needed information, the malware undergoes reverse engineering. The analysis produces several artifacts, the most important of which is the malware code. From this, a signature is created to detect the malware. The created signature is then deployed to the AV products so they can detect and remove the malware (see Figure 6-1).

Although the process is straightforward, the effort it takes for each process is directly proportional to the level of difficulty of the malware. The more advance and sophisticated the malware is, the more effort and time it takes to push out a solution to stop it. This buys more time for the malware to do more damage. To beat AV, the malware writers need to make their creation as difficult as possible to handle. To achieve this, a couple of things have to happen:

- First, the malware must be able to withstand analysis so no artifacts are produced that will lead to signature creation.

- Second, any solution that is pushed out to the AV products must be made irrelevant when it comes to malware detection and stopping the attack.

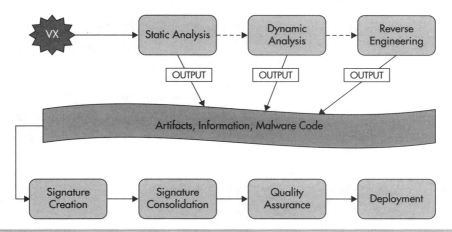

Figure 6-1   The malware incident handling process

Malware Analysis

Malware analysis is the process of gathering information from a malware short of reverse engineering. It is one of the main drivers of the development of new antivirus technologies. New malware technologies are often exposed through a combination of malware analysis and reverse engineering, and once these technologies or techniques are exposed, the development of an antivirus solution to counter these technologies is never far behind. Most of the time, all the information needed from malware can be extracted successfully through malware analysis, but in some instances where malware is proving to be difficult, reversing is needed. Malware analysis can be classified into two parts:

- Static analysis
- Dynamic analysis

Note

Malware analysis can be done without reverse engineering. Reversing malware is often the last resort if more information is needed.

Static Analysis   Static analysis is the process of extracting information while the malware is at rest. The malware file is subjected to different static analysis tools, such as PEiD, as seen in Figure 6-2, that are designed to extract as much information as

LINGO

In some circles in the industry, **malware analysis** has become synonymous with reverse engineering. These terms have been used interchangeably during conversations, but technically speaking, nothing can be further from the truth. Malware analysis does not equal reverse engineering. A lot of security practitioners can analyze malware, but only a few can really reverse it.

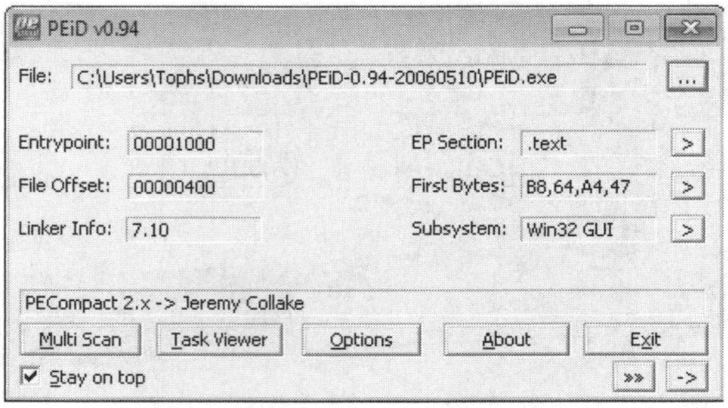

Figure 6-2   PEiD is a popular static analysis tool for gathering information from a Portable Executable (PE) file.

possible from the malware. The information collected can be as simple as a file type and as complicated as identifying maliciousness based on code.

Although static analysis is the easiest and less risky malware analysis process, it yields less promising results. It is the easiest because there are no special conditions needed for analysis. The malware is simply subjected to different static analysis tools. It is less risky because the malware is not running during static analysis so there is no risk of an infection occurring while analysis is taking place. It yields less promising results because its information gathering is based solely on what can be seen while the malware is inactive. And most of the time, there is more than meets the eye when it comes to malware. The most important stuff about it is revealed while the malware is active.

In Actual Practice

The most popular tools that are used for static analysis of Windows files can only be executed in Windows. Some AV researchers, such as myself, run these tools using WINE in Linux.

IMHO

My environment of choice for running static analysis tools is Linux, especially if I am dealing with Windows malware. Even though the malware is at rest, it is still better to take precautions and limit the risk of an infection coming from the analysis machine. One such precaution is the use of an OS that is not the target OS of the malware.

Dynamic Analysis   Dynamic analysis is the process of extracting information while the malware is in motion. Unlike static analysis's limited view of the malware, dynamic analysis offers an in-depth view into the malware's functions because it is collecting information while the malware is executing its directives.

Two things are needed to conduct dynamic analysis:

- Dynamic analysis tools
- Malware sandbox

The *dynamic analysis tools* are the ones responsible for extracting information while the malware is active. These tools monitor the different parts of the system for changes done or events triggered by the malware while it is running. These changes and events are then recorded and presented back to the analyst.

The dynamic analysis tools can be divided into two groups:

- Host monitoring tools
- Network monitoring tools

Host monitoring tools record changes that occur in the host, such as changes in the file system, modifications in configuration files, and any other relevant change that was triggered as a result of the malware's behavior. These tools also monitor the current state of the system such as enumerating the active programs running in memory that is triggered during system startup as shown in Figure 6-3.

IMHO

Sysinternals Suite contains some of the most useful host monitoring tools that are freely available, such as Autoruns and Process Monitor among others.

Network monitoring tools, on the other hand, record network events that occurred while the malware was active. The recorded information can include the ports, the protocols, the network packets, and the domains and Internet Protocol (IP) addresses the malware connected to.

A *malware sandbox* is an environment where malware is executed for the purpose of gathering information from its behavior and analyzing it. It is basically a bait system. This system is self-contained and not connected to any production systems within the company to minimize the spread of infection in case something goes wrong during dynamic analysis.

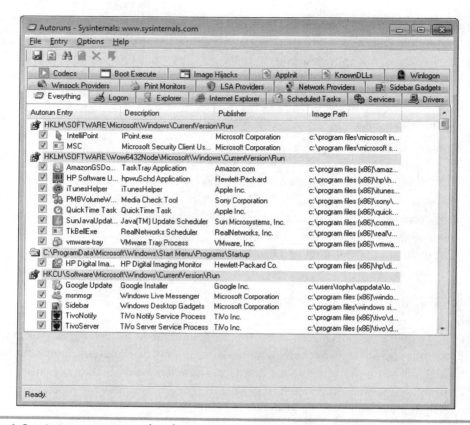

Figure 6-3   Autoruns is a popular dynamic analysis tool written by Mark Russinovich of Microsoft.

Depending on how the sandbox is designed and the selection of monitoring tools used, the output produced by a sandbox can contain some or all of the following:

- Host artifacts
  - System changes
  - Dump of malware code in memory
  - Dropped files
  - Modified files
- Network artifacts
  - Network connections
  - Packet captures

For a sandbox to be effective, the malware must run as intended. So a well-implemented sandbox needs to have everything that malware needs to execute. A sandbox can be implemented using a virtual machine (VM) or a bare-metal machine (BM). A virtual machine is an emulated environment that simulates a real system—in this case, a computer—while a bare-metal machine is the real system itself. No emulation takes place. The preferred choice mostly is a virtual machine because it offers several benefits. The OS images are easy to manage and deploy, plus restoration is quicker after each analysis session. Also in terms of hardware, it is cheaper. You can run multiple instances of it in a single system. A bare-metal system also has its advantages, one of them is that it is a real environment, which is what malware is intended to compromise.

The malware sandbox became so useful and popular that some security companies made this the core of their business. They researched and developed their own monitoring tools and sandbox implementation, which became their proprietary sandbox technology. Some of them offered this as a free online service (as illustrated here), while others offered a paid-for service in the cloud or a licensed version of their sandbox that can be deployed on site.

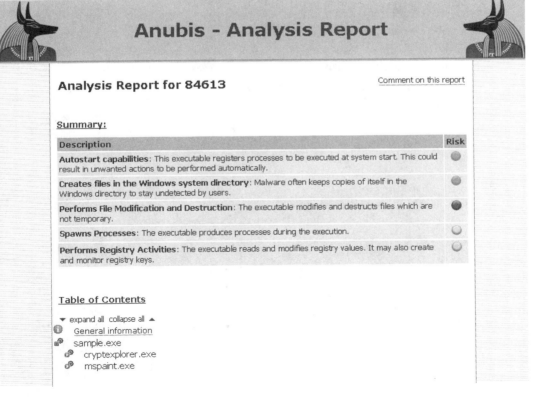

The ability to automate malware analysis was made possible by the advances in sandbox technologies. But one thing remained constant: a sandbox is still dependent on two things to be effective:

- The sandbox environment
  - Virtual machine
  - Bare-metal machine
- The sandbox technology

In Actual Practice

The number of malware samples a typical AV company receives daily from different sources that need to be processed averages almost 50,000. To handle this influx of malware samples, static analysis and dynamic analysis are done automatically. The samples are then classified to known malware families or known malware behavior based on the output of the automated malware analysis system. Most of these samples do not even reach the malware analysts' hands. If a certain sample needs further analysis and/or reverse engineering because the extracted information is not enough or it is something interesting and new, that's when it undergoes detailed attention from a malware analyst and/or reverse engineer.

Note

A sandbox in itself does not determine whether a submitted file for analysis is malicious or not. It simply tells the user the submitted file's host and network behavior.

In Actual Practice

Even though malware analysis is easily automated through the use of new sandbox technologies, AV researchers still maintain their own malware testing environment wherein they can run their own dynamic monitoring tools for longer periods of time and tweak the environment on the fly to effectively observe malware's behavior.

Malware Reverse Engineering

Even with advances in malware analysis—specifically, automated dynamic analysis utilizing advance malware sandboxing technologies—there is still no silver bullet in extracting information from malware. Some malware do escape unscathed revealing little to zero information. Although dynamic analysis offers an in-depth view of the malware while it is running, its view is still limited by the functions executed by the malware during the dynamic analysis session. If the malware has five major functions that reveal its real directives and only one is observed during analysis, the output of the analysis still does not paint a real picture of the malware's behavior. This is because if certain conditions are not met during dynamic analysis, such as any dependencies that malware needs to execute a crucial function, this behavior will not be recorded.

This is when reverse engineering is called for. Reverse engineering is the process of dissecting malware down to its code to reveal its nature. This is the most effective way of getting all the needed information, but it is not the most efficient one because it is very time consuming. To do an effective reverse engineering, reversers rely on the following important tools: disassemblers, decompilers and debuggers.

LINGO
Reverse engineers are also called reversers.

Disassemblers such as IDA Pro as seen in Figure 6-4 are tools that break down the malware into written code, typically in assembly. It is different from a decompiler; wherein the output of a decompiler is the original high-level language the binary is written from, but without the benefits of comments and highly identifiable variables. This is called the decompiled code. Debuggers, on the other hand, an example of which is shown in Figure 6-5 are tools that enable the reverser to trace the execution flow of the malware step by step and observe the changes done to the system per line of code as the malware executes.

IMHO
It is usually easier to read assembly language compared to reading decompiled code.

Malware Detection

Of all the information extracted from malware during analysis, the most important is its malicious code. Malware analysis reveals this by dumping disassembled code pointed to by the executable's entry point or by dumping code from memory. If malware analysis fails to

Figure 6-4 IDA Pro Disassembler by Ilfak Guilfanov is an essential disassembling tool for reversers, which also has its own debugger.

extract this information, reversing becomes the final resort. Access to malware code is what makes detection via signatures possible. The signature created to detect malware is based on the malware code. Without the malware code, no signature can be created.

Note
Creating signatures from malware code is not the only technology available for detecting and stopping malware. Signatures can also be created based on changes made by a malware to a system.

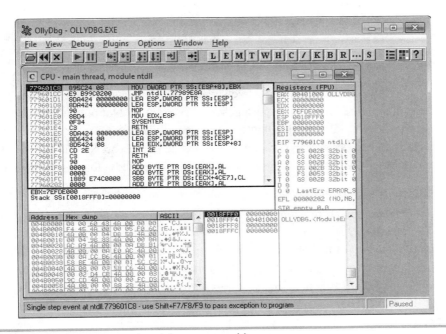

Figure 6-5   OllyDbg is a popular debugger used by reversers.

Understanding Signatures

AV products rely heavily on signatures, be it a simple hash, a collection of strings, a series of bytes representing code, or a complex set of identifying rules, to detect a piece of malware. But no matter how the signature is created, it is based mostly on the malware code. A matching signature results in a scanned file being tagged as malicious. If there are no matching signatures, then the file is assumed to be benign. The latter is what the attacker wants to achieve. To get a better understanding of signatures, let's look at how it is used by an antivirus product's scan engine.

During scanning of a binary, be it on disk or in memory, the scan engine looks for the entry point of the executable. The entry point is where the first instruction is located, and it is the key to following the execution flow of the binary. The entry point leads to the binary code itself. When the binary code is located, the scan engine compares all the detection signatures it has in its database to the binary code. If a match is found, then the binary is tagged as malicious.

Tip

For file infectors, the entry point leads to the malware code itself, because an infected file will execute the malware first before it passes execution to the host file. For packed files, the original entry point is important because it is the key to the location of the unpacked malware code in memory.

Note

Entry point only applies to executables. For nonexecutables such as Word documents and Portable Document File (PDF) files, the pointer to the malicious code is different.

So for a signature to be used effectively, the scan engine has to find the entry point of the executable first. See how important the entry point is? Not only is it important in malware analysis and reversing, but also in scanning. Scanning is an automated representation of an AV researcher's knowledge. If an AV researcher knows how to find the entry point, it will not take long for this ability to be coded into the scan engine.

Specific and Heuristic Detection

Malware detection using signatures falls into two categories: specific detection and heuristic detection. Specific detection means that there is an exact signature match that identifies the malware. The exact match can be a hash of a nonreplicating and nonmodifying malware, or it can be a series of bytes found in the malware body that represents a malicious function. Given this exact match, the antivirus product can specifically name the malware sample it detected, for example, W32/Conficker.C. If a scanned file did not match any signatures that result in a specific detection, heuristic detection kicks in. Of course, this depends on whether this feature is enabled or not.

Heuristic detection is the process of determining whether a scanned file is malicious through a set of predefined rule sets that make up a heuristic signature. This detection method does not do an exact match; rather, it searches for similarities. If it is similar enough, a scanned file is tagged as possibly malicious. Heuristic detection uses two methods to tag a file as possibly malicious:

- Heuristic classification
- Heuristic behavior

Heuristic classification is a detection method that compares the scanned file's characteristics to those of known malware families. Each malware family is represented by predefined rule sets. For example, if a scanned file's characteristics closely resemble those of Conficker's, the detection output would look like this: W32/Conficker.Generic.

Heuristic behavior, on the other hand, is applied when a scanned file does not match any known malware families. Instead, it compares the scanned file's characteristics to those of known malicious behaviors. Each known malware behavior is represented by predefined rule sets. For example, a detection name of Trojan/Keylogger.Generic indicates that the scanned file has similar behavior to an information stealing keylogger.

Specific detection and heuristic detection are designed to complement each other as seen in Figure 6-6. Specific detection covers malware that is already known, while heuristic detection covers those that are not known but have malware-like characteristics.

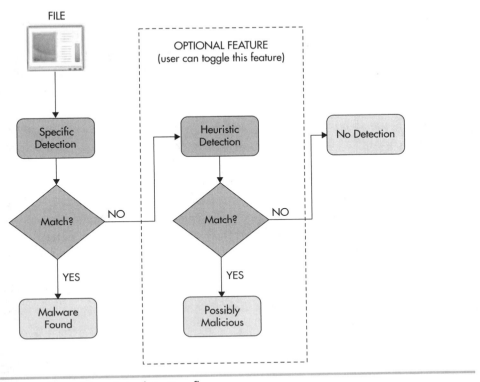

Figure 6-6   Specific and heuristic detection flow

IMHO

Heuristic detection's main aim is to detect zero-day malware. Heuristic detection tends to be slow because it uses more CPU and RAM. Although some antivirus vendors are continuously addressing this problem and have made significant improvements, some users still disable this feature. Depending on what you are protecting and the available resource of the system where the antivirus product is running, you can decide whether to have this feature enabled or not. But to help you on your decision, I would suggest leaving this on unless the performance of the system is below the threshold for it to function properly. It's always cheaper to buy RAM and CPU power compared to the cost of reparation after a system compromise.

Static and Dynamic Scanning

Armed with specific and heuristic detection, the antivirus product is now ready to scan and detect for the presence of malware in a system. Scanning takes place in two ways: static scanning and dynamic scanning.

Static scanning is the process of determining whether a scanned file is malicious or not by checking the file's physical image. A physical image is how the file appears on disk. Static scanning is also responsible for detecting the presence of malware as it is downloaded from the Internet or copied from a different media. The file's physical image does not change when it is being downloaded or copied. The file is just split up for transport and is rebuilt while being written to the disk.

Dynamic scanning is the process of determining whether a scanned file is malicious or not during runtime. Technically, some implementation of dynamic scanning simply scans the file's virtual image. A virtual image is how the file looks while it is running in memory. Depending on the OS, a file, when executed, may look similar or totally different on disk than in memory. During the DOS days, there was only one scanning technology because the file's image did not differ whether on disk or in memory. For Windows, it's totally different. The image on disk does not always equal the image in memory.

Tip
A good way to remember the difference between the two is that static scanning is used when the malware is at rest (static = not moving) and dynamic scanning is used when the malware is running (dynamic = moving).

This is the reason why a file on disk is sometimes not detected as malicious (especially when it is armored), but when it is running in memory (armors off) it is detected as malicious. This is especially true for encrypted or packed files. These files are decrypted or unpacked as they are loaded in memory. This decrypted image then triggers a match to one of the signatures, causing it to be detected as malicious.

Note
Everything in memory is decrypted. No matter how the malware is armored, for the malware code to be executed and encrypted data to be processed in memory, it has to be decrypted.

On-Demand and Real-Time Scanning

Scanning, be it static or dynamic, is utilized through two basic scanning features: on-demand and real-time scanning.

On-demand scanning is a user-invoked scanning of files in the system, be they on disk or memory. The first time an antivirus product is installed, it invokes an on-demand scanning of both disk and memory to make sure the system is clean before installation. Real-time scanning means that the antivirus product is active in memory and is monitoring both the file system and memory continuously.

Circumventing the Antivirus Product

The malware's most important asset is its source code. This is the key to everything,

LINGO
You might have noticed that I have used the term **scanning** to describe static, dynamic, real-time, and on-demand. This is because they are all related to file scanning. Their only difference is the state the scanned file is in and when the scanning occurs. Static and dynamic scanning are methods of inspection based on a scanned file's state (at rest or in motion), while real-time and on-demand dictates when the scanning occurs (always on versus upon request).

including detecting the malware. To beat AV, malware writers need to prevent access to the malware code. No malware code, no signature. No signature, no detection. The malware writers know that for AV researchers to get their hands on the malware code, the malware needs to undergo analysis and reverse engineering, which exposes its code. And when this happens, the malware must be strong enough to resist it.

To do malware analysis and reverse engineering, AV researchers rely on the following:

- Malware analysis tools
  - Static analysis tools
  - Dynamic analysis tools
- Reverse engineering tools
  - Disassemblers
  - Decompilers
  - Debuggers
- Malware test environment
  - Malware sandbox

These are the main assets that the AV researcher needs to do his job. If these assets don't work, analysis and reverse engineering will be challenging. To evade analysis, the malware must render these assets useless. To better understand how this is achieved, I have grouped the tools based on the state the malware is in when they are used.

- Tools used when malware is at rest
  - Static analysis tools
  - Disassemblers
  - Decompilers
- Tools used when malware is in motion
  - Dynamic analysis tools
  - Debuggers
  - Malware sandbox

But evading analysis is just one part of the equation of circumventing the AV product. The other part is evading detection. Analysis is driven by the AV researcher using tools, while detection is driven by the AV scanner armed with signatures. These are the two things the malware is really up against: the AV researcher and the AV scanner. The AV scanner is the digital representation of the AV researcher. Whatever the AV researcher knows about the malware, it is passed on to the AV scanner in the form of signatures and configuration files. One thing stands out when it comes to similarities between the two, that is, they both work on malware while it is at rest and in motion. While the AV researcher uses different sets of tools depending on the malware's state, so does the AV scanner. It uses either static scanning technology or dynamic scanning technology. The common denominator is the state of the malware. The malware only has two states: at rest and in motion. For malware to circumvent AV, it has to protect itself whatever state it is in.

Protecting the Malware at Rest

Malware at rest is up against the following:

- Malware analysis
  - Static analysis tools
- Reverse engineering tools
  - Decompilers
  - Disassemblers
- Antivirus scanning technology
  - Static scanning

It is often believed that malware at rest is defenseless. This is where the malware is at its most vulnerable state. It is fully exposed and ready to be sliced and diced by the AV researchers and subjected to AV scanning. It is like a body about to be autopsied. The coroner has the body in front of him, ready to be examined from head to toe and from the outside to the inside. He has his trusty scalpel to cut open the body and examine further what's inside. His assistant is beside him taking notes of everything he finds out about the body so that the information can be used to identify similar cases. Now imagine that body suddenly wrapped in aircraft-grade titanium exposing no skin. The coroner immediately finds out his scalpel is no match against the metal. His trusty tool is now useless. As a result, the coroner cannot do his job and proceed with the autopsy to gather information. Without any information, his assistant has nothing to use to identify similar cases.

Malware is exposed in the same way when it is captured. The AV researcher, with the help of his tools, gathers information to be passed on to the AV scanner in order to detect similar instances of the malware. But if the malware is armored, extraction of information will be very difficult, if not next to impossible. To protect malware at rest, the malware writers introduced malware armoring.

Since the most important asset of the malware is its code, preventing access to it renders static analysis tools and static scanning useless. This is done through code obfuscation. The most common obfuscation techniques are:

- Entry-point obscuring
- Basic malware encryption
- Polymorphism
- Metamorphism

But what about the tools used by reversers? The malware writers know that in time, no matter how long it is, reversers will be able to figure out how to beat code obfuscation. But if the reversers cannot disassemble or decompile the malware while it is at rest, they will not have any code to aid them in reversing. So the malware writers introduced antireversing techniques specifically aimed at protecting malware at rest:

- Antidisassembler
- Antidecompiler

Entry-Point Obscuring   I have already stressed the importance of knowing the executable's entry point. Without the entry point, there is no pointer to the code itself. Since scanning also makes use of the entry point to locate the malware code, hiding it is advantageous, not only for protecting against analysis but also against static scanning. Hiding a malware's entry point is known as entry-point obscuring (EPO). EPO is often used by file-infecting malware. When a malware-infected host file is executed, the malware gets executed first before the host file. This is because during infection, the malware modifies the host file's entry point to get control of the execution flow first before the actual host file. After the malware finishes execution, the control is passed back to the original host file. This behavior of file-infecting malware made it easy for AV researchers to locate the malware code. But EPO malware does things differently. The entry point does not point directly to the malware code. To illustrate this, I will use an EPO technique that uses code patching (see Figure 6-7). This technique, instead of passing control immediately to malware, lets the host program execute some of its code and then somewhere along the way a patched instruction will pass control to the malware. And once the malware is finished executing, it lets the host program finish executing. This is especially effective in fooling the AV scanner because the AV scanner is led to a set of instructions that is benign instead of the actual malware code.

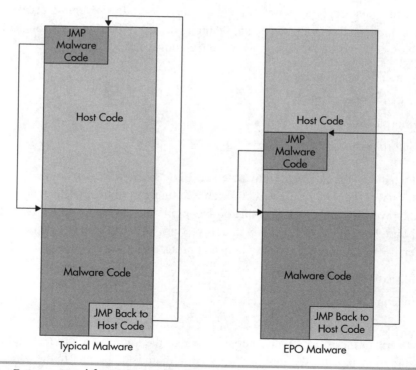

Figure 6-7 Entry-point obfuscation via code patching

Malware Encryption   Another powerful code obfuscation technique is malware encryption as seen in Figure 6-8. Unlike EPO, malware encryption protects the malware code itself. The advances in malware encryption produced a new breed of encrypted malware: the polymorphic and metamorphic malware. This new breed of encrypted malware set a new bar, not just in terms of evading analysis but also in terms of static detection evasion. And malware encryption became a new buzzword in the industry.

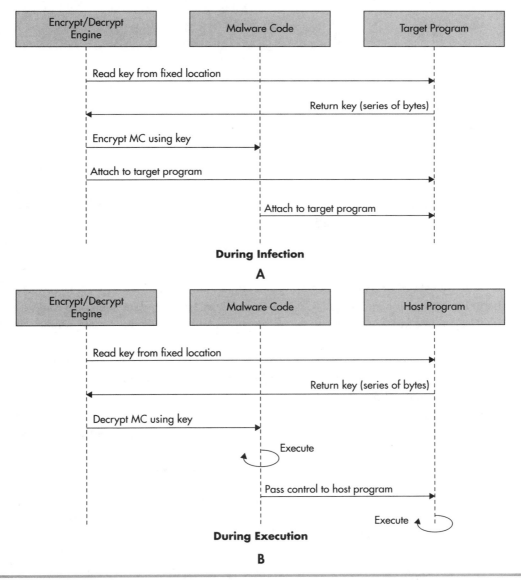

Figure 6-8   Basic malware encryption

This is one of the most important advances in malware technology because it made a significant impact in the overall threat landscape.

To better understand malware encryption and how the technology evolved, I will discuss it in the context of file infectors. An encrypted malware has three major components: the encryption/decryption engine, the encrypted malware code, and the decryption key. When the malware is executed, the encryption/decryption engine decrypts the encrypted malware code using the decryption key and then the control is passed to the decrypted malware code in memory for it to do its intended purpose. Upon infection, the decrypted malware code is re-encrypted using a different key before it attaches itself to the newly infected host program. The key can be a series of bytes from a specific location in the host program. The location is constant, but the bytes found in that location differ for every target file. This makes the keys different in every infection. Because of this, the malware code attached to different host programs differs. No two infections are exactly alike.

Although this method was cutting edge when it was first introduced, the antivirus industry was able to catch up pretty quickly because one out of the three components remained constant. The decryption key was always different, the encrypted malware code was always different, but the encryption/decryption engine remained constant. Using the encryption/decryption engine codes, antivirus products were able to create a signature to catch this basic form of encrypted malware.

Polymorphism   The malware authors, not wanting to be outdone, introduced a new malware technology known as the mutation engine. The mutation engine, which is part of the malware code, basically alters the code of another application without changing that other application's function. The mutation engine made possible the alteration of the decryption code so all of the three components are now different for every infection. This new form of malware encryption is called polymorphism as seen in Figure 6-9. Polymorphism is defined by *Merriam-Webster* as "the quality or state of existing in or assuming different forms," which aptly defines what polymorphic malware is.

But polymorphic malware is not free from weaknesses. It still needs to decrypt the encrypted malware code in memory, and every time the malware code is decrypted it is constant. It goes back to its original form. Since it is constant, a signature can be created to detect it in memory or through antivirus emulation techniques. Polymorphism is highly effective in defeating static scanning but not new advances in dynamic scanning.

Metamorphism   To counteract the AV technologies that can detect encrypted and polymorphic malware, the malware authors introduced a new form of encrypted malware called the metamorphic malware as seen in Figure 6-10. With the mutation engine on hand, the malware authors approached the problem differently. Instead of working with the three components of malware encryption, they shifted their paradigm completely.

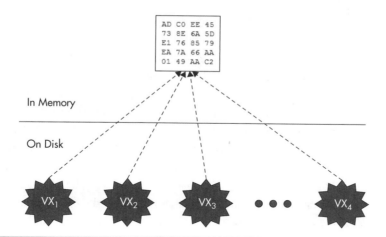

Figure 6-9   Polymorphic malware infections differ on disk, but are the same in memory because the decrypted code in all infections is the same.

They realized that with the mutation engine, they could just mutate the whole malware code itself, freeing them from the inherent weaknesses of the basic malware encryption approach. With metamorphic malware, each infection is totally different, both on disk and in memory. Metamorphic malware also has its weaknesses, because for it to morph it needs to analyze its own code to reassemble it to its new form. If it can do this, then reversers can do it as well.

Note
Metamorphism is so powerful that it is used not only in file-infecting malware but in other classes of malware as well.

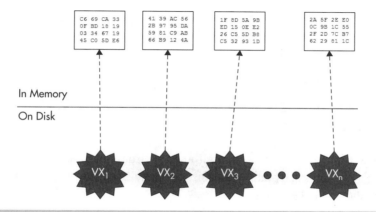

Figure 6-10   Metamorphic malware infections differ on disk and in memory.

Antireversing Going back to the coroner analogy, to continue doing his job, he needs to figure out how to cut through the metal, remove it, and expose the body. This can be done by studying the armor and looking for a weak spot that can be used to break it. Same goes for the AV researcher—he needs to figure out what to do to beat armored malware. Code obfuscation, no matter how elegant, can be beaten through reverse engineering. The only enemy is time and effort. The malware writers, not wanting to take the risk, introduced antireversing techniques to slow down or make almost impossible the process of reversing. The most common antireversing techniques for protecting malware at rest are antidecompilers and antidisassemblers. This denies reversers access to the source code of the armored malware to prevent them from figuring out how the armor works and how to beat it. The drawback of this technology is that it only works for the decompilers and the disassemblers the malware supports. This is because decompilers and disassemblers, like other software products, have their own proprietary algorithm and implementation. For example, an antidisassembler implementation in one malware might defeat the Win32DASM disassembler but not the IDA disassembler. But if the decompiler or disassembler that the malware supports is the most useful and popular with reversers, then the malware's antidisassembler feature has done its job. But still, reverse engineering can beat this, and again, the only enemy is time and effort. The more time it takes, the better for the malware. This is what the malware writers aim for. They want to buy more time for their creation to do its deed.

Protecting the Malware in Motion

Malware in motion is up against the following:

- Malware analysis tools
  - Dynamic analysis tools
- Reverse engineering tools
  - Debuggers
- Malware test environment
  - Malware sandbox
- Antivirus scanning technology
  - Dynamic scanning

When static analysis fails to extract information from malware, the malware undergoes the next stage of analysis: dynamic analysis. Dynamic analysis is the process of extracting information, through the use of dynamic analysis tools and sandbox monitoring technologies, from malware while it is running in a self-contained sandbox. If the malware does not execute, no information is extracted and the whole process fails. But malware is designed primarily to execute to do its job. To beat dynamic analysis, the malware must be intelligent enough to know whether it is running in a target system or in a malware test environment.

Anti-Sandboxing   Most malware test environments, such as a malware sandbox, are usually implemented as a virtual machine because of the many advantages it offers. So for malware to know whether it is running in a sandbox, it only needs to know whether it is running in a virtualized environment. This led to the development of what has become the most popular anti-sandboxing technology: the antivirtualization technique. If malware detects itself to be running in a virtual environment, it will exit and do nothing.

Note

Given the trend of most organizations moving to a virtualized environment, some enterprise-targeting malware uses other checks to determine whether it is running in a virtual sandbox or in a virtualized corporate environment. If it is running in a virtualized corporate environment, it continues with its execution.

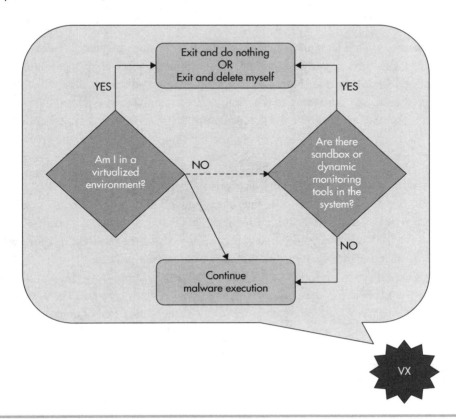

Figure 6-11   Anti-sandboxing technology in action

The bare-metal environment solves the antivirtualization feature of malware, but it costs a little more and is slower when it comes to restoration time compared to its virtual environment counterpart. But this in itself is not perfect, because the AV researcher still needs to run the dynamic tools and/or the proprietary sandbox technology of choice to gather information from malware. This gave the malware writers an opening. To beat a bare-metal environment, the malware writers concentrated on another critical ingredient of dynamic analysis: the tools used to gather information from malware during runtime. As with other software, these tools leave footprints in the system whether they are running or not. The malware writers familiarized themselves with these footprints and armed their malware creation with the ability to detect the presence of these tools via their footprints in the system. If the malware detects the presence of these tools, it will exit and do nothing.

Note

The popularity of VM-aware malware led to the belief that having a virtual system was actually safer than a nonvirtualized one. Also, some systems were made immune to malware infection by simulating the fingerprints of several tools that malware looks for before it proceeds with its execution.

Like other malware technologies, anti-sandboxing can be defeated. It can be in the form of a new virtualization technique, a new silent dynamic analysis tool, or a new sandbox technology distribution. But then again, the malware writers will simply familiarize themselves with these new technologies and enhance the anti-sandboxing feature in their malware. And the cycle repeats itself. It has become a race. The malware writers grew tired of this. So instead of playing the sandbox race game, they decided to change it.

Environment Lock   Remember my previous statement: Malware is designed primarily to execute to do its job, but it must be intelligent enough to know whether it is running in a target system or in a malware test environment. This is the ultimate goal that the malware writers want to achieve. They need a new approach to solve the problem. If they succeed, the battle against dynamic analysis will be won—at least for now.

Every time I discuss this topic, I am always reminded of an old story that was making the rounds via e-mail about a decade ago. Whether the story is an exaggerated and overdramatic version of the history behind the development of the Fisher Space Pen or not doesn't matter. It has some valuable lessons to impart.

During the space race back in the 1960s, NASA was faced with a major problem. The astronaut needed a pen that would write in the vacuum of space. NASA went to work. At a cost of $1.5 million they developed the "Astronaut Pen." Some of you may remember. It enjoyed minor success on the commercial market.

The Russians were faced with the same dilemma.

They used a pencil.

Sometimes no matter how complex the problem seems, the solution can be very simple. The malware writers were locked in a race against the AV researchers for the "Astronaut Pen." So instead of continuing into the sandbox race, they introduced a new anti-sandboxing technology: the environment lock feature. This is their "pencil." This feature makes the malware execute only on the environment it compromised. It does this by taking environment-specific markers, such as hardware ID, media access control (MAC) address, or anything that is unique to the system, as variables and then adds this information as conditions for its execution. If the malware is moved to another system, these variables will not match; therefore, the malware will not execute. So catching this type of malware and submitting it into a malware sandbox for dynamic analysis will not yield any result. This was essentially a win for the malware writers. It virtually defeated dynamic analysis.

Anti-AV Scanning   But for malware to undergo analysis, it has to be captured first. Usually the malware is captured in a target system that the malware compromised. These systems often have AV products installed. So the first real encounter the malware has is against the AV product. To avoid being detected, captured, and analyzed, the malware has to avoid the technologies used by AV products.

Malware writers know that the AV product can only defend systems from the threats that they know of. This knowledge is represented by the detection signatures it has that can specifically detect and identify the malware. For malware that is totally new and not covered by specific detection, the AV product uses heuristic detection. Depending on how the heuristic signatures are written and the amount of data sets from which they are based upon, it can be effective or not. And to ensure that the system is always protected, AV products scan in real time. This means that the products reside in memory, keeping a watchful eye on the file system on disk and the programs loaded in memory.

Depending on how the malware arrives in a target system, it undergoes scanning immediately. If it is downloaded from the Internet or arrives as an attachment in e-mail, it undergoes static scanning. But we already know that static scanning is easy to defeat, so almost all the time, malware is executed in a target system. Once malware is running, the AV product uses dynamic scanning to inspect the malware during runtime. Depending on the current signature database of the AV product, the malware might get detected using specific detection or heuristic detection. But before being matched to any existing signatures, the AV scanner must be able to find the malware code. No matter if it's static scanning or dynamic scanning, the flow of scanning is the same. The only difference is that in dynamic scanning, the one being scanned is the malware's image in memory.

Since the flow is the same, some code obfuscation techniques that worked in protecting malware at rest also work in protecting malware in motion. The most effective techniques that work for both states of malware are entry-point obscuring and metamorphism. These techniques also help in delaying analysis and reverse engineering in case the malware is captured.

Another technology used by malware writers to avoid dynamic analysis is to turn off the AV product altogether and deny access to AV vendors' websites. The same concept as the one used in detecting the presence of dynamic analysis tools is used to detect the presence of AV products. But instead of exiting, the malware turns off the AV product that is running.

In Actual Practice

Most malware undergoes not only automated analysis, but also automated signature creation. If the malware that is processed happened to be metamorphic, the automated system has no way of determining this. As a result, the signature from the system can detect only a specific form or generation of the malware, while the others that are totally different slip through AV.

Armored Malware

The development of malware technologies that protect malware at rest and in motion produced a new generation of armored malware that is able to effectively evade analysis and detection, making conventional AV solutions irrelevant. An armored malware can contain any combination of the following technologies:

- Anti-analysis technology
  - Code obfuscation techniques
  - Antidisassembler/decompiler
  - Antidebugger
  - Antimonitoring tools
- Anti-sandboxing technology
  - Antivirtualization/emulation
  - Anti-sandbox (publisher-specific, e.g., anti-Anubis, anti-GFI)
  - Environment lock

- Antidetection technology
  - Code obfuscation techniques
  - Disable AV

The Need for an Army of Malware

The development of AV evasion technologies shows how heavily the attackers are invested in their malware. But they know that sooner or later, the malware will get caught, and if the malware gets caught, that's the end of the attack. But what if one malware picks up the slack if the other is captured? This makes captured malware dispensable. As AV pushes out new signatures to detect and eliminate malware, new malware takes over, which is not detected by the newly deployed AV signature, rendering the AV solution irrelevant. It is irrelevant because even though it stopped the malware, it did not stop the attack. The system remains compromised.

To achieve this, an army of malware is needed whose members are totally different from each other in form but not in behavior. An army of malware is a cluster of malware that is totally unique from each other. No two samples are exactly alike. The only thing that is the same is their purpose.

Next-Generation Malware Kits

The malware writers already have existing malware technologies in their hands to create an army of malware. They just need to put them together. One technology is the mutation engine found in metamorphic malware. The ability of metamorphic malware to change its form on every infection made it the first ever real malware army. It takes on different forms, with each of these having the same purpose. The only downside is that the production of new forms is relatively slow because it depends on the infection process. Another technology that is already in existence is the malware creation kit. The malware creation kit is a convenient way to create an army of malware because it has the ability to produce malware in bulk, much faster than metamorphic malware. The downside is that the malware produced by early malware creation kits is easily detected because they do not sufficiently differ in form.

The mutation engine made possible the ability to modify code without sacrificing its functionality, while the malware creation kit enabled the ability to create malware samples in bulk. Both of these technologies have the capability to create malware with the same purpose. Individually, they have their own advantages and disadvantages, but together they form a very powerful technology that preserves their advantages and virtually eliminates their individual disadvantages. The result is a new malware kit that can produce malware samples in bulk that are unique in form, but with the same purpose. But this is not enough.

A battalion commander will not let his soldiers go to the battlefield without any protection. They are not only armed to the teeth, but also have with them the most advanced protective gear to protect them from enemy fire. Same with an army of malware—malware that is deployed for infection, no matter how many and how different they are, without the proper armor, when captured, can be easily analyzed. The army needs armor.

Before, the process of armoring malware was done by coding the features into the malware itself. But with an army of malware, this is not feasible anymore. Imagine coding all these features one by one into thousands of malware samples every day. This is not smart. The answer is coding the AV evasion technologies into the malware kit itself. This is the next generation of malware kits (see Figure 6-12). It's an all-in-one kit that endows each created malware with the most advanced AV evasion technologies. The result is an armored army of malware.

Stand-Alone Armoring Tools

The next-generation malware kits gave attackers a powerful and dangerous weapon. But this is not the only weapon they have. Why? Because even though the malware creations have the ability to make AV irrelevant, an AV researcher getting his hands on a malware

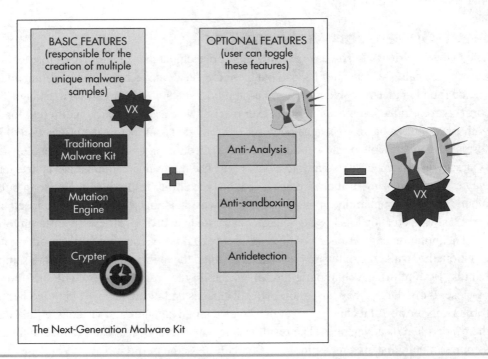

Figure 6-12   The next-generation malware kit

kit and reversing it will have with him the knowledge on how to detect and eliminate the creations of that malware kit. The other weapons prevent this from happening.

The other weapons attackers have are stand-alone armoring tools (see Figure 6-13). These tools can be applied on both the next-generation malware kit to protect it from being reversed and the kit's malware creation to further enhance its AV evasion capabilities. There are many stand-alone armoring tools, but the most popular are the following:

- Crypters
- Real-time packers
- EXE binders

The crypter is the stand-alone tool version of the malware encryption routine. Its main purpose is to encrypt the malware to avoid detection. Real-time packers, on the other hand, do not only encrypt but also compress a binary, making code reversing much more difficult. The original technology behind real-time packers is primarily used to hide proprietary code from the competition. But like any other tools or technologies, if it serves the attacker's purpose, it will be used with malicious intent. They have been used extensively to encrypt and compress malicious codes. The end result is a self-executing compressed and encrypted file.

Note

Some real-time packers, such as NeoLite, have the ability to change the malware code itself, similar to a mutation engine.

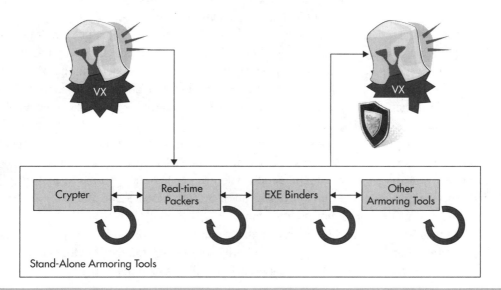

Figure 6-13   Enhancing the malware further with stand-alone armoring tools

While crypters and real-time packers already pose a challenge to the AV products and essentially kill static analysis, the use of the EXE binder makes it more difficult. The EXE binder is the stand-alone tool version of the malware infection routine. It binds a malware with a benign binary—hence the name EXE binder. This saves the attacker time in making a noninfecting malware enticing. The attacker does not need to follow the route of the early Trojan horse authors; instead, he just needs to find an interesting executable, such as a game, and then bind his malicious code to that. This tool is special because it plays a major part in social engineering. Individually, all these tools are effective in AV evasion, but together they make the malware much more slippery and dangerous.

> **LINGO**
> **Packed file** pertains to binaries that are packed using real-time packers. Do not confuse this with self-extracting archive files that are a product of compression tools such as ZIP and RAR. A packed file decompresses and decrypts itself in memory; then the unpacked code executes immediately after that. A self-extracting archive is an executable that dumps the decompressed file to the hard disk for later use without invoking the software associated with the compressed file.

The Impact of an Armored Army of Malware

Stopping an army of armored malware is never easy. AV researchers often take two types of approaches: a quick fix and a right fix. The quick-fix approach to stopping an army is the deployment of multiple specific signatures for detection. This is a one-is-to-one detection. Each captured member of the army has its own signature. The right-fix approach concentrates on the deployment of a single "catch-all" signature aimed at detecting not just the members in the possession of the AV researchers but the whole army. Obviously, the first approach is not feasible and scalable. It is not an effective and efficient solution. It is ineffective because it only covers what the antivirus researchers were able to capture; and it is inefficient because it will dramatically increase the size of the signature database being pushed out to AV products. But sometimes AV companies resort to this shortcut or quick fix due to response time constraints. A detection signature has to be deployed immediately to stop the infection. There is just not enough time to analyze and reverse the malware to find a better solution. Researchers need to quickly stop the bleeding first while working on a better cure.

The second one is the right approach, but it requires a lot of work in malware reverse engineering. This is usually done after the initial solution to stop the bleeding has been deployed. But even if this is the right approach, it still has its limitations:

- First, the "catch-all" signature is based on a finite data set of captured malware samples. It is only as good as the number of captured malware samples.

- Second, if the malware is sporting a new technology in AV evasion, the AV product must have the appropriate technology to address it.

- Third, this approach relies heavily on reverse engineering. So before anything else, reverse engineering must be successful.

If the malware is too difficult, it will take a long time to come up with a solution, and the AV product is stuck with the quick fix. By the time a solution is discovered, the attackers are already using a new army of malware. This gives the attacker another advantage. An army of malware not just renders the pushed AV solutions irrelevant. It also renders the AV companies' response ineffective and inefficient.

In Actual Practice

The influx of a high number of malware samples increased the reliance of AV companies in automated signature creation systems. Although it helped to some degree in addressing quantity, the quality of signatures has suffered greatly. It fails to address metamorphic and armored malware and false positives, such as those on known system files that have been an issue in recent years.

The Malware Factory

The stage is set. The AV evasion technologies, the next-generation malware kits, and the stand-alone armoring tools are now all available to the attacker. The availability of these tools in the attacker's arsenal made the attacker much more dangerous. It gave the attacker the capability to create an army of highly resilient malware. And with a little scripting and automation know-how, the attacker is able to create thousands of malware a day using an assembly line approach that I call the malware factory.

The Malware Assembly Line

The malware assembly line approach has streamlined the process of creating an army of armored malware. It also made possible the recycling of old detected malware binaries and codes to produce a new army of armored malware. See Figure 6-14.

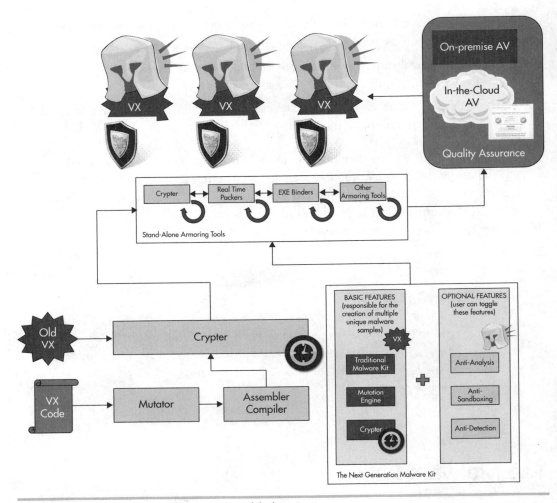

Figure 6-14 The malware factory assembly line

The assembly line is divided into three stages:

- Base malware sample creation
- Stand-alone tools armoring
- Quality control

Base Malware Sample Creation

An assembly line always starts with a base malware built from a next-generation malware kit, some examples of which are shown in Figure 6-15, or derived from an old binary or an old malware code. The first stage is where the base malware samples are created.

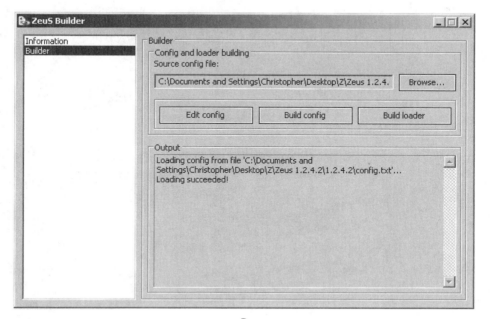

Figure 6-15   Two of the most notorious malware kits known today are SpyEye and Zeus.

This is where an old malware binary is being recycled, where an old malware code is being mutated and then compiled or assembled into a new malware binary, and where the next-generation kits are producing an armored malware. A recycled malware and a newly assembled binary, before going to the second stage, pass through a crypter first, since these two types of base malware do not have the technical capability of kits to create an infinite variation of malware samples. One way a crypter solves this problem is by using date and time, down to the microsecond, as key.

Stand-Alone Tools Armoring

The second stage is where the fun begins. This is where the base malware samples undergo different armoring. The second

LINGO
Armored malware is also called highly resilient malware.

stage may include one or a combination of the following tools: crypters, code obfuscators, packers, AV evasion tools, and EXE binders. The end result is a highly resilient armored malware. Figure 6-16 shows some examples of stand-alone armoring tools.

In Actual Practice

Not all stand-alone tools are local or on-premise. Some services are offered online, such as the Indetectables-Crypter, shown here.

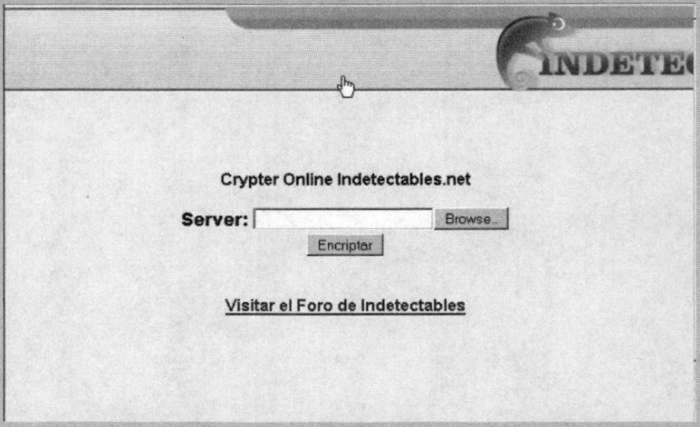

INDETE

Crypter Online Indetectables.net

Server: [_____] Browse...

Encriptar

Visitar el Foro de Indetectables

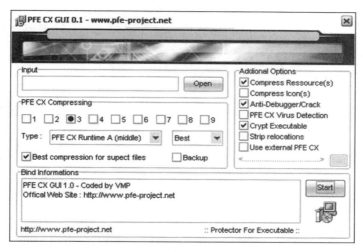

A

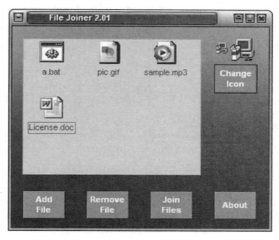

B

Figure 6-16   Some of the most common stand-alone armoring tools.

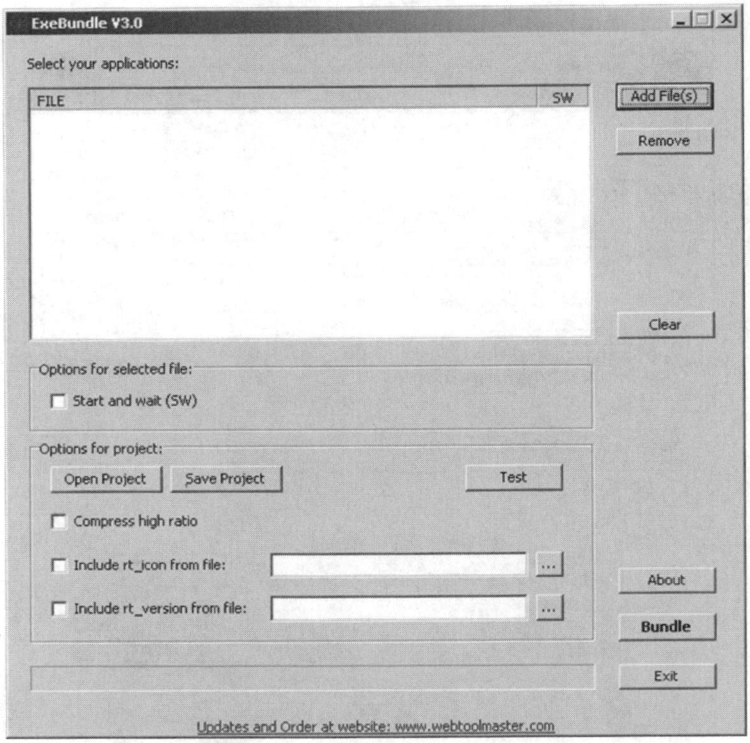

C

Figure 6-16   Some of the most common stand-alone armoring tools. *(continued)*

Quality Control

The third stage makes sure that the newly created army of malware will succeed. The malware samples produced by the malware factory undergo quality control before they are deployed for their mission. The quality target is almost always antivirus evasion. So the final step in the process is to check whether the end product is detected by AV products or not. Some malware factory implementations have their own multiscanner (see Figure 6-17), while some use free online malware scanning services such as NoVirusThanks (see Figure 6-18). The advantage of using NoVirusThanks compared to other scanning services is that it offers the option not to distribute the submitted files to AV vendors. Once the samples pass this quality assurance step, they are now ready for deployment.

Figure 6-17   An example of a multi-AV scanner tool used in a malware factory.

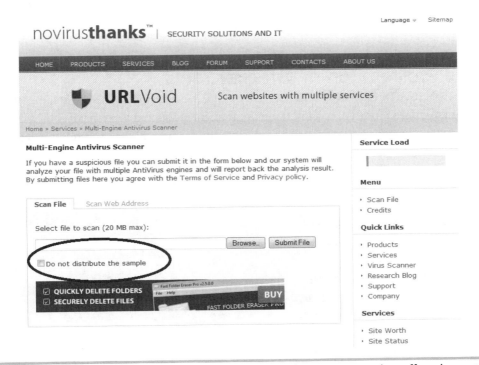

Figure 6-18   NoVirusThanks.org is a popular online malware scanner that offers the option not to distribute submitted samples to AV companies.

Tip

Submitting a sample to online malware scanning services is often avoided by the attackers because the sample gets submitted to antivirus companies. Online malware scanning services are usually used for hash searches.

Note

There are two types of online malware scanning services. One type is the one I discussed wherein you submit a file or query via hash and it tells you whether that file is malicious or not. The other type is like an online antivirus product that scans your disk for malware.

In Actual Practice

Not all malware samples need to be undetected by all antivirus products to be deployed. This depends on the antivirus products used by the target company. For example, if the target enterprise uses Symantec, the attackers will consider the malware samples ready for deployment if Symantec does not detect the samples even if other antivirus products do.

The Proliferation of Attacker Tools

The tools used in the malware factory are not that hard to find. Although some of these tools are offered for sale, most of them are free, including old versions of tools that were previously for sale. And even those new versions that are still for sale are often leaked to the public because of fierce competition in this underground economy. So someone with the motivation and know-how to use a search engine can get a hold of these tools (as illustrated here), assemble his very own malware factory, and create an army of highly resilient malware under his control. Did somebody say disgruntled employee, opportunistic hacker, or script kiddy?

Malware Population Explosion

The ability to create an army of armored malware by using the malware factory approach gave the attackers enormous advantage, resulting in the increase of the success rate of an attack. Almost all attacks involving malware came with an army of thousands of malware. It's a surge. It's like thousands of zombies running after you with one purpose, and that is to eat your brains.

The malware factory is one of the reasons why the number of unique malware samples seen in a given time period has increased throughout the years. The other reason is the proliferation of attacker tools on the Internet, giving anyone with malicious intent the ability to create his own army of armored malware.

According to AV-Test.org, they processed an average of 54,000 unique samples per day in 2010, up from an average of 33,000 unique samples per day in 2009. A decade ago, they were just processing roughly 500 samples per day. Figure 6-19 shows year-over-year growth of unique malware samples.

If you do the math, that's one unique malware sample created every 1.6 seconds. And these figures only show the number of malware samples that have been seen or discovered. It does not take into account the thousands more that are lurking out there that were not caught. It is expected that this number will continue its exponential growth in years to come, causing a massive malware population explosion.

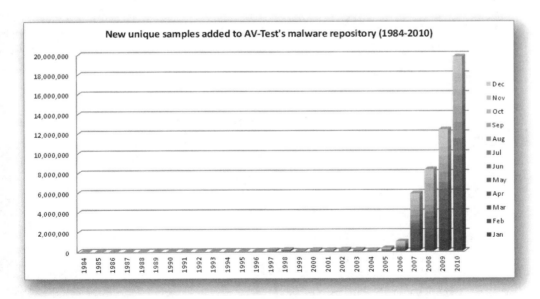

Figure 6-19   Year-over-year growth of unique malware samples added to AV-Test.org's repository.

It seems that the malware factory is in full swing. This is one factory that will not be closing down anytime soon.

We've Covered

- The malware incident handling process
  - Malware analysis
    - Static analysis
    - Dynamic analysis
  - Malware reverse engineering
- The basic antivirus product functions and features
  - Malware detection through signatures
  - Specific and heuristic detection
  - Static and dynamic scanning
  - On-demand and real-time scanning
- The different malware technologies for evading malware analysis and antivirus detection
  - Entry-point obscuring
  - Malware encryption, polymorphism, and metamorphism
  - Antireversing
  - Anti-sandboxing
  - Anti-AV static and dynamic scanning
- The different tools for evading malware analysis and antivirus detection
  - Crypters
  - Real-time packers
  - EXE binders
- The assembly line approach to building an army of malware
  - Base malware sample creation
  - Stand-alone tools armoring
  - Quality control

CHAPTER 7

Infection Vectors

We'll Cover

- The different ways malware is delivered or deployed to a target system

- The common social engineering tactics employed by infection vectors

- The characteristics of infection vectors that attackers take into consideration when deciding the deployment method for their malware

- The different URL obfuscation techniques employed by attackers

- The common buffer overflow techniques to get control of program execution

- The characteristics of a technology that gives it a potential of becoming an infection vector

The rate at which malware is produced is staggering. With the capability of automatically producing an armored army of malware with advanced antivirus (AV) evasion capabilities, the attackers have virtually beaten antivirus solutions. Chapter 6 showed us how the attackers achieved this through the development of different malware technologies, the advancement in attacker tools, and the development of the assembly line approach to building new and recycling old malware called the malware factory. This resulted in a massive malware population explosion.

    With an armored army of malware at the attacker's disposal, this chapter will show the different techniques attackers use to deliver their malware into a target system.

Infection Vectors

To deliver or deploy malware into a target system, attackers utilize what is called an infection vector. It is the means by which malware is able to infiltrate a target system. It is the malware's transport system. To be able to compromise a system, the malware installer must install the malware components successfully. But before this can happen, the malware installer must find its way to the target system. It does this through the use of an infection vector.

    As seen in Figure 7-1, infection vectors deliver one or a combination of any of the following: the malicious binary

> **LINGO**
> Infection vectors are also known as attack vectors.

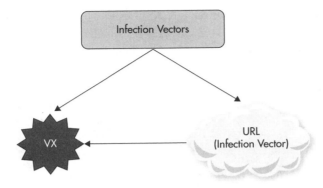

Figure 7-1   Infection vectors and their payload

or a Universal Resource Locator (URL) link that hosts the malicious binary or the exploit that enables malware to be installed. URL links are special because even though other infection vectors deliver it, it is also an infection vector itself.

The following are common infection vectors utilized by attackers:

- Physical media
- E-mail
- Instant messaging and chat
- Social networking
- URL links
- File shares
- Software vulnerabilities

In Actual Practice

Not all attacks utilize an installer to install the malware components. In some cases, the one that is deployed through the different infection vectors is the malware itself. Once executed inside the target system, it installs itself to the proper location and makes the necessary changes to the host to ensure its continuous survival. This is especially true in old malware families. But not all malware needs to install itself in the system to thrive. Take, for example, the infamous MS-SQL Slammer that exists only in memory.

No matter what type is used, these infection vectors have one important mission and that is to have the malware installer or the actual malware, if it is the one being deployed, execute in a target system. This is the measure of success of an infection vector. Aside from the infection vector's technical aspect, social engineering also contributes to the success of an infection vector. Some of the most common social engineering tactics employed by infection vectors are listed here. An infection vector can utilize one or a combination of any of these:

- Coming from a trusted source
- Has a sense of urgency and importance
- Arouses the interest

Each infection vector has its own unique quality. A certain infection vector might be well suited for a certain attack but not another attack. Or it might work well with a specific malware installer but not with other malware installers. The choice of which infection vector or a combination of any of them to use depends on the result of the information-gathering stage of an attack as discussed in Chapter 5 and the characteristics of each infection vector as described here:

- Vector coverage
- Vector speed
- Vector level of interaction
- Vector shelf life

The coverage of an infection vector is a measure of how many targets it is able to reach the moment it is deployed. It can be limited to a single target at a time, or it can cover a multitude of targets. Vector coverage takes into consideration only getting the malware within reach of the targets. It does not take into account whether the malware being delivered by the infection vector is able to execute in the target system. So, for example, if an attacker sends out e-mail with a malicious attachment to one million e-mail addresses, the attacker is able to reach a million targets in a click of a button, but that does not mean that all those one million recipients will open and read the e-mail.

The speed of an infection vector is a measure of how fast the infection vector reaches a target. Some infection vectors take a long time to reach a target because it involves human movement, such as getting from point A to point B, or it can be as fast as a mouse click because it travels solely in cyberspace where speed is only limited by the bandwidth the target system has. Same with vector coverage—vector speed only takes into consideration getting the malware within reach of a target.

The level of interaction of an infection vector is a measure of how much human involvement is needed to get the malware installed on the target system once the vector reaches its target. Some vectors need a certain level of human interaction to get their malware installed, while some totally eliminate the need for this. For example, malware delivered through e-mail as an attachment needs a human to execute it for it to be installed in the target system, while malware delivered through a vulnerability can be installed in the target system without any need for human action.

The shelf life of an infection vector is a measure of how long an infection vector remains effective in deploying the malware it is carrying. Some infection vectors depend on a small window of time to be effective. Once that window of time closes, the infection vector's chances of deploying the malware diminish or even vanish. A vector's shelf life takes into consideration the vector alone and not the malware. Even if the vector has a very long shelf life but the payload it is carrying is detected by AV solutions, then no matter how sophisticated the vector is, it will fail.

Physical Media

Physical media was the first widely used infection vector of malware. During the dawn of personal computers, data was transferred from one system to another using floppy disks. So this was the main vehicle of choice for malware during that time. Early file infectors were written with the aim of infecting files within a single computer. The only ability they had of moving to another system was when an infected file found itself in a disk and that disk was used in another system.

The coverage of this vector is limited to those who have physical contact with an infected media. Because of this, infection is usually confined to a single geographical setting, such as a neighborhood, a school, or an office, unless the infected media finds itself in another location. In this case, the malware will have a new local chapter of infected computers in that location.

As for its speed, it is very slow because it depends on human movement. For this vector to reach an intended target, it has to be physically passed on to the target.

The level of interaction of this vector is high. For the malware to be installed in the system, the user or the attacker has to manually insert the physical media into the target system and execute the malicious file it is carrying. Now with physical media, a malicious file can be executed manually, which is considered a high level of interaction, or it can be executed automatically, which is considered a low level of interaction. Files in physical media can be executed through auto-execution capabilities offered by the OS. Depending on the setting of the operating system of the target system, a newly inserted physical media can automatically execute a file that it is carrying just by inserting the media into the target system.

Regarding its shelf life, as long as the physical media is supported by the target system, it will never expire. As long as computers use physical media, this vector will be around.

You might think that, with some of the characteristics I described regarding physical media as an infection vector, attackers will abandon it as a choice for spreading their malware. But in fact, they still use it today, both in targeted and opportunistic attacks. All it takes is a little social engineering to make it work.

Consider the two scenarios here. The first is one way the vector can be used for targeted attacks and the second is one way it can be used for opportunistic attacks.

A person standing outside a building of a well-known software company with

> **LINGO**
> **Opportunistic attacks** are attacks that do not have a specific target. The main goal is to have as many system infections or compromises as possible.

a bag full of free Universal Serial Bus (USB) sticks, passing it around to employees going in and out of the building, is all it takes to get an infected physical media inside a target organization. Offering it for free is already enough to get it into the hands of employees, but adding labels such as "30-day trial of Online Game X" or "90-day trial of AV Software X" can make it more enticing, thus, increasing the chance that the employees will stick it into their work or home PCs. Now, some companies have protection in place against unauthorized physical media being used in company assets, but the majority of them don't. If you are able to copy to and from a USB stick fresh from the store in your work PC then your company is vulnerable to this infection vector.

Another scenario is someone planting malicious binaries in CD-ROMs containing bootleg software. The buyer will surely get more than what he bargained for. It's like the attackers are saying, "You can get the full line of Software X for just $9.99. But wait, there's more!!! It also comes free with keyloggers and data stealers!!!"

E-mail

The potential of an e-mail vector in terms of coverage and speed makes it very attractive to an attacker. But to get the malware running in the target system, some level of human interaction is still needed.

The coverage and speed of this vector far exceeds that of physical media. An e-mail vector's coverage is massive. Anyone with an e-mail address is a potential target. In terms of speed, the malware is delivered to the target in seconds after it is deployed.

For this vector to be successful, some level of interaction is needed, unless the e-mail is packing technology that will enable the malicious binary it is carrying to execute and install silently in the system. Some technologies that make this possible are embedded script that is triggered just by previewing or opening the e-mail and code that exploits vulnerability in the e-mail client. But without these technologies, the reader must open the e-mail, read it, and do as the message recommends. Before, malicious attachments are compressed and password-protected to avoid detection, but given its high level of interaction, the e-mail has to be convincing enough for the potential target not to be too lazy to take the time in decompressing the password-protected file with the password supplied in the e-mail and execute it. But with advancements in AV evasion techniques and the capability of producing an army of malware, the attackers are now doing away with password protection to avoid detection and simply deploying nonpassword-protected compressed files, as seen in Figure 7-2. One positive side effect of this for the attackers is that it is lowering the level of interaction needed for the vector to be successful. But even if human involvement is lowered, the e-mail still has to be believable enough for the potential target to take action.

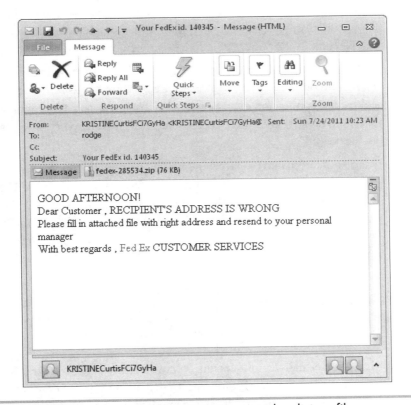

Figure 7-2   A sample e-mail vector carrying a compressed malicious file

In Actual Practice

AV products cannot scan a password-protected compressed file. This is why malicious sample exchanges between researchers use this method to ensure that the malware sample being exchanged reaches its intended destination without being detected and blocked by AV products.

To make sure that this happens, attackers make their e-mail vector enticing by using social engineering tactics:

- **The e-mail appears to come from a trusted source**   The FROM address shows a person or entity that is known or trusted, at least in some level, by the recipient. Or the SUBJECT line pertains to a topic that is familiar to the recipient, an example of which is "Feedback Needed for Recently Attended Management Conference."

- **Urgency and importance**   The message body contains something that needs immediate attention or all hell will break lose. Take a look at this sample message: "Install the attached application to ensure continuous access to your corporate e-mail account. Failure to do so might block access and result in deletion of all e-mail messages in the server."

- **Arouses interest of the receiver**   Imagine getting an e-mail with the SUBJECT "ILOVEYOU" and with an attachment name that is visible as "LOVE-LETTER-FOR-YOU…" from someone you work with or you have not seen for a very long time. Will it arouse your interest or curiosity to read the e-mail and open the attachment?

Note

The ILOVEYOU virus, aka LoveLetter worm, spread itself through e-mail using an enticing message that aroused the interest and tickled the curiosity of the receiver. It also appeared to be coming from a trusted source because it used the e-mail account of the infected individual to send out copies of itself to that individual's contacts.

The shelf life of an e-mail vector depends on how fast a specific e-mail is identified as a vector by antivirus and/or antispam solutions. The advantages in coverage and speed that it offers also contribute to its downfall. Its speed and immense coverage causes saturation, making the sample e-mail available to anyone, including AV researchers.

The thing about e-mail vectors is that they need e-mail addresses. Because of this, one question comes to mind. Where do the attackers get the e-mail addresses? Here are some of the answers:

- E-mail addresses can be scraped from the Internet. E-mail address is one form of identification in the Internet. It is used as a login name and an index of your profile. If an e-mail address is entered into an online form or posted anywhere online, it becomes available for scraping.

- E-mail addresses can be bought. Websites you registered at that ask for e-mail addresses, especially those that offer free services, are prone to selling your information unless their privacy policy states otherwise. But there are other sources aside from these legitimate websites that offer e-mail addresses for sale. One such source is e-mail spam providers.

- E-mail addresses can be guessed. This method is often applied in targeted attacks. Organizations usually follow a certain format for their e-mail addresses. Some common formats are <firstname>.<lastname>@company.com and <lastname><letter_of_first_name>@company.com. An attacker can simply use trial and error to guess which format is used. Or if the attacker has access to an e-mail message coming from someone in the targeted organization, a business card, or a directory of employees, the attacker can easily guess the e-mail format based on any one of these pieces of information.

- E-mail addresses can be collected. The malware can do this from the address book of the compromised system and send itself automatically to those collected e-mail addresses. In the case of the Melissa mass-mailer worm, it was sent to a handful of people originally. When their system got infected, the Melissa worm sent a copy of itself to the first 50 e-mail addresses found in the infected system's e-mail address book. So for every successful infection, the coverage increases 50 times more.

Although e-mail vector is a popular choice for the attackers because of its coverage, it is a different story when it is used as an infection vector for a targeted attack. In targeted attacks, the e-mail vector is sent only to a group of targets that work for, executives of, or members of the same organization, or in rare cases, only one. This avoids saturation that leads to discovery by AV researchers. For targeted attacks, an e-mail vector borrows from the playbook of its e-mail phishing brethren. It uses the same tactics for spear phishing to target specific users and whale phishing (see Figure 7-3) to target users that hold high positions in an organization such as executives. But instead of deceiving the receiver into giving out information, the receiver is fooled into installing the malware in the targeted system, either through the malicious file being carried by the e-mail or through

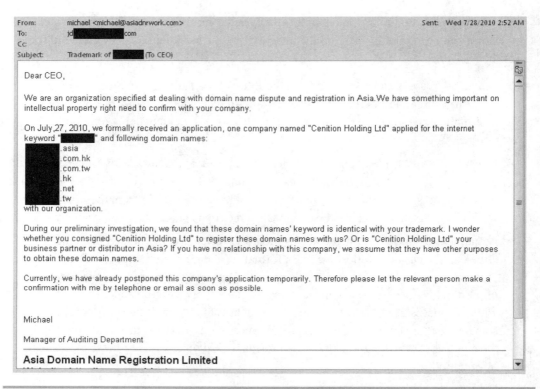

From: michael <michael@asiadnrwork.com>   Sent: Wed 7/28/2010 2:52 AM
To: jd███████.com
Cc:
Subject: Trademark of ██████ (To CEO)

Dear CEO,

We are an organization specified at dealing with domain name dispute and registration in Asia. We have something important on intellectual property right need to confirm with your company.

On July,27, 2010, we formally received an application, one company named "Cenition Holding Ltd" applied for the internet keyword "██████" and following domain names:

.asia
.com.hk
.com.tw
.hk
.net
.tw

with our organization.

During our preliminary investigation, we found that these domain names' keyword is identical with your trademark. I wonder whether you consigned "Cenition Holding Ltd" to register these domain names with us? Or is "Cenition Holding Ltd" your business partner or distributor in Asia? If you have no relationship with this company, we assume that they have other purposes to obtain these domain names.

Currently, we have already postponed this company's application temporarily. Therefore please let the relevant person make a confirmation with me by telephone or email as soon as possible.

Michael

Manager of Auditing Department

Asia Domain Name Registration Limited

Figure 7-3   A sample e-mail vector using the whale phishing technique

a URL link that is found in the e-mail. In this case the URL, deployed by the e-mail, is another infection vector that points to a compromised domain or another vector that will ultimately deploy and install the malware in the target system. A vector that uses several vectors to deploy the malware is called a multistage infection vector.

Instant Messaging and Chat

The exchange of information is instant in instant messaging (IM) and chat. Like e-mail, it also has the capability of sending not just texts but also files. But when used as an infection vector, it usually delivers malicious links. But this does not mean that it is also not used to deliver malicious files. In some cases, it does.

The target usually receives a chat message from an unknown contact. Some messages just contain a link, while some messages contain texts that are convincing enough to warrant visitation to a link. But not all chat messages containing malicious links come from unknown contacts. Some can come from known contacts. This is made possible by an infected system where chat software is installed or by the chat account itself being compromised, probably because the owner of the account logged in to an IM phishing website or unknowingly used a Trojanized instant messenger application that not only logs chat messages but also the user's chat login credentials. In situations such as this, the likelihood of the link being clicked by the receiver becomes really high because it came from a trusted source, which is one of the social engineering tactics used by attackers to increase the success rate of their infection vectors. This is also one instance wherein the attacker can choose to send a malicious file instead of a link. The likelihood of someone accepting a file transfer request from a known contact is higher compared to an unknown contact.

The coverage and speed of this vector are comparable to that of an e-mail infection vector. Anyone with an IM or chat user account is a potential target. When it comes to the speed of delivery, it is as fast or instant as pressing the RETURN key.

The shelf life of this vector depends on the discovery of the malicious chat message that is going around. The chat message is almost impossible to block. This is usually addressed via advisory from security companies. But for those who do not read advisories or keep themselves abreast of what's going on in the security field, this does not really help. To solve this, the AV companies do not just send out advisories—they also block access to the malicious links and create signatures to detect the malicious files being delivered through instant messaging and chat, assuming that they have access to the malicious link and file.

As for the level of interaction, the target user has to click the link or accept the file transfer for the delivery of the payload to be successful. This is why some social engineering tactics similar to those used in e-mail infection vectors are also at play in IM and chat vectors. But not all require human interaction.

One example, as discovered by Pure Hacking, is by exploiting vulnerability in Skype in Mac OS X. The affected versions are those that are earlier than 5.1.0.922. In this example, a specially crafted instant message in Skype can result in redirection to a website. So if an attacker wants to redirect a target user to baddomain.org, he simply sends a specially crafted instant message, as seen here:

```
http://www.example.com/?foo="><script>document.location='http://
baddomain.org';</script>
```

The result is automatic redirection of the target user to baddomain.org. The webpage is rendered by Skype as seen in Figure 7-4. It did not require any human interaction from the target user. This automatic redirection to an attacker-controlled website opens lots of possibilities for the attackers that includes malware installation in the target system. But given Skype's default setting of instant messages coming only from approved contacts, the attacker must have access to a compromised Skype account to do this.

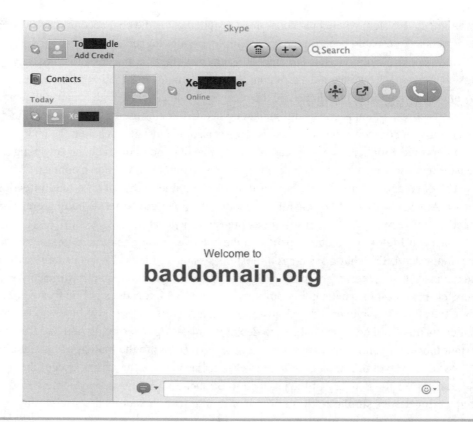

Figure 7-4 The target user is redirected to baddomain.org as a result of the specially crafted instant message sent from a compromised contact.

Getting access to IM and chat account credentials can be a result of IM phishing or a Trojanized IM application as discussed previously. These collected credentials are then sold or posted publicly for free in paste sites, as seen in Figure 7-5, making them searchable in the Internet.

Social Networking

The popularity of social networks prompted the attackers to use them as an effective tool to deploy their malware. The more popular a social networking site is, the higher the number of its registered users, thus, greatly improving the target coverage of this vector. The user population of some very popular social networks actually exceeds those of certain countries, as seen in Figure 7-6.

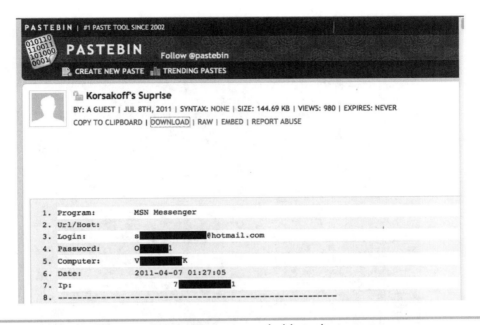

Figure 7-5   A list of compromised chat accounts searchable in the Internet

The capability of social networks to send instant messages or updates in the form of feeds that are visible not only privately to known contacts but also to the public, depending on the user's privacy preference, makes this a desirable infection vector. One advantage this has over IM and chat is that these instant messages remain hosted in the compromised user's public-facing feeds unless the user or the social networking site removes it. So it stays there waiting for an unsuspecting victim. In IM and chat, the instant messages disappear once the chat software is closed, assuming automatic message logging is disabled.

The coverage of this vector is the immediate contacts of the registered user account under the attacker's control. The more contacts the registered user has, the larger the coverage. If the registered user's updates are visible to the public, anyone who stumbles upon a malicious feed is also a potential target, thus increasing the coverage of potential victims.

The speed of this vector depends on when a potential target sees the malicious updates. For a target that is currently online and is a direct contact of the registered user under the attacker's control, that target will immediately see the malicious update and may act upon it immediately. But for those that are currently offline, it might take some time, even days, before they see the malicious updates. And the older the updates, the further down it is pushed in the potential target's news feeds.

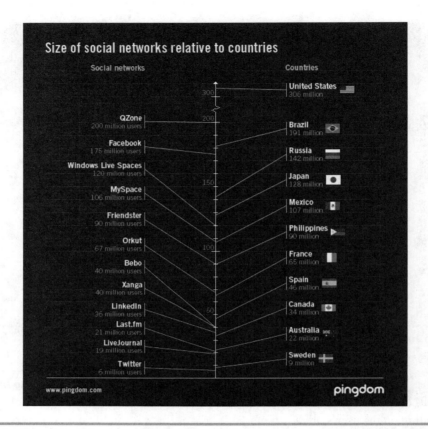

Figure 7-6 Population size of social networks relative to countries (Source: www.pingdom.com)

For this vector to work, some level of human interaction is needed. The potential target must be enticed through social engineering means for the vector to be successful.

The shelf life of this vector depends on it being discovered by AV researchers. Once discovered, the social networking site can remove it and take the necessary steps to suspend the account of the compromised registered user or give it back to its rightful owner.

To effectively utilize this vector, the attackers must have access to a registered account that has a multitude of connections, friends, or followers; or they can create a public profile or page that will host their payload.

Getting access to a registered account is not that hard. A simple Google search can do the trick. Figure 7-7 shows a list of compromised Facebook accounts that is searchable on the Internet. This list of compromised accounts was compiled as a result of phishing, system compromise by a keylogger, or simply poor choice of password.

```
Program:        Fir
Url/Host:       htt    www.facebook.com
Login:          mit    @hotmail.com
Password:
Computer:       GEC    PC
Date:           201    -24 09:48:11
Ip:                    9            9

Program:        Fir
Url/Host:       htt    www.facebook.com
Login:          bir    @hotmail.de
Password:
Computer:       CAR    -6028FD7
Date:           201    -24 10:04:48
Ip:                    8

Program:        Fir
Url/Host:       htt    de-de.facebook.com
Login:          bir    @hotmail.de
Password:       Fir    eg
Computer:       CAR    -6028FD7
Date:           201    -24 10:04:50
Ip:                    8

Program:        Fir
Url/Host:       htt    /login.facebook.com
Login:          bir    @hotmail.de
Password:
Computer:       CAR    -6028FD7
Date:           201    -24 10:04:52
Ip:                    8
```

Figure 7-7   A list of compromised Facebook accounts searchable on the Internet

Once the attacker gets hold of a registered user's login credentials, he can post messages on that user's public-facing updates, wall, or tweets. The attacker can also send messages to that compromised user's connections, friends, or followers, and since that message came from the recipients' known contact, there is a big chance that ample attention will be given to that message.

What I described here is done with the active participation of the attacker manually logging into a compromised social networking account and then posting updates, but most of these tasks can be done automatically by malware when a user logs in to a social network site using a compromised system.

Social networking sites such as Facebook give a registered user the capability to create a page that is visible to the public. This page can represent an individual, a brand, a topic, or an idea. And instead of having friends, a page compiles "likes." These are users who like the page and express it by clicking the page's "like" button. Once a Facebook user likes a page, subsequent updates on that page will appear in the user's news feeds. The more likes a certain page has, the more popular it becomes and the more potential targets there are for the attacker. Pages are becoming popular with attackers because there is no need for a compromised account. An attacker can simply create his own page that will host malicious updates.

Attackers take advantage of a Facebook page by creating a page that represents something that will arouse the public's curiosity. Usually it has something to do with a recent event. Take, for example, the recent killing of Osama bin Laden. After the announcement by President Barack Obama that the terrorist leader had been killed, a Facebook page claiming to have a video of Osama bin Laden's death went up, as seen in Figure 7-8.

The page is designed to lure the curious public (arousing their interest) into following the direction posted on the page, believing that the video of Osama bin Laden's death will be shown, but instead, the process results in a malware infection. But how was the curious public able to find this page? Usually, when something newsworthy happens, the masses flock to their favorite search engines to search for relevant content regarding it. With the help of search engine optimization (SEO), the URL links to these malicious pages often appear as the top search result.

LINGO
SEO, or **search engine optimization**, is a process of increasing a link's reputation through gaming of a target search engine, resulting in the link having a high rank and thus displayed first in a search result.

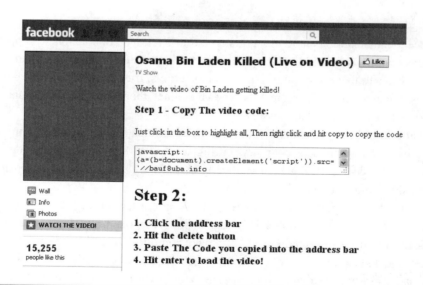

Figure 7-8 Facebook page claiming to have access to a video of Osama bin Laden's death

URL Links

A URL link is a special kind of infection vector. It is both an infection vector and a payload of another infection vector. Infection vectors that have URL links as their payload are considered infection-vector-hosting infection vectors. But URLs do not rely solely on these other vectors, such as e-mail, instant messaging, social network postings, or documents with links, to be delivered. They can also be reached or stumbled upon by unsuspecting users through fat finger typing or typos.

All of us, in one way or another, has typed a wrong address in a browser. For example, instead of typing www.citibank.com, we sometimes type www.citibsnk.com. Since the letter A and S are adjacent to each other on a QWERTY keyboard, it is easy to commit this typo. Attackers take advantage of typographical errors such as this through typosquatting.

Typosquatting is the process by which another entity will register a domain that is a typo of a legitimate domain. So in this example, an attacker can register www.citibsnk. com and then make it appear like the original by copying the exact look of the original website. The attacker can then use this website in many malicious ways, which can include phishing for financial credentials or as an infection vector for spreading malware.

Links that are used as infection vectors can be any of the following:

- Direct link to a malicious file (e.g., www.baddomain.info/malware.exe). The malicious file can be an executable or a malformed file with an exploit.

- Direct link to a page containing malicious scripts.

- Direct link to a page that hosts an exploit for a certain browser.

Drive-By Download

Wherever the links point to, the motivation of each is to install malware on a target system. To accomplish this, a URL visited by a potential target must succeed in downloading a malware to the target user's system with little to no human interaction. This method is known as a drive-by download. Common drive-by download is made possible through ActiveX control (exclusive to Internet Explorer), Java applets embedded in a Hypertext Markup Language (HTML) page, or via browser vulnerability that enables the automatic download of malware without the user's knowledge.

Once a user visits a drive-by download site, either by accident or through another vector, a pop-up often appears claiming to be security software or a fake update. This is the social engineering component of a drive-by download. Because of technologies now in place that protect against drive-by downloads by limiting software installation to those that a user explicitly allows, the attackers use social engineering to make sure that after successful download, the malware package will also be executed and installed in the system. This is why the download is often presented as software update or security software.

Fake Antivirus   Fake AV hosting drive-by download URLs display a pop-up that simulates scanning of the user's system. It scares the user into downloading and installing fake antivirus software, believing that it is the real thing, bypassing technologies, such as User Access Control (UAC) in Windows or its equivalent in other OS platforms, that are meant to protect users from installing unwanted software.

> **LINGO**
> **UAC**, as defined by Microsoft, is a security component that allows an administrator to enter credentials during a nonadministrator user session to perform occasional administrative tasks.

Fake AV also has a side business in addition to installing malware in a target user's system. Most fake AV, like the one that posed as a Mac security product seen in Figure 7-9, even asks user to enter their credit card information as payment for downloading and installing the supposedly genuine antivirus product. This results in a TKO win for the attacker:

> **LINGO**
> **Fake AV** is also known as scareware because it is primarily designed to scare the user into installing the software.

- The attacker gets paid by the user to install malware on the user's system.

- The user's credit card credentials were handed to the attacker freely during placement of the order.

- The malware is installed on the user's system.

Fake Software Update   The modus operandi of fake software updates is the same as the fake AV. The only difference is that it tries to pass itself off as a legitimate software update. Unlike fake AV, fake software updates do not ask for credit card information because they are always passed as free updates of popular software. See Figure 7-10.

Tip
Since Adobe Flash Player update is one of the most spoofed by attackers, I would advise to get updates for this software from http://get.adobe.com/flashplayer/.

URL Obfuscation Techniques
Like malware, URL links also utilize evasion techniques through link obfuscation to avoid being detected by security products. These techniques are often applied when a URL is delivered by another infection vector such as e-mails, IM, or social network feeds. Some

Figure 7-9   A sample screenshot of a fake Mac security product that victimized Mac users on May 2011

of the techniques employed by the attackers to protect their URL from being detected and eventually blacklisted are the following:

- Homographic obfuscation
  - ASCII manipulation
  - IDN manipulation
- Subdomain obfuscation
- User name obfuscation
- Anchor element obfuscation
- URL shortening

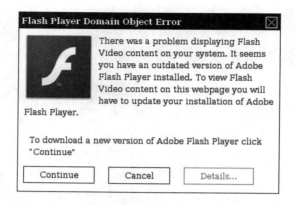

Figure 7-10   A sample screenshot of a fake software update claiming to be Adobe Flash Player

Homographic Obfuscation   A homograph, as defined by *Merriam-Webster*, is a set of words spelled alike but different in meaning, derivation, or pronunciation. The word "bass" for example is a homograph. It can be a fish or it can be a low-pitched sound. The spelling is the same, but the meaning and pronunciation are different. But in URL obfuscation, homographs are used to make a fake URL appear to look as close to the original as possible. This is known as homographic obfuscation.

> **LINGO**
> Homographic obfuscation, homographic **attacks**, and **homograph attacks** are all one and the same thing.

The main idea of this attack is to deceive the user into thinking that the URL in front of him is the original one. The spelling appears to be or is exactly the same as the original but in fact they are not. The two common ways that this is accomplished is through:

- ASCII manipulation
- Internationalized domain name (IDN) manipulation

ASCII manipulation is as simple as replacing a character with a similar-looking character. Take, for example, www.bank0famerica.com and www.damba11a.com. The letter O has been replaced by the number zero in the first example and the small letter L has been replaced by the number one in the last example. As you can see, some character replacement can be easily spotted, as in the first example, while some might be a little challenging as in the second example.

A weakness of ASCII manipulation is that the replacement is limited to similar-looking characters because the attacker is working with characters from the same set.

But with IDN manipulation, the attackers are given the ability to replace characters with exactly the same-looking characters. This is made possible because the replacement characters being used belong to a different alphabet system, which consists of a whole new set of characters.

An *IDN* is a domain name that is written using characters from another alphabet system. For example, a Chinese domain will contain Chinese characters. But since Domain Name System (DNS) is restricted to using ASCII, some sort of transcription has to happen from IDN to ASCII before the domain is resolved. The transcription is done through punycode.

> **LINGO**
> **Punycode**, as defined in RFC3492, is an encoding syntax designed for use with IDN in applications (IDNA).

Punycode uniquely and reversibly transforms a Unicode string into ASCII string. For example, the Chinese domain 克里斯托弗.COM, as displayed in the browser's address bar, is equivalent to the punycode XN--74Q394ANPCYVEJ36E.COM. Given its equivalent ASCII form, the Chinese domain can now be resolved by DNS.

IDN manipulation replaces characters in a URL with exactly the same-looking characters taken from another alphabet system. One often-used alphabet system for this kind of manipulation is the Cyrillic alphabet. As seen in Figure 7-11, the Cyrillic alphabet has characters that look exactly the same as our alphabet's lowercase C and lowercase A. This makes it easy for an attacker to craft a convincing and effective homograph of an original domain. For example, the attackers can craft a URL that looks like www.citibank. com/login. This is exactly how it will appear in the browser. But the reality here is that the letter C is not the ASCII C we know so the URL will not point to the real login page of Citibank, but instead it will point to www.xn--itibank-xjg.com/login, which is the punycode equivalent of the crafted fake URL by the attacker. You can check this out by converting the punycode into its native character using the conversion tool found in http://api.webnic.cc.

Subdomain Obfuscation   As defined in RFC1034, a domain is a subdomain of another domain if it is contained within that domain. Seeing if the subdomain's name ends with the containing domain's name can test this relationship. For example, A.B.C.D is a

Аа Бб Вв Гг Дд Ее Ёё Жж Зз
Ии Йй Кк Лл Мм Нн Оо Пп
Рр Сс Тт Уу Фф Хх Цц Чч
Шш Щщ ъ ы ь Ээ Юю Яя

Figure 7-11   The Cyrillic alphabet

subdomain of B.C.D, C.D, D, and " ". Based on this definition, spoof.baddomain.org is a subdomain of baddomain.org.

Subdomain obfuscation is the process of creating a subdomain name based on another domain that the attacker is trying to spoof. The link bankofamerica.com.baddomain.org is one example. It is really a subdomain contained in the baddomain.org domain. It is clearly designed to trick users into thinking that they are visiting Bank of America's website, but in fact they are going to a website controlled by the attacker. Although this looks pretty obvious, some users are still duped into clicking the link.

User Name Obfuscation   Another popular way of deceiving the users into believing that they are clicking a legitimate URL is through user name obfuscation. It applies the same principle as the subdomain obfuscation, but instead of using subdomains to spoof a website, it uses user names. This method is originally used for authentication to access a website. The format it follows is http://<username>:<password>@<domain>. But the attackers are able to use this format to their advantage by creating a user name exactly the same as the domain they want to spoof. For example, clicking www.bankofamerica .com@member.baddomain.org will bring the user to baddomain.org instead of the bank's website. One powerful feature this has is that any character with the exception of the forward slash (/), semicolon (;), and question mark (?) can be used before the @ symbol. So the attackers can greatly improve on the previous example by adding numerous "_" symbols between the user name and the @ symbol, effectively hiding the @ symbol and the real domain name. But browsers nowadays are able to warn the users about this, as seen in Figure 7-12.

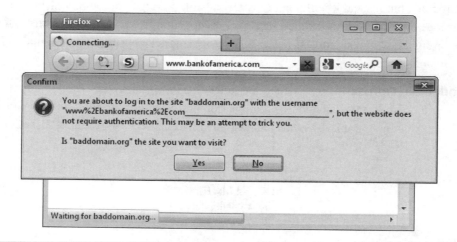

Figure 7-12   User name obfuscation using numerous underscore characters to hide the @ symbol and the real domain name revealed by browser security feature

Anchor Element Obfuscation   In HTML, an anchor element is used create a link pointing to a resource depending on its attributes. It is written as <a>, which is known as an "a" tag. The attribute that is interesting to our discussion is the href attribute. This attribute points to a URL. The following is example code that uses the <a> with an href attribute:

```
<html>
<body>
<a href="www.elisan.org">Visit My Site!</a>
</body>
</html>
```

The value assigned to href is the URL where the anchor is pointing, while the text, "Visit My Site!" is what will be displayed on the HTML page.

Attackers take advantage of this by feeding a URL value to href that points to their malicious website and changing the text to the website they want to spoof. The result of the code is shown here, and how it looks in a browser window is shown in Figure 7-13.

```
<html>
<body>
<a href="http://baddomain.org">www.bankofamerica.com</a>
</body>
</html>
```

Although the malicious site is obviously displayed when the mouse cursor hovers above it, it's still able to infect users, especially those that are not that tech savvy.

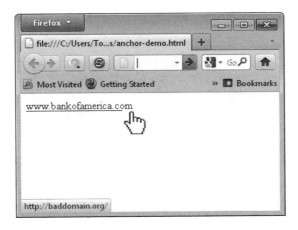

Figure 7-13 The link on the webpage is different from the real link it is pointing to, as shown in the mouse hover.

URL Shortening   With the popularity of short messaging services limited to 140 characters like Twitter and Heello, the text real estate is limited and has to be used as efficiently as possible. So sharing long URLs is almost out of the question. This is where URL shortening comes in. URL shortening is a technique that significantly reduces the number of characters in a URL, in effect, shortening it. For example, a URL containing 263 characters can be shortened to only 13.

Long URL version:

- http://www.thelongestlistofthelongeststuffatthelongestdomainnameatlonglast.com/wearejustdoingthistobestupidnowsincethiscangoonforeverandeverandeverbutitstill lookskindaneatinthebrowsereventhoughitsabigwasteoftimeandenergyandhasnorealpoint butwehadtodoitanyways.html

Shortened version:

- http://bit.ly/2EnEgk

The URL shortening service I used in the preceding example is provided by Bitly as illustrated here. Bitly is a free URL shortening service. There are lots of URL shorteners available out there. Google even has one.

It didn't take long for the attackers to abuse this service because it offered so many advantages for them. The service is free and there is no need to register, so it minimizes the digital trail that will lead to them. It is easier to use this service compared to the other obfuscation techniques, and it is a lot less obvious because it clearly masks the real link. Moving the mouse cursor over the link, when delivered via other infection vectors, does not reveal the real link it is pointing to, making it ideal for the attackers.

File Shares

The Internet is full of files. It is becoming the number-one distribution method for files. A user who purchases software does not need to get her hands on a physical media—the file can simply be downloaded from the Internet. This method is fast and convenient. It's immediate gratification. But not all files that are downloaded from the Internet come from trusted sources. Some are hosted in different file-sharing sites, while others are shared through peer-to-peer (P2P) file-sharing clients. These file-sharing methods do not have the necessary security checks utilized by trusted sources to ensure that what is shared is really what the user is getting. Anyway, most of the shared files are free. This is what makes it a hit to users. The popularity of these file-sharing methods makes it attractive to the attackers in terms of potential target coverage and in terms of speed of how their creation is able to reach a potential target. The attackers take advantage of this by spreading their files via these methods. To make their file interesting, they give it a name that is enticing to potential targets.

Note
Some malware families, like the bot agent SDBot, drop enticingly named executables into popular P2P applications' share folders to deceive other peers into downloading and executing the bot agent into their system. Some sample names include "Angelina Jolie Sex Game crack.exe," "Ahead Nero Burning Rom 5.5.10.20.keygen.exe," and "All ID Software serial.exe." This is one method it uses to spread.

Tip
Some file-sharing websites will post the hash of the file they are sharing so the user can check whether the file that was downloaded into the system is the one shared by the website.

Software Vulnerabilities

No software is perfect. All of them have bugs and some have flaws. Some are known, while others are not. Some are critical, while others are minor. Depending on the severity of the bug, it can have unpredictable and unintended results. The attackers, with some of them being software developers themselves, recognized the value of an unknown or undiscovered critical bug waiting to be exploited in certain software.

The advantage of using software vulnerabilities as an infection vector over other infection vectors is that it significantly lowers, if not totally eliminates, the need for human interaction as we have seen in the exploited vulnerable version of Skype for Mac OS X in the previous section.

LINGO
Software bugs are different from software flaws. A **software bug** is an issue with a feature that is not functioning as intended, while a **software flaw** is an error in the design and architecture of the software itself. A patch can fix a bug, while a flaw only can be fixed by a complete redesign and overhaul of the software.

There are lots of materials that cover software vulnerabilities already. With this in mind, we will focus on those that are used to install malware on a system.

To take advantage of software vulnerabilities, the attackers use an exploit. An exploit can be a piece of code or a chunk of malformed data that causes the target software to behave in a way not intended by the software manufacturer. The most common exploit is the one that takes advantage of buffer overflow.

LINGO
A **buffer** is a contiguously finite space in memory.

Buffer Overflow

Software is made up of two distinct components: code and data. Code is the set of instructions that makes use of data. During data manipulation, software often makes use of a temporary data storage called a buffer. A buffer is created to hold data and nothing more. But sometimes, due to programmatic error, more data is written to the allocated buffer. This results in data overflowing to adjacent buffers. This condition is called a buffer overflow. Attackers take advantage of this by overflowing the buffer with code instead of data. The buffer is overflown in such a way to transfer the control to that code, thus executing it. The often-used buffer overflows are

- Stack overflow
- Heap overflow

Note

A buffer overflow can be triggered using a malformed file. The malformed file is the one that is deployed by the attacker. And once this seemingly innocent-looking file is opened by a vulnerable application, the data from the malformed file overflows the buffer.

Stack Overflow   The stack is a LIFO (last in first out) data structure. This means that the data that is pushed last into the stack is the one that is popped out first. It is aptly called a stack because it is stacking data on top of one another. Think of it like a stack of plates. The last plate that is put on the top of the stack is the one that is used first. Because of its LIFO nature, the stack is often used to store temporary variables, making it efficient to use with program functions.

Stack overflow is the result of overflowing the buffers on the stack to get control of the execution flow of the program. This is made possible by overflowing the buffer enough to overwrite the value stored in RET (return address). To understand this concept, let's look at how the stack is used by program functions.

A program function is like a small program within a program. It's an independent, compartmentalized program that performs specific operations using data passed to it and then returns the result back to the main program. Since data has to be manipulated by a function, it utilizes the stack as a temporary storage for this data. When a function is called within a program, it pushes all the data into the stack, including the return address. To see what the stack looks like, see Figure 7-14. The return address is where the instruction pointer is currently pointing when the function is called. This is important, because after the function has finished processing, the execution flow has to go back to that return address so the main program can continue its execution flow. This value is stored in RET. When the function finishes, the value stored in RET is passed to the instruction pointer so the main program can go back to its execution flow before the function was called. So, if the attacker is able to

LINGO
In a program execution flow, the **instruction pointer** points to the memory address that is going to be executed next.

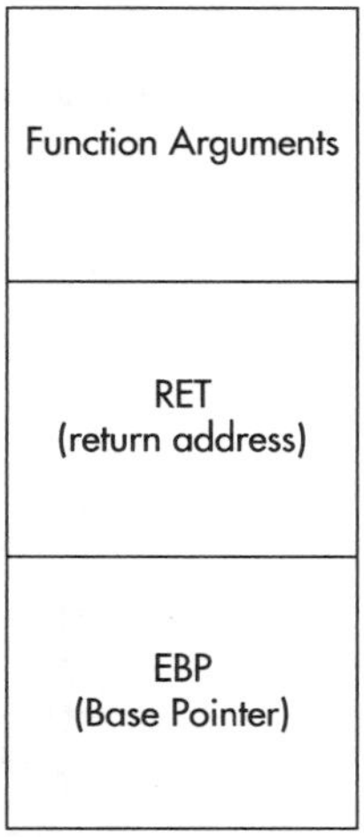

Function Arguments
RET (return address)
EBP (Base Pointer)

Figure 7-14   What the stack looks like during a function call

overflow the buffer and as a result overwrite the value stored in RET with an address value that points to malicious code, the instruction pointer will point directly to the malicious code, resulting in the code being executed.

Heap Overflow The heap is a dynamically allocated memory space. The logic behind this is that the amount of memory needed by a program is not known in advance; therefore, memory has to be allocated as needed and freed up when not needed. The difference between a heap and a stack is that a heap does not have return addresses similar to a stack's. This makes the technique used to control execution flow in stack overflow useless. Overflowing a heap instead results in data and pointers to other data or program functions to be overwritten. As a result, the attacker can overwrite these pointers to point to malicious code instead of the original location it was pointing to.

Privilege Escalation

The ability of a software vulnerability to deliver and install malware in a system depends on its ability to get privilege escalation. Privilege escalation is the process of gaining access to system resources that are accessible only to a super-user or system administrator. With this, the attacker can do pretty much everything with the system, including installing malware.

Privilege escalation is achieved when the exploited vulnerable software already is running on escalated privilege or it has access to system resources or functions running on escalated privileges.

Zero-Day Vulnerabilities

The knowledge of a program's vulnerabilities that can be exploited is often kept private by the attacker. This is known as a zero-day vulnerability. A zero-day vulnerability is an exploitable hole in an operating system, software, or even hardware that has been discovered by those other than the manufacturers or publishers of the vulnerable object. If an independent researcher has discovered a zero-day vulnerability, the next step is to report this to the manufacturer or publisher so a patch or a new minor version can be released that fixes the vulnerability. Some software manufacturers even pay for this kind of information, making vulnerability

LINGO
Zero-day is a term used to describe something that is new and totally unknown. The day these holes are discovered by or brought to the attention of the manufacturers is called day one. Zero-day was coined to give the impression that it is already known, usually by the attackers, even before that day. Before, zero-day was only used to describe vulnerability, but now it is also used to describe new and undetected malware as zero-day malware. The term zero-day malware is also used to describe malware that utilizes a zero-day vulnerability.

discovery a good independent business for software hobbyists. But it's a different story if an attacker discovers it. It is usually kept secret to be used in future attacks or to be sold to other cybercrime groups. Keeping it a secret is where the vulnerability's immense value lies, because this vector's shelf life depends on how long it is kept a secret and how long before a patch is released to fix it.

There are cases where a vulnerability has been known to be public already, but still the patch to fix it is pending release; thus, any malware that utilizes this vulnerability still enjoys some level of success. Unfortunately, the only way to prevent vulnerable software with no available patch or fix from being exploited is to uninstall or not use it, but in cases where the software is vital to an enterprise's operation, this is usually out of the question.

Tip
A good way to stay abreast of the latest vulnerabilities is by visiting http://cve.mitre.org.

The Potential of Becoming an Infection Vector

Not all infection vectors are or can be covered in this chapter. There may be technologies that are being utilized by the attackers today that neither I nor the security industry in general is aware of. There is always the possibility of something that you least expect becoming an infection vector. Aside from the familiarity with common infection vectors, another thing that is important to take away in this chapter is the ability to recognize a technology's potential of becoming an infection vector. To do this, let's look back at the previously discussed infection vectors. Some of them have one or a combination of certain capabilities that enables them to be utilized as effective vectors for attack. These are:

- The ability to process data from an external source
- The ability to move data to a chosen destination
- The ability to share data

If a technology is able to process, move, or share data, then that technology has the potential of becoming an infection vector.

We've Covered

- The different ways malware is delivered or deployed to a target system
  - Physical media
  - E-mail
  - Instant messaging and chat

- Social networking
- URL links
- File shares
- Software vulnerabilities
- The common social engineering tactics employed by infection vectors
  - Coming from a trusted source
  - Has a sense of urgency and importance
  - Arouses the interest
- The characteristics of infection vectors that attackers take into consideration when deciding the deployment method for their malware
  - Vector coverage
  - Vector speed
  - Vector level of interaction
  - Vector shelf life
- The different URL obfuscation techniques employed by attackers
  - Homographic obfuscation
  - Subdomain obfuscation
  - User name obfuscation
  - Anchor element obfuscation
  - URL shortening
- The common buffer overflow techniques to get control of program execution
  - Stack overflow
  - Heap overflow
- The characteristics of a technology that give it a potential of becoming an infection vector
  - The ability to process data from an external source
  - The ability to move data to a chosen destination
  - The ability to share data

CHAPTER 8

The Compromised System

We'll Cover

- The malware infection process

- Types of malware installation locations

- Ways of hiding installed malware files

- Ways of passing control to malware

- The main directives of an active malware

- The common series of malware-initiated communications

Malware is made with one purpose and that is to exist in a target system executing the relevant functionalities the attacker bestowed on it to fulfill its mission. For this to happen, the malware must first reach the target system it is intended to compromise. Chapter 7 showed us how different technologies were utilized to serve as infection vectors to deliver malware to a target system. The previous chapter also stressed the point that some infection vectors require a level of human interaction to install the malware and that the success of deployment often hinges not only on the different characteristics of the infection vectors but also on the social engineering tactics employed by the attacker to further deceive the targeted user.

In this chapter, we will take a look at what happens next after the successful delivery of the malware by its infection vector. The chapter covers how malware infects a system and how it behaves once the system is compromised.

Have you ever experienced executing a binary or double-clicking a file? Nothing obvious happened, and then suddenly it disappeared? If you did, chances are you just executed a malware and your system is now under its control.

Note

In this chapter, I will use malware as a general term to describe both malware installers and malware components, unless a topic specifically applies to one of the two. This is due to the fact that not all malware is deployed using malware installers and not all malware that is deployed needs other components to function, as described in previous chapters.

The Malware Infection Process

Now that the malware has reached the target system via its infection vector, its first directive is to establish a foothold on the system through infection. Depending on what infection vector was used to deploy the malware, system infection happens automatically or through the aid of human interaction. If the case is the latter, then the malware installer or the malware itself, if it is deployed without the aid of an installer, utilizes superficial disguises to reinforce the social engineering tactics utilized by the infection vector and to further deceive the target user into installing the malware. The most common disguises are:

- The use of fake icons
- The use of long extension names

These disguises are aimed at deceiving the target user's eyes, a sort of an optical illusion. The delivered malware is trying to appear as something that it is not. It's like a wolf in sheep's clothing. So it might gain trust instead of fear. The shepherd, believing that it is a lost sheep, brings the disguised wolf to join his flock only to discover in the morning that all of his sheep have been slaughtered and feasted upon by the wolf.

Since file browsing is graphical user interface (GUI)-based, the two things that a typical user sees in determining the file type without much investigation is the file icon and the file extension. So these two things are often manipulated to mask the malware file's real nature. For example, an executable file with a JPG icon gives the impression that it is a graphic file instead of an executable; couple that with a fake JPG extension to stress the point and it becomes more convincing as a JPG file.

Note

Windows relies on the file's extension and not its internal structure to determine how the file should be handled. So if a file has a JPG extension, Windows will attempt to open it as a graphic file. If the file has an EXE extension, Windows will treat the file as an executable and run it. Conversely, an EXE file that is renamed will not be executed. This is why malware file extensions are renamed in malware collection sets so none of them will be executed accidentally.

Since Windows relies on extensions to handle the file, an executable with a JPG extension will not work. It will not be executed by Windows. It must have an EXE extension to work. The attackers need to find a way to attach an EXE extension to the fake JPG file without making it obvious to the target user. But since Windows has a limitation on displaying long filenames in a GUI-based file browser, the attackers rely on this to attach the EXE extension to the fake JPG file and hide it from view of the target user. A sample of abusing this limiation is seen in Figure 8-1.

ImportantReport.pdf

.exe

Figure 8-1   An example of a malware file utilizing fake icons and long extension names

This limitation has to do with handling of long filenames. A long filename is only partially displayed because the browser only displays a certain length of characters and then truncates the rest. The attackers take advantage of this limitation by creating long extension names for the malicious binary. For example, a file with a filename of "InnocentLookingFile.JPG._____.EXE" will be displayed in the browser as "InnocentLookingFile.JPG" or "InnocentLookingFile.JPG.___." The long extension name has been truncated. Depending on the font configuration of the target system, the filename might be displayed exactly as the attacker wants it, wherein the name ends exactly with the last character of the fake extension name without any characters trailing it. But no matter how it is shown ultimately in the browser, the most important thing here is that the trailing characters after the JPG extension, including the real extension, which is EXE, are truncated from view. This gives the user the impression that the file he is looking at is indeed a JPG file. But since the real extension name is still EXE, the system will assign it a default icon for executables unless the attackers assign an icon to it that looks like an icon for JPG files to complete the disguise. This is why the use of fake icons and long extension names are always used together because they complement each other, and as a result reinforce the social engineering tactic used by the infection vector.

Tip
A nonexecutable file that is delivered through e-mail is not a guarantee that it is not malicious. JPG files, and any other data files for that matter, can be malformed to exploit vulnerability in the software that takes them as an input.

To illustrate how these disguises reinforce the social engineering tactic employed by the infection vector, take, for example, this scenario. If the malware is delivered via e-mail and it says that the file is a photograph of a famous person, the malicious file will be made to look like a picture file to add credence to the e-mail's deceptive message. It will have a JPG file icon. Its filename might end in ".JPG_____.EXE" or a similar variation as long as the JPG file extension is immediately after the filename and a long trail of characters ending up in ".EXE." The malicious file tries to look the part the e-mail says it is: a picture file instead of a malicious executable.

A quick way to know a file's nature is by using Windows' File Properties context menu as seen in Figure 8-2. If a long filename ends with an EXE extension, it will show up as an executable. But this should not be the absolute basis of determining the nature of the file in question.

Tip
Using Windows File Properties menu to determine the nature of a file is not reliable because malware can manipulate this.

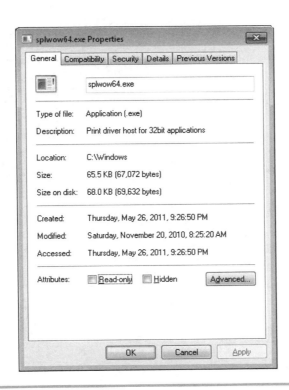

Figure 8-2   The File Properties Window

Once the user is convinced through the collaboration of the infection vector's social engineering tactics and the disguise employed by the malware file to execute the delivered malware, infection begins. But depending on the malware's need and the technology it possesses, it can get around infecting a system with nonadministrator permission. Otherwise, it would need escalated privileges to infect the system. If the user is running under the context of an admin user, such as the default installation of Windows XP, the malicious file will already have escalated privileges. This works really well for disguised files. But if the user is not running under the context of an admin user, the user would need to explicitly grant the executable escalated privileges for it to successfully infect the system.

In Windows, the user will be alerted by the Windows User Account Control (UAC) (see Figure 8-3) if an executable needs to be granted escalated privileges. As I previously stated, a user running in administrator mode works well for a disguised file. But in this instance where escalated privilege needs to be granted, a disguised file might not work, because if a user is alerted to something being installed and needs escalated privileges just by clicking a supposedly picture file then this will raise suspicion, unless the disguised file has technologies that will enable it to bypass UAC and still get escalated privileges.

LINGO
As defined by Microsoft, **User Account Control (UAC)** is a feature in Windows that can help prevent unauthorized changes to your computer. UAC does this by asking you for permission or an administrator password before performing actions that could potentially affect your computer's operation or that change settings that affect other users.

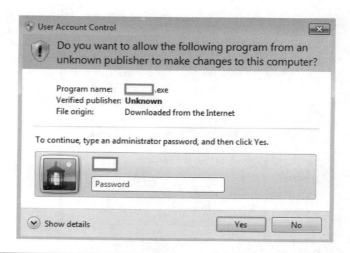

Figure 8-3 The Windows UAC

Tip

Log in only as administrator or as a user with administrator privileges when installing software or managing a system. For any other purposes, such as everyday, operational computing, always log in as a standard user.

The weakest link in this feature, as with other security features, is the user. If the user is already convinced that what he is executing is legitimate, the granting of permission is almost a sure thing. The file is executed and escalated privilege is granted, paving the way for the malware to infect the system. This is why scareware is a favorite of attackers because it does not need to use sophisticated technology to bypass UAC. It is effective enough to deceive or scare users into granting it escalated privileges.

Note

Not all malware needs escalated privileges to infect a system.

Now that the malware is running with escalated privileges, it proceeds in its infection routine. Generally, the infection process can be divided into the following steps:

LINGO

Malware persistency refers to a condition wherein malware is always active in an infected system even after reboot or shutdown.

- Installation of malware files
- Setting up malware persistency
- Removing evidence of the malware installer
- Passing control to the malware

Installation of Malware Files

Before anything else, the malware does some preinstallation checks for its own protection and to ensure successful infection. Depending on whether it is being installed by a downloader or a dropper, the necessary steps as discussed in Chapter 5 are performed to ensure that the malware being installed is up-to-date and has all the necessary components and instructions needed to fulfill its mission. Its protective features, based on malware technologies described in Chapter 6, are activated to check whether the environment is suitable for infection and there is no risk of the malware being analyzed or monitored. If any of these checks fails, the installation aborts. Otherwise, installation continues.

Two Types of Malware Installation Locations

After all the preinstallation checks are done, the installation of the malware files proceeds. The malware components are copied into their respective locations in the system. There are two types of locations where copies of the malware are installed:

- The operational location
- The staging location

The Operational Location   The operational location is where the malware components that will be active during system compromise are dropped. In Windows, the most utilized locations are the following folders:

- Windows folder
- System folder
- Programs folder
- User settings folder

Note
The most utilized locations where malware files are installed are what antivirus (AV) products scan under "Quick Scan" mode.

The Staging Location   The staging location, on the other hand, is where copies of the malware are dropped that will be used for infecting other systems. A staging location can be any of the following:

- Removable storage media
- Location in the local drive
- Network share

Some malware look for attached storage media and drop a copy of it there. This can happen during initial installation of the malware files if a removable storage media is plugged in to the system, or when a removable storage media is plugged in while the malware is active or has total control of the system.

Another staging location, and the most utilized, of course, is the local drive. Malware drops a copy of itself in interesting areas in the hard drive. One popular location is the public folder of peer-to-peer (P2P) file-sharing applications. This folder contains the files that are shared publicly by the application. Copies of the malware are usually placed there so they will be available for copying by other peers.

Also, for infected systems that are connected to a local network that has write access to a public network drive, the malware drops a copy of itself to this network share, making the malware available to other users who also have access to that network share.

Hiding the Installed Malware Files

The installation of malware files is not just simply copying the malware components into their respective locations; the malware writers also take into consideration how to hide these files from simple browsing. The most common ways the malware components are hidden without the use of any rootkit technology are the following:

● Hiding using attributes

● Hiding in plain sight

Hiding Using Attributes   In Windows, the easiest way to hide a malware component from being enumerated via simple browsing is to give it the HIDDEN attribute. A file or folder with a HIDDEN attribute does not appear during file browsing, either through command-line browsing or GUI-based browsing.

Hiding using attributes is not limited to giving the malware components HIDDEN attributes; the use of HIDDEN folders is also utilized. This is done by placing the malware components with the HIDDEN attribute into a newly created HIDDEN folder. The HIDDEN folder can be located in the following:

● In the root directory

● In another folder, such as Windows or any other common folders where malware is usually placed

● In an obscure location that nobody will bother looking at

This technique of hiding is not limited to using a single folder. Multiple layers of subfolders can be utilized as well. Some of them can have the HIDDEN attribute, while others do not. An upper-level subfolder can have multiple subfolders under it that are a mix of HIDDEN and non-HIDDEN folders. The malware file can be in any of those subfolders. This adds to the obscurity of the location.

Also, some malware components have the SYSTEM and READONLY attributes enabled. These other attributes carry with them certain advantages such as protection from deletion and removal of the attributes without escalated privileges.

Although it is easy to reveal hidden files and have them visible in Windows Explorer, as seen in Figure 8-4, by simply enabling the Show Hidden Files, Folders, And Drives option in the GUI browser, it is a little bit more challenging to identify which of the thousands of files in the hard drive is the malware component, especially if you do not

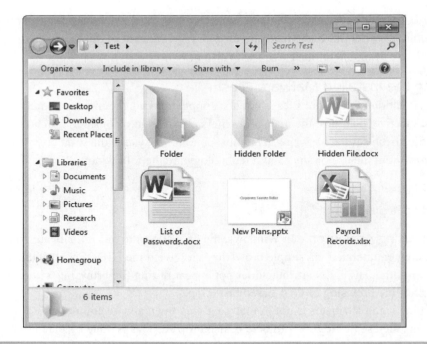

Figure 8-4 Hidden folders appear lighter when displayed in Windows Explorer.

know what you are looking for. But the attackers are not taking this for granted, so they also take precautions that enable them to hide the malware components in plain sight.

Hiding in Plain Sight   Another way of hiding malware components without the use of any attributes or when the attributes have been stripped from the files is to hide them in plain sight. Hiding in plain sight means that the malware files must be able to blend in with other files to avoid standing out like a sore thumb. This is very useful, especially when the malware component is copied to a location that contains lots of files, such as the Windows\System32 folder, which is full of thousands of EXE and DLL files.

To hide in plain sight, the malware utilizes the following obfuscation techniques:

- Filename obfuscation
- File date and time obfuscation

The dropped malware can have any name it wants. As Shakespeare wrote in *Romeo and Juliet,* "A rose by any other name would smell as sweet." So no matter how it is named, its nature does not change. But for malware, strategic naming, although superficial, helps in its ability to hide in plain sight.

Depending on the role, the location, or the utilization of the malware components, the following are common naming schemes utilized by malware to hide in plain sight:

● Homographic names

● Fake names

If the malware components are going to be copied or installed in operational locations, they can utilize either of the two naming schemes to hide in plain sight. For example, can you see the difference between "ntdll.dll" and "ntd11.dll?" One of them is real, while the other one is a homographic equivalent name. How about the filenames "asferror.dll," "kernel32.exe," "kernelBase.exe," and "kernel64.dll"? Which of them is a name of a real file? Only one is real; the others are fake names. Now imagine these files together with thousands of other files inside a folder and you have no idea what you are looking for. It becomes a little bit challenging to spot which file is the odd one out, right?

For malware components that are going to be copied or installed in staging locations, they utilize enticing fake names such as "Office2007Crack.exe," "MyTaxReturn.pdf," "WarcraftKeyGen.exe," or "AVProductFullVersion.msi." If these files are copied to a removable storage media, public network drive, or a public folder of a P2P file-sharing application in a local drive, chances are somebody will see one of these malicious files, get interested, and then execute it.

Also since all of the malware components dropped in staging locations are meant for infecting, whenever possible, they also utilize the same techniques used by malware installers to hide their true nature. To review, these are:

● The use of fake icons

● The use of long extension names

In Actual Practice

If the compromised system does not have any file-sharing programs installed, some malware installer creates the folder and drops multiple copies of the malware there. All have different enticing names and are either exact copies or a different generation of the malware. The advantage of this is that if ever the target user does install a file-sharing program in the future, the malware components will be there already. But one disadvantage is that this method can raise suspicion, because how can a system have a public share folder of a file-sharing program that is not installed? Other malware installers don't do this; instead, they check first for the presence of any file-sharing programs and then drop the malware to the appropriate folder. If none are installed, then no action is taken.

Figure 8-5   A malware file hiding in plain sight in a Windows/System32 folder

Filename obfuscation works well in locations where the files have varying date and time stamps, but for locations that contain files that have uniform date and time stamps, the malware that is copied also modifies its file date and time to coincide with the other files located in that folder. This helps in keeping the malware under the radar. Can you spot which file in Figure 8-5 is bogus?

Setting Up Malware Persistency

After all the malware components have been installed in their respective locations, the next step of infection is for the malware installer to manipulate the target system's configuration settings to facilitate malware persistency. The malware must remain active at all times for it to operate as intended by the attacker. Since being active in a system means living in volatile memory, to achieve malware persistency the malware must be able to survive shutdown and reboot. So to be persistent, the malware must be able to autostart.

In Chapter 2, we saw how different types of classes of malware autostart in Windows. They make use of any of one or a combination of the following: Master Boot Record (MBR), the boot sector, batch files, INI files, Task Scheduler, StartUp folder, the registry, and by piggy-back riding on other processes.

Tip
The Autoruns tool by Microsoft reveals the different autostarting locations in Windows. This is a good tool to use if you want to know what executables are launched automatically during bootup.

Aside from configuring the system to enable the malware to autostart, the malware installer also disables another threat to the malware: the Windows System Restore.

As described by Microsoft, System Restore helps the user restore the computer's system files to an earlier point in time. It's a way to undo system changes to the computer without affecting the user's personal files, such as e-mail, documents, or photos. This is useful in times where an installation of a program causes unintended results and uninstallation of the program did not do the trick. With this feature, the user can restore the system to an earlier point in time before the installation of the program when everything was working properly. Restore points can be created manually or automatically through a feature called System Protection.

Disabling System Restore is done by deleting the System Volume Information folder located in the root directory. This folder contains all the system restore files. Without these files, the user will not be able to restore the system back to a previous state, thus, preventing the removal of the malware.

Removing Evidence of the Malware Installer
After all the needed malware files have been installed and all the necessary changes to the system have been made to facilitate malware persistency, the malware installer makes like a tree and leaves. Since the job of the malware installer is done, there is no more need for it to linger in the system. Plus, making itself scarce after the infection process prevents the AV researchers from capturing the malware installer sample. To accomplish this, the malware installer removes any evidence of its presence in the system by deleting itself.

Technically, the malware installer does not delete itself in the system. A file cannot be deleted while its process is running, which is why an executable cannot delete itself. To solve this, malware installers typically make use of scripts such as a batch file. A batch file is created, usually in a temporary folder, by the malware installer with the appropriate codes to delete the malware installer and then the created batch file itself. Unlike executables, scripts such as a batch file can delete themselves.

This technique works by making the batch file launch after the malware installer drops it and have it repeatedly attempt to delete the malware installer until it is successful. This is done through a conditional loop in the batch file code. Since the malware installer remains active in memory until it has finished everything it needs to do, the batch file will not be able to delete it. It will always fail while the malware installer is active in memory. But once the malware installer exits, it is no longer active in memory. Therefore, the batch file will be able to successfully delete it. Once this is done, the batch file then deletes itself. As a result, the malware installer is deleted, the batch file is deleted, and thus, no evidence of the presence of a malware installer is left.

The following is a sample batch file code that is used for this purpose, assuming the malware installer and the created batch file are located in the same folder:

```
:Repeat
del "malware_installer.exe"
if exist "malware_installer.exe" goto Repeat
del "this_batch_file.bat"
```

Note
Batch file is the script of choice of malware installers, especially for those targeting Windows, because it does need any special scripting interpreters or applications. It is native to Windows as a carryover from DOS.

The same technique is also used by some malware that does not utilize any malware installer for system infection. This kind of malware has checking mechanisms to determine whether it is in the proper location or not. If not, it copies itself to the appropriate location and makes the necessary changes to the system to make itself persistent. It then deletes itself using the same batch file technique utilized by malware installers.

Passing Control to the Malware

The last thing a malware installer does before it exits execution and then eventually gets destroyed is pass control to the malware to make it active. Passing control to the malware is usually done by:

- Invoking the malware immediately after installation
- Letting a benign application invoke the malware
- Postponing until the next bootup

Invoking the Malware Immediately After Installation

Passing control to the malware can be done simply by invoking the malware after installation. This method does not require any system reboot. This is similar to a software installer asking the user to "Run application X" immediately after installation. The user can choose either Yes or No. The same technology is used here. The only difference is that in the case of the malware installer, the user is not prompted. The malware is invoked immediately.

Letting a Benign Application Invoke the Malware

There are cases where control is passed to the malware by a benign application. This happens when an application loads different resources it needs to function and one of these resources is compromised.

One example is a compromised DLL being utilized by most applications. Once an application loads the compromised DLL, the malware executes. Another example is malicious browser plug-ins that get executed every time the browser is used.

Postponing Until the Next Bootup

Since the malware has already been made persistent during the installation process, another method of passing control to the malware is waiting for it to start during bootup instead of immediately invoking it.

It might not make sense at first—why wait for a reboot when the malware can easily be invoked immediately? But if the malware is targeting a specific user to infect and not all users of the machine, this is where this method becomes useful. To better explain this, let's take a look at one of the differences between HKEY_LOCAL_MACHINE (HKLM) and HKEY_CURRENT_USER (HKCU). HKLM affects all users while HKCU only affects a specific user profile. Therefore, modifying keys under HKCU enables the malware to infect a specific profile, enabling it to pinpoint a specific target if needed.

Another thing that makes this method useful, regardless of whether the target is a specific user or all users in a machine, is avoiding sandbox analysis, especially those that do not monitor or execute dropped files in another sandbox session. Postponing the passing of control to the malware until the next reboot does not give the sandbox the chance to monitor and capture host and network activity of the newly installed malware. The sandbox was only able to capture the malware installer's activity, which is not as useful compared to that of the installed malware.

In Actual Practice

Automated malware analysis systems monitor all dropped files by the malware installer, collect these, and resubmit them to the sandbox for processing. But some malware files do not have the ability to install themselves on the system; reliance on system changes made exclusively by the malware installer usually fails and the malware does not function as intended.

The Active Malware

When the malware has fully established its grip on the system through successful infection and is fully operational and active in memory, it now has the needed system resources at its disposal to fulfill its mission. Once it is active, it immediately goes into action and executes its main directives. Depending on the type of malware and its mission, the directives can vary. But whatever combination of directives a malware has, they can be any or a combination of the following:

LINGO
Active malware is malware that is currently running in memory.

- Maintaining its foothold on the system
- Communicating with the attacker
- Executing its payload

For example, malware that is utilized for a "hit-and-run" mission that does not call for continuous access to a compromised system and does not need to communicate back to the attacker for instructions only has a single directive, and that is the execution of its payload.

LINGO
A **"hit-and-run" mission** is a campaign that happens in a short period of time. If it is an information-stealing mission, the malware will collect whatever it can in a given time frame, send the information out, and destroy itself. If it is on a mission of destruction, it will simply execute its Trojan payload and destroy what it needs to destroy, including itself.

Maintaining the Foothold

Now that the malware has fully established its foothold on the system, one of its directives is to maintain this grip. It must continue to own the system for as long as it needs to. To do this, the malware must be capable of doing the following:

- Hiding its presence
- Updating itself
- Maintaining exclusive access to the compromised system

Hiding the Malware's Presence

When a malware infection occurs, several changes happen to the compromised system, as we have seen in the previous section. These changes can include any of, among others, the following:

- Addition of installed malware files
- Changes to existing files
- Deletion of existing files
- Changes in the registry settings of Windows
- Changes in other configuration files

If you know what to look for, these changes can serve as telltale signs of the presence of malware. But these changes are not the only telltale signs of malware presence. Evidence of malware activity is also a major indicator. So in order to maintain a foothold on the system, the malware must not only be able to hide these changes made during infection but also any evidence of its activity. Hiding these changes is one thing, and hiding the malware while it is active is another. Active malware, or malware in motion, reveals signs or traces of its activity while it is running. Plus, if it has network capabilities, it will also reveal its network activities. So to effectively hide its presence, the malware tackles two kinds of evidence that can prove its existence:

- Evidence in the host
- Evidence in the network

Evidence in the host includes added, changed, and deleted files during malware infection; changes in the registry settings and configuration files; and the active malware's footprints while running. Evidence in the network includes the network footprints or traces resulting from network connections initiated by the malware.

Hiding Evidence in the Host   During installation, the hiding of installed malware files was already taken care of by using simple optical techniques. Changes to and deletion of existing files require no effort from the malware to hide because it is hard to determine which, among the hundreds of thousands of files in the system, were modified or deleted without ample knowledge of the malware's behavior.

But when it comes to changes in the registry settings and other configuration files, hiding them effectively requires a bit more effort since manipulating any settings for the purpose of obfuscation might render the configuration useless. So when it comes to concealing this particular host evidence, certain technologies must be employed by the malware. The same thing goes for hiding active malware activity. Since these certain technologies can only function while the malware is running, the malware must be active, making the hiding of this evidence dependent on the malware being persistent in the system.

The capability to hide while active in memory can range from the simplest method to the most complex. The simplest method can take the form of a homographic disguise of a process name to thwart simple enumeration, or it can be as complex as the utilization of new, sophisticated rootkit technologies. This depends on the malware's mission. If the malware needs to be in the system for a short period of time, hiding usually is not needed. But if it plans to be a permanent resident of the system, hiding becomes a must.

Having a rootkit technology affords the malware an effective way of hiding its footprints in the host while running. For malware that does not utilize any rootkit technology, it hides by applying the old but tried-and-true method of stealth as discussed in previous sections.

Hiding Evidence in the Network   It is always easier to hide host activities than network activities. Network connections always leave a trace. Malware handles this by making the connection less suspicious. It does this by regularly connecting to benign domains, some serving legitimate purposes for the malware, while others are just diversions, and sparingly connecting to its malware resource domain.

And if data is being exchanged between the malware and its resource domains, the malware takes steps in preventing access to or deciphering the data by using data encryption or by embedding the data inside nonsuspicious files during transport.

> **LINGO**
> A **malware resource domain** is a domain that malware utilizes for its purpose. It's an encompassing term for command and control (C&C), malware-serving domains, domain drop zones, and any other domains used for malicious purposes.

Updating the Malware Itself

Malware can only do so much when hiding itself. Eventually, its technology will be revealed and a solution will be formulated. If this happens, the malware simply updates itself with a new generation with the same functions and capabilities, but armed with new technologies to evade detection, as discussed in Chapter 6. The new solution will work on the old malware version but not on the new version, thus ensuring the continuity of the compromise.

But usually, the malware does not wait for it to be discovered to update itself. Updating can be done regularly to fix a malware bug or to introduce a new functionality to the malware. The malware checks for updates by connecting to its malware-serving domain on a scheduled basis. Depending on the configuration of the malware, the update checking is done regularly or sparingly.

Maintaining Exclusive Access to the Compromised System

There is nothing more telling that something might be wrong than a slow system. A system that is slow often raises suspicion of an infection. A system slowdown can be a result of too many resident programs running or a nasty malware infection. Whatever the cause, it often raises a red flag, and malware that wants to maintain a foothold on the system does not want red flags.

Tip

A system slowdown is not only caused by too many programs (benign or malicious) loading during startup and running in memory, but also by conditions such as a defragmented hard drive and a cluttered registry, especially if the operating system is Windows. It is always advisable to regularly optimize a system using tools that came with the operating system and to remove unwanted programs that use up system resources.

Malware can take up too much system resources, especially if it is poorly designed and written. It can take up too much memory and CPU time that causes the system to crawl. But if the malware is designed well enough that it results in efficient utilization of resources, it is able to function effectively without raising any red flags due to system performance issues, unless it finds itself in a system with multiple malware infections or in an already slow system because of too many active resident programs.

Note

In the days when computing power was not as fast as we have now, malware writers took extra care in refactoring their code, even counting how many CPU cycles were needed to execute one assembly instruction. The less CPU cycles an instruction needs, the better. This is because well-performing malware that does not hinder system performance has a higher chance of surviving in a system because it does not raise any suspicion.

Multiple infections in a system, even if the other malware inhabiting the system are efficient in using resources, can still add up. The same thing goes for a system with too many resident programs hogging up memory space and computing power. No matter whether it is other malware infections or legitimate resident programs, having too many programs in one system can contribute to a system slowdown. Unfortunately for the malware, it is ill advised for it to deactivate other legitimate programs, even if it can, because it might break something in the system and thus trigger suspicion. However, it can surely prevent the system from being infected with another malware or even remove it from a system.

A malware can either patch an existing vulnerability, such as the one it used as an infection vector, so no other malware can use it, or it can detect and remove another malware attempting to infect the system or that is already existing in the system so it can have exclusive access to the system. And once it eliminates the possibility of another malware inhabiting the system and ensuring its own exclusivity, it can continue to operate silently under the radar without raising suspicion.

Note
In some cases, the malware installer does vulnerability patching before passing control to the malware.

Communicating with the Attacker

The need to interact with the attacker depends on the malware's purpose. If the malware is on a "hit-and-run" mission, then interaction with the attacker is oftentimes not needed because most malware involved in this kind of operation already carries with it the instructions to fulfill its mission. But for those campaigns wherein continuous malware residency is needed on a system, the malware must be able to reach out and interact with the attacker. This ensures that the malware has the updated instructions needed to fulfill its mission.

Two Kinds of Malware Communication

There are two kinds of communication between the malware and the attacker:

- One-way communication
  - Malware-initiated
  - Attacker-initiated
- Two-way communication

One-Way Communication   Either the malware or the attacker can initiate one-way communication. Malware can simply send information to the attacker as programmed. This kind of malware already has the instruction it needs to carry out the mission. The attacker simply sits back and waits for information coming from the malware. Some keyloggers use malware-initiated one-way communication. The malware does what it is programmed to do and then communicates back to the attacker all the data it has stolen without the attacker ever reaching out to the keylogger.

When the malware simply waits for instruction and acts on it without sending anything back, this is attacker-initiated one-way communication. Most distributed denial-of-service (DDOS) malware is like this. It waits for a target from the attacker and then proceeds with its DDOS functionality. The attacker does not need to receive any information from the malware to know whether the attack is happening or whether it is successful; the attacker simply tries to access the service of the target and if it is unreachable, he knows that the attack has succeeded.

Two-Way Communication   Two-way communication is when there is an interaction between the malware and the attacker. This is a more robust way of communication because the attack can be modified and tailored based on current conditions or situations. The malware sends out information to the attacker, and the attacker sends out commands to the malware based on this information.

Reasons for Communicating with the Attacker

Whether the communication is one way or two way, malware communicates with the attacker to accomplish one or a combination of the following:

- Report its status
- Get commands
- Send information

Just like an obedient servant, malware reports back its status to the attacker as needed, such as the infection status and whether it is successful or not. If the malware has different functions that it needs to accomplish, the outcome of which is important to the attacker, the status of each is reported back to the attacker. It can range from a simple pass or fail status or a detailed report of the outcome of each.

Based on the status reports sent by the malware, if the malware is equipped with this functionality, the attacker in return sends commands to the malware as needed, especially after a successful status report of an infection. Getting commands from the attacker is the most important reason for communication. Without this, the malware loses its purpose and thus becomes useless. It might still function based on the current command configuration it has, but unless it is designed for a "hit-and-run" mission, the malware will lose its relevance in the attack. The commands from the attacker not only include new directives that influence the malware's behavior but also updated information regarding the malware's resource domains.

Note

Getting commands from the attacker is not dependent on the ability to send status reports since not all malware are equipped with this functionality. It is nice to have but not critical to an attack.

Aside from status reports, the malware also sends relevant information to the attacker that can include information about the compromised system, especially immediately after infection, and, of course, most important of all, the stolen data.

Series of Malware-Initiated Network Communications

When malware communicates with the attacker, not all connect immediately to the malware resource domains. Instead, connecting to the malware resource domains is just part of a series of network communications that some of these malware initiate. The purpose of the other network communications is for the malware's own protection.

The following are the common series of the network communications initiated by the malware:

- Check for connectivity by using known good domains such as google.com
- Check for real date and time using Network Time Protocol (NTP) servers
- Check for updates by connecting to malware-serving domains
- Check for commands by connecting to its C&C
- Drop stolen data to its drop zones

Before anything else, the malware checks whether the system it has infected has Internet connectivity. If there is none, the malware does not proceed to the next communication steps. This ensures that the malware does not leave any network communication footprint. Once connection is established, it checks whether the system time of the infected system is accurate. This step is an attempt to defeat a sandbox that manipulates system time. If everything is in order, the malware then checks whether an update is present in the malware-serving domain. If there is, it takes the necessary steps to update itself. If there are none, it proceeds to connecting to its C&C and waits for a command from the attacker. The malware can listen continuously to its C&C or it can poll it every once in a while to avoid suspicion. The polling period can range from a millisecond to days.

In the case of information-stealing malware, if the stolen information is ready to be sent out to the attacker, the malware connects to the drop zone if it is a domain. If it is anything other than that, it sends out the information as described in Chapter 5.

Executing the Payload

This is the most important directive of the malware. This is the reason why the malware exists in the first place. Everything that was done was in preparation for this moment. As we have seen in Chapter 2, each malware class has its own payload. For example, a backdoor's payload enables the attacker to have continuous access to a compromised system, while that of a keylogger's results in the collection of user credentials that was logged from the user's keystrokes. But whatever the payload is, each of them can be characterized using three dimensions:

- Payload severity
- Payload execution cycle
- Payload trigger

Payload Severity

The severity of the payload depends on its nature. Whatever the payload is, it can range from something as harmless as displaying a message on the computer screen to a more destructive Trojan payload that results in the compromised system being unusable, and a complete restoration is the only way to put it back into action.

Payload Execution Cycle

The execution cycle of the payload, on the other hand, is the number of times the payload needs to execute to see or fully capitalize on its results. The execution cycle can be once or it can be recurring. For example, a destructive Trojan payload that causes complete wipeout of an entire system only needs to be executed once, like a nuclear detonation wherein one explosion wipes out the entire area it covers. It does not need to explode over and over again to see the effects of its damages. Another example that needs only a one-time execution cycle is malware involved in local pharming. The malware simply needs to modify the hosts file once to facilitate persistent information theft through local pharming. While the payload of a backdoor, which provides the attacker continuous access to a compromised system, needs to be executed in a recurring manner.

> **LINGO**
> **Pharming** is an attack that redirects traffic intended for a legitimate website to a fake one through the modification of hosts files, network router compromise, or poisoned Domain Name System (DNS).

Payload Trigger

Execution of the malware payload can be instant or it can be conditional. Instant execution means that the malware immediately executes its payload during runtime, while conditional execution means that certain conditions have to be met first before the payload is executed. For example, the malware might wait for a certain date to activate its payload. The most recent malware that grabbed headlines because of a mysterious payload that was supposed to trigger on a certain date is the Conficker worm, which pegged its trigger date on April 1.

Tip

To check whether you are infected by Conficker, use the Conficker Eye Chart located at www.confickerworkinggroup.org/infection_test/cfeyechart.html.

In Actual Practice

Most malware analysis systems have date and time manipulation features to trigger a payload that is dependent on these factors. But this only works for malware that does not check NTP servers or does not utilize any time-checking mechanisms to determine the real date and time.

Malware can use different payload triggers aside from dates. These can include the presence of a software installation, an active process in memory, Internet connection (Wi-Fi versus local area network [LAN]), or any other condition or information that the malware can gather and make sense of. The only limitation is the attacker's imagination.

LINGO

Payload condition is also known as payload trigger.

We've Covered

- The malware infection process
  - Installation of malware files
  - Setting up malware persistency

- Removing evidence of the malware installer
- Passing control to the malware
- Types of malware installation locations
  - The operational location
  - The staging location
- Ways of hiding installed malware files
  - Hiding using attributes
  - Hiding in plain sight
- Ways of passing control to malware
  - Invoking the malware immediately after installation
  - Letting a benign application invoke the malware
  - Postponing until the next bootup
- The main directives of an active malware
  - Maintaining the foothold
  - Communicating with the attacker
  - Executing the payload
- The common series of malware-initiated communications
  - Check for connectivity by using known good domains such as google.com
  - Check for real date and time using NTP servers
  - Check for updates by connecting to malware-serving domains
  - Check for commands by connecting to its C&C
  - Drop stolen data to its drop zones

PART III

The Enterprise Strikes Back

CHAPTER 9

Protecting the Organization

We'll Cover

- The value of a system in the realm of digital threat
- The value of a system relative to the organization
- The value of a system relative to the attacker
- The different characteristics of a system that give it its value
- The cost of compromise
- The threat modeling process
- Basic threat modeling artifacts
- Security solutions coverage
- The process of choosing appropriate solutions
- Types of honeypots
- Honeypot deployment locations
- How to create and maintain an incident response plan

A system compromised by malware poses a great risk to the organization. As we have seen in the previous chapter, a system under a malware's control can be used to achieve the attacker's malicious directive. We have also seen in Part II how easy it is to create and deploy malware to the attacker's target of choice and that conventional solutions are oftentimes rendered powerless against the deployed malware. So the risk is always there that you will become infected.

In a home setup, the owner is responsible for either a single system or a handful of systems connected to a home network, so responding to and fixing a compromised system is easy. But in an organization where there are hundreds or even thousands of systems connected together, the challenge is greater. It's not just the number of systems that makes it more challenging, but also the complexity of the requirements to support the network needs of each system. To effectively protect an organization's network, there must be a full grasp of the characteristics of the systems within the network and the network itself. Understanding the systems under your watch is key in facing the different waves of attacks that you and your organization will face.

In this chapter, I will discuss how to understand your system through the different characteristics that make them valuable. As a result, you will be able to prioritize these systems based on their value so in case of multiple system compromise, it will be easy to determine which systems have to be attended to first. We will also take a look at how prone the systems and the network are to a malware infection and what to do about it. The chapter will then conclude with the introduction of an incident response plan that takes into consideration the system priorities and the current security posture of the network. Basically, this chapter lays down the foundation that will enable you to handle and overcome the ever-persistent threat of malware infection.

The Threat Incident Responders

The rise of digital threats gave birth to a new breed of IT professionals that are not only experts in system administration and networking but also in digital security. They are the ones who respond to, investigate, and mitigate security-related issues that arise in an organization's network, which include hacking and malware infection among others. They are trained in or

LINGO
Threat incident responders and malware incident responders are generally known as **incident responders**.

have knowledge of computer forensics, malware investigation, hacking techniques, and different existing security solutions. They are the threat incident responders.

The incident responders are like the SWAT team of the IT department. Everyone is responsible for making sure that the network is secure and functioning. But in the event of malware infection, they are the ones who are called to clean up the mess.

Having a team of highly skilled incident responders in an organization that is equipped with the proper tools to do their job is a big plus, especially if there is a process in place. This is where the importance of having an incident response plan comes in. A well-thought-out and well-written incident response plan goes a long way, especially in a real malware crisis situation.

Tip
Procrastinating on creating an incident response plan because nothing has happened so far is a very bad idea. A serious malware incident always occurs when you least expect it.

Organizations sometimes fall into the trap of complacency, especially if nothing exciting is happening on the security front. And if something does happen, people often find themselves not knowing what to do. Even with a team of highly qualified incident responders but with no guidance, the response to deal with the threat might be all over the place. The problem will still be solved, but not as effectively and timely as everyone wants it to be. With a plan on hand, everybody will know exactly what to do instead of making something up on the fly, resulting in an effective and quick solution to the malware incident. And the first step to having a plan is to understand the systems under your watch.

Understanding the Value of the System

What makes a system valuable? Is it the system's hardware cost? Is it the cost of the software that makes the system operational? Is it the critical function that the system performs? Or is it the data that the system hosts? Any of these can dictate a system's value. But when it comes to the realm of digital security, understanding the system's value means going beyond the usual value of the system as its owner, the organization, sees it. We have to understand that there are two parties involved here: the attacker and the target. In an attack, the target can be an individual, an organization, or another attacker. So we need to recognize that a system's value is relative to the two parties. We need to take into account the following:

- The value the organization places on the systems it owns
- The value the attacker places on those systems that make them a target

Therefore it follows that a valuable computer system, as defined by its owner, does not necessarily equate to becoming a valuable target. Becoming a valuable target depends on the attack being waged by the bad guys. Depending on the attack, the system's relative value to the attacker can increase or decrease. For example, an attack that is focused on stealing information will find systems holding sensitive data to be more valuable targets compared to critical systems. On the other hand, an attack that is designed to cripple an organization will see critical systems as more valuable targets, as opposed to systems hosting sensitive data.

Value to the Organization

The value of an organization's system in the realm of digital security often boils down into two parts:

- The function of the system
- The user of the system

The Function of the System

Every system running in an organization has a purpose or specific function that is important to an organization's daily activities. The function is what gives the system its value. The function of a system can be classified into the following:

- Operational use
- Data host

Operational Use   Systems used for day-to-day operations include servers and workstations that are used to fulfill a specific function. Some of these functions are critical, while some are not. A system performing a critical function for an organization needs to be available and functioning as intended at all times except for scheduled downtime or maintenance. Otherwise, the impact to the organization might be detrimental. A critical function might include controlling and monitoring a computerized production line, maintaining safety systems to ensure that no unwanted incidents occur, or providing important service infrastructure to an organization's customers and partners. In general, unexpectedly knocking offline systems that perform a critical function can have significant adverse impact to an organization's business.

LINGO
Systems performing critical functions are also called **critical systems**.

These systems are what drive the organization to function. If any of these systems bog down or are attacked, it can cause a denial of service, which greatly affects not only the organization but also its customers.

Imagine queuing up to get your license in a Department of Motor Vehicles (DMV) satellite office. When it is your turn to be processed, the computer systems suddenly go offline and you have no choice but to wait until the problem is fixed. The wait time can be short or long, depending on the problem. And the most frustrating part of this entire incident is that the people behind the desk don't even know how long it will take to fix the problem.

Note
The more critical the system is, the higher its value.

Data Host   Data needed by organizations to operate are housed on systems called data hosts. Depending on the type and sensitivity of the data being hosted, access to these systems is controlled. Access is only given to users or other systems that need the data for their activity. This is a commonsense practice that should be adhered to by every organization. Although this is a choice for some and not for others, for businesses or organizations belonging to certain sectors, this is a compliance requirement. For example, health care organizations must abide by the Health Insurance Portability and Accountability Act (HIPAA) privacy and security rule. As defined by the government, the HIPAA privacy rule provides federal protections for personal health information held by covered entities and gives patients an array of rights with respect to that information. At the same time, the privacy rule is balanced so that it permits the disclosure of personal health information needed for patient care and other important purposes. The security rule, on the other hand, specifies a series of administrative, physical, and technical safeguards for covered entities to assure the confidentiality, integrity, and availability of electronic protected health information.

For enterprise systems, servers host the most important data in the company. They can be private information of people working in the company, customer data, source code, trade secrets, and so on. And usually, servers are very well protected, and access to the server itself and the data is limited to those who are authorized. But in reality, not all important data resides on the servers. Some of this data is worked on, processed, or generated by people in their workstations and laptops. And sometimes copies of this data are left in these systems, unchecked.

Tip

Always consider a very good DLP (data leakage prevention) solution.

Note

The more sensitive the data being hosted by the system is, the higher its value is.

The Users of the System

A system's function is not the only basis of a computer system's value to an organization; another aspect that gives it value is the user or users of that system. Oftentimes, the access right of a system within the company and the data it holds are dependent on who uses the system. This gives a system with high-profile users immense value compared to other systems in the organization.

How often do we see scenes in movies that involve a character trying to get information using another character's PC? A lot. Especially in scenes found in action and spy movies. One that comes to mind immediately is in the *Iron Man* movie. Pepper Potts snuck into Obadiah Stane's office so she could get information using his system. Another good example is from the movie *Unknown* starring Liam Neeson. But I will let you figure out which part of the movie shows this.

So who are these users and how are they different from one another? I commonly divide users of different systems within an organization into the following:

- Executives and senior management
- Technical users
- Human resources (HR) and finance
- Marketing and sales
- Noncritical users

Executives and Senior Management   Systems used by executives and senior management can contain the most sensitive data pertaining to the business of the company. This data can include future company strategy; release roadmap of a flagship product; and confidential correspondence with partners, business contacts, and people within the company. Since these are the people who are responsible for steering the company to success through their decision-making based on various company data they have, this shows how important the data residing in their systems is. Having this data stolen and sold to a competing company can be detrimental to the company's future business.

Attackers usually target these users through e-mail infection vectors. They send out whale phishing e-mails specially crafted for these head honchos to either get them to divulge their network logon credentials or trick them into executing malware in their system. Either way, the end result is enabling the attacker to have access to confidential data reserved for higher-ups' eyes alone and also to enterprise resources the executives have access to.

HR and Finance   Systems used by HR and finance can contain a wealth of information about the employees and the overall financial health of the company. An attacker can gather a lot of information about an individual based on his employee record. This can include not only work-related information, such as work history, performance appraisals, and salary information, but also personally identifiable private information, such as Social Security number, credit information and history, citizenship and immigration status, family information, and residence history. This information can be sold easily to identity thieves or can be used to blackmail an employee into doing something like planting malware inside the organization.

Other data that is up for grabs is the enterprise's financial information. Financial information not intended for public consumption that falls into the wrong hands could be used as a tool against the organization. One example of this is financial dealings between the organization and a favored client. This favored client gets massive discounts on the services and products offered by the organization that are not being offered to other clients. Information like this can tarnish an organization's relationship with other clients not given the discount, and if ever the organization does offer the discount to all clients in an effort to keep their business after this unauthorized disclosure, the organization's bottom line will be affected.

Technical Users   Technical users include research and development (R&D), IT, customer support, and any user groups that are involved with the technology of the company. Systems used by technical users are attractive targets because they usually hold the most valuable proprietary data and intellectual property of the company, like source code, new concept research, and detailed information about a company's technology or the company's systems.

Having access to this information can give a competing organization a significant advantage technology-wise. This is especially true in technology-based companies. Unauthorized access to their specific technology algorithms or system designs that gives them advantage over their competitors could hurt them badly to the point of destroying the whole company. Also, if the information about the company's systems and its network architecture gets into the wrong hands, the organization might find itself compromised.

Marketing and Sales   Systems used by marketing and sales can contain customer leads, customer information, marketing strategy, and confidential sales figures. It can also contain aggregate customer data that can be used to strategize sales effort and marketing.

Just how important this data is can be seen through the monitoring of customer spending habits. Membership cards that retail stores offer that let you collect points for your purchases and exchange them for rewards is one example of monitoring customer spending habits. This information can be used to come up with targeted ads for that specific customer, or aggregate this data together with other customers' data to formulate which products are trending and when. This information is so useful and valuable that Barnes & Noble bought Borders' customer data as part of the deal of acquiring their intellectual property. The data contains customer purchases like books and DVDs, customer names, addresses, phone numbers, and e-mail addresses.

Tip

Nothing is free when it comes to retail membership cards. For the perks you enjoy, you are paying for it with your information.

But with the introduction of Intel's Audience Impression Metrics (AIM) Suite, there is no need to offer membership rewards to understand an organization's target customers. As reported by CNN last November 2011, Intel's AIM Suite is used at digital signs to produce targeted ads. For example, a young lady might see ads for a beauty care product, while a young man might see ads for sports gear. According to Intel, the AIM Suite adds powerful data collection and audience measurement tools to an organization's signage network. By providing valuable metrics that were previously unavailable, the organization can better understand audience characteristic such as actual impressions, length of impressions, potential audience size, and gender and age range demographics. These metrics can help the organization determine the best location for displays, tailor screen content based on audience characteristics, and understand audience engagement levels. The software uses facial detection cameras to determine characteristics of the faces that help determine age and gender. It is worth mentioning that the software does not record any facial images, but it does send data back to the organization according to the same CNN report. This information that is sent back can be beneficial not only to the organization collecting it, but also to a competing organization that sells the same products and services.

Noncritical users   Noncritical users are those who have no need to access any sensitive data in the organization. If they do need to access data, they only access those that are in the lowest spectrum of sensitivity. One example of this certain type of user is a receptionist. Usually the system a receptionist uses has limited access within the network and the data it holds pertains to visitors and their scheduled appointments only.

Value to the Attacker

As discussed previously, a system's value as far as the attacker is concerned is dictated by the attack type. A system becomes a potential target if it fits the bill of enabling the attacker to fulfill the purpose of the attack. If the main purpose is to steal proprietary data, systems that hold data or are used by individuals or groups that have access to data are the best targets, while systems that perform critical functions are the best targets when it comes to an attack that is aimed at an organization's operational disruption or destruction.

Therefore, a system's value for an attacker can be summed up into the following:

- The operational value of a system
- The potential monetary value of data that can be skimmed from a system

The Operational Value of a System

The operational value of a system is very important to an attacker, especially if the attack involves either of the following:

- Taking down a competing organization
- Sabotaging a competing organization

These attack types call for targeting critical systems. Critical systems always have the highest operational value in an organization and in this situation, also for attackers. Sabotaging these systems with false data or taking them down through system destruction or a denial-of-service attack can adversely affect an organization's operation. It can cause a stop in production, an interruption in service, or total system loss. Whatever the effect is, it will cost the organization money.

The Potential Monetary Value of Data

An attack type that involves stealing information always looks at the potential monetary value of stolen data. Stolen data, whatever it is, is only worth what the buyer is willing to pay for it.

For widespread, opportunistic attacks the targeted data is whatever can be easily sold to the public, such as credit card numbers and online banking credentials. This data is so liquid in the underground malware economy that the most popular malware families such as Zeus and SpyEye specialize in stealing online banking information. Since these are widespread attacks, they do not discriminate systems based on function or operational use or the data they host. Every system is a potential target. The attacker assumes that any system, whether it is a home PC or an enterprise system, will, in one way or another, be used for online banking and if that happens the malware will be there waiting to collect the user's banking credentials.

> **LINGO**
> **Liquid data** is data that can easily be sold to the public.

For targeted attacks, the systems that offer most value to the attacker are those that host sensitive data and those that users who work on and have access to sensitive data use. The sensitive or proprietary information found in these systems is what the sponsor pays for when contracting a cybercrime group to wage a targeted attack against an organization for the purpose of stealing data. Most of this data cannot be sold publicly because, relatively speaking, it has no value to them. Otherwise, this would be a very good candidate for an opportunistic, information-stealing attack. In most cases, the data is valuable only to its owners and the criminal sponsor.

For example, the system schematic of a gaming console is kept under lock and key. For the organization, obviously, this is valuable to them, which is why they protect it from being accessed by others who are not authorized. If this information gets stolen, it will not sell as quickly in the underground malware economy because an average criminal will not know what to do with it. But if a certain individual understands the schematics and has the ability to reverse engineer the console using the stolen schematic so a cheaper knock-off version of the console can be sold, or a modification to the original console can be made so it can run pirated games that happen to be distributed by this certain individual, then this schematic will prove valuable to this person. And if this person has the means and the resources to sponsor an attack so he can get his hands on the schematics because it will mean big money for his piracy business, then that schematic will have a monetary value for the attackers that is equivalent to the amount the sponsor is willing to pay for it, minus the cybercrime group's operating expenses. And as a result, any systems that host or have access to this data are now a potential target by the contracted attackers.

Oftentimes a system is targeted solely because of its users. In this instance, the attackers recognize that certain users have access to systems or are using systems that are authorized to connect to data hosts and process this data locally. Think of malware being delivered via an e-mail sent directly to the chief executive officer (CEO) of a targeted company. A perfectly crafted infection vector that uses an effective social engineering technique might just do the trick.

Tip

An organization must be ready to defend against targeted and opportunistic attacks.

One such example is a high-profile attack conducted against EMC. The infection vector utilized for the attack against EMC was phishing e-mail. According to EMC, two different phishing e-mails were sent out over a two-day period to two small groups of employees (see Figure 9-1). Although, the e-mails ended up in the Junk folder, the subject line, "2011 Recruitment Plan," caught the eye of one employee and resulted in the e-mail being read and the Excel file, "2011 Recruitment plan.xls," being opened. Unknown to the employee, the Excel file contained a zero-day exploit through an embedded Adobe Flash file that enables the installation of a backdoor, assuming the exploit will work properly as expected. The vulnerability utilized by the exploit was an Adobe Flash Player vulnerability (aka CVE-2011-0609), which allowed remote execution of arbitrary code.

IMHO

The way EMC handled this attack attempt is commendable. Instead of sweeping it under the rug, they informed their customers and made the necessary moves to address the threat, which should serve as a model for every organization.

Figure 9-1 Phishing e-mail sent to EMC by the attackers

Understanding the Characteristics of the System

Now that there is some level of understanding of what gives a system value in the context of digital threats, it is time to utilize this knowledge and apply it to properly prioritize computer systems within an organization. The purpose of this prioritization is to help in the decision-making process and determining which asset or sets of assets the incident responders must focus on first in cases of multiple malware incidents.

> **LINGO**
> The term **digital asset**, or simply asset, is another word for a system or a computing machine.

In an ideal world, organizations have resources to cover all incidents as they occur, even if they happen at the same time. But in the real world, resources are limited. There are only a finite number of hands in the organization that are responsible for responding to and fixing malware incidents. Therefore, it is imperative that systems are prioritized so the most important systems will be taken care of first. In this way, the manpower is best utilized.

Understanding the different systems under your watch is key in prioritizing which one should be worked on first in case of a compromise. The following are some of the system characteristics that can be used to determine a system's priority:

- System type
- Operational impact
- Sensitivity of hosted data
- Users of the system
- Network location
- Accessibility to the asset
- Asset access rights
- Recovery
- System status

Note

These characteristics are merely suggestions. Depending on your specific need or setup, you might add more to the list. The most important thing here is that you are able to identify characteristics of the system under your control. These characteristics must describe the system's value not only to the organization but also to the attacker.

System Type

A system can be classified into the following types:

- Server
- Workstation
- Mobile device

A server, as we all know it, is a system that processes requests and provides data to other systems. Simply put, these are systems that serve other systems. Workstations, on the other hand, are systems that users use to perform their computing tasks. In this context, we will limit the definition of a workstation to a system that is on site and does not leave its geographical location. In short, this is the desktop in your cube. A mobile device, which technically is a workstation, is a system that is or can be used outside of work premises. A mobile device can be a laptop, a tablet, or a mobile phone.

Usually, systems classified as mobile devices carry the highest risk of being lost and compromised because they can be stolen or accidentally left behind. If the device contains sensitive data and there is no data encryption or remote-wipe functionality, chances are this data will find itself being touted for sale or used to gain access to the organization. Because these systems connect to networks outside of work, they can be compromised. These networks can include the user's home network and public Wi-Fi hotspots. From the point of view of the organization, there is no way of knowing whether these networks are safe. Connecting to these networks carries the risk of the data going through the wire or over the air, being sniffed. It also carries the risk of the mobile device being infected, since most of these networks do not have any protection in place to make them secure.

In Actual Practice

Mobile devices, especially laptops, usually have the most stringent endpoint security and data protection solution.

In addition, mobile devices are prone to rogue wireless network attacks. Mobile devices need to connect to the Internet at some point. Travelers often utilize Internet connections offered by airlines. A laptop user can go online and do some work or simply pass the time surfing while flying to his destination. The most popular airline Internet provider is Gogo. It's SSID (Service Set Identifier), "gogoinflight," is uniform in all flights. Typically, after the first connection, this SSID is remembered by the laptop. This makes it convenient for the user so that every time he boards a flight that offers the Gogo service, his laptop will automatically connect to the network and the user only needs to provide his credentials so he can surf while cruising in an altitude of 30,000 feet.

The same thing goes also for your mobile phone. For example, AT&T iPhone users enjoy free Wi-Fi in certain hotspots such as coffee shops and bookstores. The user simply needs to connect to "attwifi." This is AT&T's free Wi-Fi hotspot's SSID. Once the iPhone connects to it and the user chooses to remember the network, every time the user finds himself in a place that offers AT&T's free Wi-Fi, he will be automatically connected. This is the same behavior as any mobile device. The same feature is at work when you connect to your wireless network at home. You do not need to connect manually and input your credentials all the time to establish a connection. It's very convenient.

But unfortunately, function and security often find themselves at the opposite ends of the spectrum. This feature of remembering and automatically connecting to known networks through their SSID was designed to make it convenient to reconnect to supposedly trusted networks. But this feature leaves a lot to be desired. Its main checking feature of using just the SSID is a flaw in its design. This is a weak method that opens it up to abuse. The attacker can simply put up a rogue wireless infrastructure and give it an SSID of "gogoinflight" or "attwifi." Since most mobile devices have these SSIDs remembered in the network settings, these devices will automatically connect to these rogue networks. The attacker can then conduct a lot of malicious deeds on these connected devices, such as a man-in-the-middle (MITM) attack and the utilization of a rogue Domain Name System (DNS) server that can be used to conduct phishing and install malware on these devices by answering resolution requests with an IP that hosts a remote code execution exploit that can result in a malware installation.

Tip

It is always a good practice not to choose the option of remembering a public network. This will ensure that your mobile device only remembers networks that you know for a fact are safe. It is also a good practice to disable SSID broadcasting in your wireless router so the attacker cannot spoof the SSID.

Operational Impact

Is the system critical or not? This is where that distinction is made based on the operational impact of the system, as discussed in a previous section. The operational impact can be ranked based on the following:

- Production impact
- User impact
- Business impact

Production Impact

Will a system's downtime affect the organization's production? Does the sytem control any processes within the company that are vital to the production of goods and services?

Into Action

To determine whether there are mobile users in your organization that are prone to this attack, you can set up an open wireless network using popular SSIDs such as attwifi and gogoinflight and check whether there are any mobile devices connecting. Those that establish a connection are prone to attack and must be warned about this risk.

If so, will production totally or partially stop if the system is taken offline? What's the effect of this downtime in terms of cost?

User Impact

What users will be affected? Are they customers, business partners, or employees? How many will be affected? Is it only one, a hundred, a thousand, or all of them?

Business Impact

How will the compromise affect the business? Will it cost damage to the company's brand and reputation? Will it affect the organization's existing deals and those that are in the pipeline?

It usually follows that if the user impact includes customers, there is also impact to the organization's business—for example, an incident where the customers are the ones heavily impacted because the system compromised by a hacker or by an information-stealing malware hosts customer information. This incident can have a negative impact to the customers because their information is exposed, and it will also have a detrimental business impact, both in brand reputation and in cost. One recent case was the Sony hacking in early 2011 where customer data was compromised. This was not caused by malware, but it illustrates the impact of user data being stolen, not only to the users but to the company as well. Aside from the cost of reparation, Sony offered all the affected customers free downloadable games and one year's worth of credit monitoring.

Another example of business impact is a defaced company website caused by a compromise. It can put a ding into an organization's reputation, especially if the organization is a security company.

Sensitivity of Hosted Data

Does the system host or contain any data? If so, how sensitive is it? Is the data encrypted or not? How liquid is the data? Can it be sold easily to the public or is it only valuable to a specific group or audience? For example, a system that contains credit card information of customers contains very liquid data.

Tip
Stored data must be encrypted if possible, so, even if it is stolen, the bad guys won't be able to use or sell it. The data will prove useless to the attackers, unless, of course, they have the ability to decrypt it.

Users of the System

As previously discussed, the access rights to a system within the company and the data it holds are dependent on who uses the system. Each user or set of users processes different kinds of data for their daily activities and this data varies in sensitivity depending on who the user is.

Network Location

Is the system located in a production network? Or is it located in a test network? Organizations can have different network tiers, and each tier can be more restrictive than the one below it. The highest tier can be a super-secret network that includes systems that are most critical and host the most sensitive data. Each tier might also have its own security solution in place. The higher the tier, the more protected it is.

Accessibility to the Asset

Can the asset be accessed from outside the organization's network? If yes, how and what are these solutions? Given how easy it is to telecommute and the growing number

Your Plan

How to identify the tier level of your network:

1. Identify and enumerate the critical systems within the organization.

2. Identify and enumerate the systems hosting the most sensitive data.

3. Identify and enumerate the networks they are in.

4. If the systems are spread out, restructure your network appropriately to have them in the same network if possible.

5. Rank these networks based on how critical the systems are and how sensitive the hosted data is in those networks. The highest tier will have the highest number.

6. Once you have ranked the networks, identify and enumerate the other systems connecting to those networks.

7. Do these systems need to be there? If not, place them into the appropriate networks if possible.

8. The other systems that remain in the same network as the critical systems and data hosts will have the same network tier ranking, even if they are not critical, while those that were moved out and transferred to a different network tier will inherit the ranking of that network tier.

9. Make sure the highest-tier systems have the appropriate protection.

of employees doing this, there is always the need to access systems from outside the organization. The most common way of achieving this is by using a virtual private network (VPN).

Aside from VPN, there are lots of other solutions available in the market today that make connecting to computer assets easier and faster. The challenge for IT operations is to identify the risks of using these other solutions and then decide whether to allow these solutions to be used within the company. Also, what other precautions are needed to make sure these solutions will not be abused that might end in a system compromise?

Asset Access Rights

Does an asset have access to other systems or other networks? If an asset is compromised, will it spread infection to other systems?

Aside from an asset's network location, the access rights of an asset, regardless of who uses it, should also be taken into consideration so in case of a compromise, the movement of a possible malware spread can be tracked immediately.

Recovery

System recovery is very important. The system has to be restored back to its last known good and working state before the compromise. This is included in the characteristics because the incident responders need to know whether the system can be restored or not. This saves time and manpower because if a compromised system cannot be restored, attending to it will just be a waste of time. Simply cutting off the compromised system from the network will do the trick. And when everything is back to normal, this system can be rebuilt from scratch because of the unavailability of recovery.

To determine whether the systems can be restored or not, two recovery variables must be taken into consideration:

- Recovery availability
- Recovery time

Recovery Availability

The availability of recovery depends on whether the system has restore points, either locally or backed up somewhere in the network.

Recovery Time

Even if recovery is available, another variable that needs to be considered is the recovery time. How long will the recovery take place? Will it be minutes, days, weeks, months, or even longer?

System Status

Is the system nearing its end of life? If it does, restoring this system is probably not needed. Usually, a compromised asset that is nearing its end is replaced by a new one and no effort is wasted to recover and fix that asset.

Tip

Always keep regular backups of systems nearing their end of life.

Prioritizing the Systems

After the characteristics have been identified and written down, the next step is to put weights on these characteristics. A weight is a numerical value assigned to each characteristic. For example, a system that does not host sensitive data will have a zero weight in its "sensitivity of hosted data" characteristic, while a server that hosts proprietary information will have a higher weight. The weight can range from zero to any number. It can be as low as 10 or as high as 100. This will depend on the range you come up with based on your understanding of your system.

Once the weights are identified, they must be assigned to the system's characteristics. You can then employ a sophisticated mathematical equation or simply add the characteristic weights of the system. Those that have the highest sum are the highest priority systems. If there is a deadlock, you have to sit down and assess which one should be prioritized first. After this process, you will have a prioritized list of systems, which will serve as your prioritization guide to deal with multiple system compromise.

Aside from the prioritized list of systems resulting from documenting each of the system's characteristics, you also have in your hands full documentation of the systems under your watch, which can be used as a reference not only for troubleshooting or solving system and network-related issues, but also for new IT professionals that will join the company. Since the document also defines network location and tiers, IT staff members will only be given access to documentation on systems that are directly under

Into Action

The weights are not set in stone. As the system changes, so does its weights, so if any changes are made to the system, like new data being hosted, its location changed, or adding more users that have access to it, its weight should also be modified appropriately.

their responsibility. Someone who is not cleared to access information on systems located in high-level network tiers will be denied access to resources and documentation containing this information.

The Organization's Security Posture

Knowing the systems through their characteristics enables you to determine each of the system's risk of getting infected, the current state of network security, and the overall security posture of the organization.

An organization's security posture is defined by its overall attitude toward security. Is the organization taking security seriously? Does it have the appropriate security solutions in place? If yes, does the organization treat it as a checklist and simply buy the cheapest solution, or does it do a thorough research and evaluation of existing solutions to determine the most effective one? Does the organization invest in security awareness training? Does it have a security plan and a safe computing process in place? If yes, are they just words written on paper, or are they alive in action? The answers to these questions define an organization's security posture. This will give you an idea of the current state of the organization's security posture and what needs to be done to improve it. A good first step in this direction is to make sure that the systems under your watch are secure. Failure to do so risks costing the company greatly.

Understanding the Cost of Compromise

Every system compromise carries with it a dollar amount. It costs organizations money to deal with the effects of a system compromise. Some of these costs are easily computed, while some are not. Making people, especially the budget approvers, aware of this and openly discussing this stresses the importance of improving an organization's security posture.

There are basically two types of cost when it comes to dealing with a system compromise:

- Direct cost
- Indirect cost

Direct Cost

Direct cost is easily itemized and computed. This usually involves the following:

- Remediation cost
- Business cost

Remediation Cost

Remediation costs include the following:

- Man-hours needed to fix the compromise
- Software and hardware cost needed to fix the compromise

To deal with a compromise means man-hours consisting of incident responders' time and that of other people who will be needed to help in removing the malware or mitigating the threat. Instead of them doing other productive work, their time is spent in fixing a compromise. Also, the incident responders will be using tools that can either be software based or hardware based to conduct forensics investigation, analysis, and detection of the threat. Some of these tools are probably free, while some might cost a little bit.

Business Cost

Business costs include the following:

- Lost revenue due to downtime
- Lost productivity or man-hours due to system unavailability

Since we rely heavily now on digital infrastructure to function inside the workplace, having systems temporarily out of commission because of an infection will cost the organization money in lost revenue that could have been earned if there had been no production stoppage and also lost productivity or man-hours. The people, even though they are not working, will still get paid for simply waiting to have the compromised system back online.

Indirect Cost

Indirect cost is associated with a compromise that everybody recognizes is there but is challenging to estimate. For example, a compromise that went public is sure to affect how the victimized organization is viewed by its partners and prospective clients. A number of prospective clients that are still on the fence might decide against doing business with the company and go to a competing organization. Although these is still unrealized business income, one can only imagine what might have been if the compromise did not happen and some of these prospective clients were in the pipeline.

Another thing about indirect cost is that the financial impact is not exclusive to the organization alone. For example, a banking Trojan that steals financial credentials and information might already be in the process of emptying the checking account of the users who conducted online banking on a compromised system. The stolen money is paid for by the account owner initially and then by the bank once the antifraud guarantee kicks in and the account owner gets his money back.

Protecting the Systems

Protecting your systems and making sure that the network is secure contributes largely to the improvement of an organization's security posture. The information collected from documenting each system's characteristics will serve as a good reference in determining what solutions are needed to protect the hosts and the network.

Threat Modeling

A good way to determine how prone the systems and the network are to an attack is to conduct threat modeling using the information from each of the system's characteristics. Threat modeling is the process of determining the different ways of how a system or network can be compromised based on a solid understanding of the network and the systems in it.

Note
Threat modeling is not limited to systems alone. It is a process that applies to everything that needs to be hardened or secured, like your home. The main idea is finding security issues so they can be mitigated. In software, for example, it is integrated into the software development process. Threat modeling is done during the design phase of the development cycle to ensure that the software being developed is secure.

Threat modeling is not a one-time thing. Before implementing any changes to your systems and network, a threat model is warranted to ensure that the organization's systems and network retain their level of security. This is also a good way to determine if you have missed something during your initial or previous threat modeling. Sometimes it happens that things get missed or not covered in the first pass of threat modeling.

Threat Modeling Process

Threat modeling can be broken down into the following stages:

- Identify the systems.
- Map the network.
- Identify the threats.
- Rate the threats.

Identify the Systems   All systems that require threat modeling or that are part of the network where threat modeling will be conducted need to be identified. The artifact resulting from the process of creating a prioritized list of systems based on their characteristics covers this.

Map the Network The organization or corporate network must not be a mystery to anyone. It must be clearly mapped. The physical and logical layout of the network must be documented.

Identify the Threats With the systems identified and the network mapped, a simulation of possible attacks can be made. In this process, assume the mind of an attacker. Find as many holes as you can and write them down in detail. The description of the threat must be as accurate as possible. What is it? What infection vectors might be used to achieve compromise? Are there any dependencies? If yes, are they found in the organization's systems or network? These are some of the questions that must be answered by the documented threat description.

Rate the Threats Once the threats have been identified, the next step is to rate them based on severity. If the threats directly affect a high-tier network, it is rated high on the severity scale. There are many factors, aside from this, that affect a threat's severity and they are relative to different organizations. Some organizations might think one threat is a major factor, while another might see it differently.

Some of the factors are:

- Affected network
- Affected systems
- Likelihood of occurrence
- Likelihood of success

As previously mentioned, what network tier is affected is a major factor in rating the threat. The types of systems also affect the threat rating. But it is not only the network or the systems—the likelihood of a threat occurring and whether it has the chance to be successful in compromising a system are also taken into consideration when rating the threats.

Threat Modeling Artifacts

The threat modeling process produces documentations or artifacts that can be used throughout the hardening of the organization against threats. These artifacts must be updated if anything changes in the system or in the network to keep it fresh. The artifacts are only valuable if they contain up-to-date information.

A threat modeling must produce at least the following artifacts:

- Systems description
- Network diagram
- Rated threats

Identifying the Appropriate Solutions

Based on the result of the conducted threat modeling on the organization's systems and network, the different security holes that an attacker can take advantage of are identified and rated. This should already give the organization an idea of what appropriate solutions to implement. Some of these holes can be solved by the organization itself, while some will need expert help. The solutions can be as simple as updating outdated software or as complicated as a complete redesign of the network. Once all the security holes are plugged and the other concerns raised by the threat modeling are addressed, the organization should also consider deploying security solutions to protect its environment.

IMHO

Bear in mind that no security solution is perfect, but having the right ones that complement each other deployed in an organization can help lessen the blow of a compromise. It's like vitamin C. You take it to increase your resistance against a cold, but it does not guarantee 100 percent that you will not get sick.

Security Solutions Coverage

The main thing with a security solution or a combination thereof is coverage. Security solution coverage can mean different things depending on what security solution provider's literature or brochure you are looking at. It can mean coverage against specific threats, such as against zero-day vulnerabilities, against botnets, or against mobile malware. Or it can mean coverage of protection for an asset, such as all hosts connected to a network or all mobile devices as they leave the network. These are all good to know, especially when deciding which security solution to get, but the most important security solution coverage that must be addressed includes the following:

- Before infection
- During infection
- After infection

Note

Not all of these will be covered by one security solution alone. To get full coverage, a combination of different security solutions is needed.

Before Infection   Security solutions that have the capability to detect unknown threats should cover this. The main goal of having this covered is to prevent infection from happening in the first place. This is considered the first layer of protection. Some security solutions that fall into this category are host solutions with heuristic detection mechanisms and host and network intrusion prevention systems.

During Infection   Malware always finds a way in no matter what. If this happens, it means that the malware has already compromised at least one system. When the first layer of defense fails, there must be a way to at least warn the user of a compromise. Security solutions that monitor host and network anomalies fit this category. Solutions that detect malware communication also fit this category.

After Infection   Cleaning up the mess is very important after a system compromise. Security solutions that offer malware cleanup, backup, and restoration fall under this category.

Tip

Make sure that the promise of cleanup works. Given how entrenched the malware is in the OS after a successful infection, sometimes a complete restoration is the only way to remove it.

Process of Choosing the Appropriate Solutions

After taking into consideration the coverage areas of security solutions, it's time to go through the process of choosing the appropriate solutions. The following actions are included:

- Identify the security features.
- Research available solutions.
- Evaluate and negotiate.
- Decide, propose, and purchase.

Identify the Security Features   This first and most important part of the process is knowing what security features are needed to protect the organization. To identify the security features, one must look back at the result of the threat modeling session and look at the security deficiencies that were brought to light. Take a look also at the risk of getting infected based on the system's nature and function. All of these will be the basis in coming up with a list of needed security features. For example, if there is not a policy that does not allow the use of external storage to be plugged into any endpoint, you must have a security feature that protects against malware that takes advantage of this vector.

Budget Note

Most of the time, people fall into the trap of looking at available solutions first instead of identifying the security features that they really need. As a result, the organization sometimes pays for and ends up with solutions that it does not really need. Instead of having the solution fit the organization, they are making the organization fit the solution. This is why most budget proposals to purchase security solutions are not approved. There is no concrete data to support the purchase. Identifying the security solutions first gives you the data showing that there is really a need and that it must be addressed.

Research Available Solutions   Knowing what you need makes you a smart security solution shopper. This information can be used to look for available solutions. This is the time to engage vendors and talk about your security needs without divulging any critical information. Read reviews of the security solutions you are considering or they are recommending. Talk to previous and current users of those solutions. Get as much information as you possibly can. After you've made a solid determination that a certain solution is what you need, mark it as your first choice and then identify a backup or a second choice or even a third choice so you will have something to fall back on if the first solution fizzles out.

Tip

There are lots of free security solutions out there. If you plan to consider any of these, do the research and make sure everybody understands the risk of using free or open-source security solutions.

Evaluate and Negotiate   Once you've zeroed in on a specific set of solutions, evaluate each and every one of them, including the backup choices. Run different compromise scenarios and simulate an attack, as was done in the threat modeling session. These use-cases will serve as the success criteria during evaluation.

If based on the evaluation, the security solution passed, then it's time to negotiate the price and other contract terms.

Tip

Price is not the only thing that is negotiable. Some security vendors are also open to negotiating concessions like longer support periods, faster response time, and money-back guaranteed service-level agreement (SLA).

Budget Note

Always have the negotiated price documented. Ask the vendors to provide an official quote that reflects the new price. This document will be used when asking for the budget.

Decide, Propose, and Purchase   After a decision has been made on which solutions to purchase, next comes the challenging part: asking for the budget. In an organization where security is top priority, asking for the budget might be met with little resistance compared to those who see security as something that can be put off. But it doesn't matter which kind of organization one belongs to—the same amount of effort must still be exerted when it comes to preparing a budget proposal. Approval comes if the work is done right and everybody understands the importance of having the solutions in place. Having a well-crafted budget proposal is key.

Budget Note

When budgeting for security solutions, divide the needed solutions according to network tier. If the budget is tight, propose purchasing solutions that will protect the highest network tier first and the critical systems in it, and then the rest of the solutions needed to protect the other tiers can be spread across the different budget cycles. Always propose the purchasing of solutions for the next level network tier. Also, always propose two sets of solutions per network tier: the preferred solution and minimum required solution.

Expect a lengthy discussion and lots of questions during the budget proposal meeting. But if everything falls into place and the approval is given, then a step in the right direction has just been made.

Proactive Threat Detection

Protecting the organization with the appropriate solutions is already a very big step in improving an organization's security posture, and implementing proactive threat detection takes it even further. It offers the following significant advantages. First, it lets the

Your Plan

During the preparation of the proposal to purchase security solutions, the following information must be included in the budget proposal:

1. Preferred solution total cost and its breakdown

2. Minimum required solution total cost and its breakdown

3. Pros and cons of preferred solution and minimum required solution

4. Risk of not buying any solutions or buying only the minimum required solution

5. Cost of compromise that includes restoration cost, manpower cost, and lost business opportunity

Into Action

Budgeting proposals usually happen annually and are reviewed every quarter for proposals that can be removed or added. Even if it is not a budget period, you can create a budget proposal as you go through the process of understanding and protecting your systems. Having a prepared budget proposal early will give you the time to review and refine it for the upcoming budget proposal period. The following is a simplified example of a typical budget proposal.

Network Level 1 Security Budget Proposal

Cost of compromise: 500,000

Cost of manpower to restore: 10,000

Customer restitution cost: 410,000

Estimated lost business opportunity: 80,000

Option 1–Preferred Solution

Preferred solution total cost: 156,000

Network security: 96,000

Host security: 6,000

Security appliance subscription: 54,000

Pros: Full protection is achieved, etc.

Cons: None

Option 2 – Minimum Required Solution

Preferred solution total cost: 96,000

Network security: 96,000

Pros: Network is protected

Cons: Host is not protected

---

incident responders know the different kinds of threats attacking the organization or that it is susceptible to. Second, it gives incident responders the upper hand in analyzing and dissecting the threat even before it becomes successful in attacking the organization's network.

This can be achieved through the following:

- Implementing security solutions with proactive threat detection
- Utilizing honeypot technologies
- Deploying network monitoring tools

Solutions with Proactive Threat Detection

Implementing security solutions that go beyond signature-based technologies to detect threats is always a plus. These solutions often contain technology that utilizes heuristics, data mining, and machine learning. Although not perfect, these solutions will fare better in detecting zero-day threats compared to other traditional solutions.

Honeypots

A honeypot is a monitored resource that serves as a trap or a decoy against an attack or a threat. It is a security tool that helps prevent, detect, and gather information about a threat. It prevents the threat from compromising its intended target by deflecting the threat from real systems to the honeypot. It does this by appearing to be or have characteristics of the threat's desired target. It detects the threat through anomalies or unusual behaviors exhibited by the honeypot, and these behaviors can be used as a signature to identify the threat. The honeypot gathers information by observing the attack or threat as it functions in the honeypot. It does this by monitoring host changes and network traffic. It's the same concept as a sandbox, but instead of running a malware and capturing information as a result of that execution, the honeypot continuously monitors for changes and captures information so it can be reviewed to determine whether an attack has taken or is taking place.

Depending on the depth of information gathered, it can be used to preemptively stop the attack. Since honeypots are designed to be baits, their deployment must not impede or in any way affect production systems and the network.

A honeypot can be any resource. It can be a virtualized machine, a bare-metal box, a network drive, a network service or an e-mail address. No matter what type of resource it is, as long as it is monitored and deployed with the purpose of it being a sacrificial lamb for attacks, it is considered a honeypot.

> **LINGO**
> When two or more honeypots are deployed as a system or a host and are connected to each other to simulate a production network, it is called a **honeynet**. Lance Spitzner of Honeynet Project first introduced this concept.

Types of Honeypots There are two types of honeypots:

- Passive
- Active

A *passive honeypot,* or a low-interaction honeypot, just sits there and waits to be attacked. It can simply be a system set up with low-level security and tons of vulnerable applications sitting in a network just waiting to be compromised. Some of these honeypots utilize deception techniques to simulate user behavior, like logging in and out of websites and opening applications. This makes the honeypot appear like a real workstation.

Another example is an e-mail address that says ceo@your_company.com, which is used as bait for spear and whale phishing. Collected e-mails sent to this address might include information phishing attacks or spear and whale infection vector e-mails.

An *active honeypot,* or a high-interaction honeypot, actively seeks out the threat. This honeypot is similar to a passive honeypot that simulates user behavior, but instead of just mimicking a normal user behavior, it actively crawls and clicks links of dangerous websites that will likely result in an infection. One example of this is Microsoft's HoneyMonkey, aka Strider HoneyMonkey Exploit Detection System. As defined by Microsoft, Strider HoneyMonkey is a Microsoft Research project that detects and analyzes websites hosting malicious code. The intent is to help stop attacks that use web servers to exploit unpatched browser vulnerabilities and install malware on the computers of unsuspecting users.

Honeypot Deployment Locations These honeypots are often deployed in two types of settings:

- Production
- Research

Production honeypots are deployed within an organization as part of their security initiative. They are designed mainly to prevent and detect an attack. Take, for example, a bare-metal machine deployed in a production network that simulates user behavior. The only difference this system has with other workstations or servers in the network is that it has security holes in it. Since most of the real systems in the company are hardened and this is the weakest of the bunch, then the likelihood of this system becoming the initial target within the organization for compromise is very high. Think of a cheetah chasing a herd of gazelles. Gazelles are not just fast; they are also very nimble, making them a challenge for the fastest mammal on four legs. Even though, a cheetah can outrun them, the gazelles' ultimate weapon is its agility, so it is still paramount for the cheetah to choose the weakest among the herd so she can enjoy her lunch with less effort. Same with an attack: the machine that offers less resistance is highly susceptible to getting infected.

Research honeypots are used specifically for the purpose of research. Their main goal is not to deflect an attack, but rather to capture and analyze it. These honeypots are usually deployed in a lab setting where experiments on threats and new technologies are conducted, with the end goal of learning as much as possible from the attack so the appropriate solutions to prevent it from victimizing targets can be formulated. When it comes to actual deployment, these honeypots tend to be much more complex compared to their production counterpart since they utilize technologies, some of which are experimental, to effectively gather as much information as possible from an attack.

Network Monitoring Tools

Having the right network monitoring tools that make sense of what's going on in the host and in the network and that alerts incident responders on a possible threat can stop the threat at its earlier stages. This will be tackled further in Chapter 10.

Creating an Incident Response Plan

To effectively respond to a malware incident, it is not enough to have a list of prioritized systems that will serve as a guide on which systems must be attended to first in case of a multiple system compromise. The organization must have a well-documented incident response plan in place to serve as guide to the incident responders once they are in the trenches. This solves so many "Now what?!?" situations. Nobody wants to have someone deployed to solve an incident and in the middle of the mitigation process be faced with a situation that he is not totally prepared for and suddenly gets stuck on a problem or stops for a long time to think about what the best next move will be. Usually, this causes unwanted disarray and takes a lot of time, and time is very precious when it comes to incident response.

An incident response plan can cover everything from malware infection, system breaches through hacking, to system crashes. Our concentration will be more on responding to incidents involving malware, but that does not mean that the concepts that I will present are not applicable to other incidents. In fact, some of them are.

When creating an incident response plan, consider the following:

- Identify different compromise scenarios.
- Identify solution patterns.
- Define roles and responsibilities.
- Establish protocols.
- Conduct periodic dry-runs.
- Review and improve.

Note
An incident response plan is a plan of action, a guide on what the right move is. It is not a step-by-step manual that an incident responder must follow blindly.

Identify Different Compromise Scenarios

Although nobody can really anticipate everything that might happen, identifying likely compromise scenarios is a good mental exercise in threat prevention. It forces everyone to think at least two steps ahead of the attacker. It's like a game of chess. Your opponent is about to make a move. Given the current position of the pieces, what will happen if your opponent moves a certain piece into a certain location? Will it result in a checkmate? Will it result in one of your important pieces being eaten? Or is it strategic positioning that will leave you no choice but to move your pieces in a specific way your opponent wants you to? You have to take into consideration the different pieces and locations they can be moved to and then predict the possible outcome of the different combinations resulting from this.

Tip
Findings from conducting threat modeling help in identifying crisis scenarios.

Identify Solution Patterns

One advantage of identifying the solutions to the different compromise scenarios is that it gives the incident responders the opportunity to solve the problem in a relaxed and calm state of mind. It takes away the pressure and time constraint that comes with solving a malware infection as it is happening. Going back to our chess game. After anticipating your opponent's every move and the possible outcomes of those moves, you're able to think of a countermove for each scenario. You are now in the position to give an appropriate response to your opponent's next move. In a chess game, you have to act and think really fast because the game is timed. So all of the mental work done anticipating the opponent's every move and coming up with a countermove all happened in the heat of the moment. Oftentimes the result is favorable but sometimes it is not. You'll know when you made a mistake and then come to realize that you missed something and that is what your opponent took advantage of. But what if you can go back in time before you made your countermove, press pause on the remote control of space and time to get rid of the pressure of having a time limit, and then analyze the different move combinations your opponent can take? By considering all the different countermoves you can answer with, you can make sure that you do not miss something and that your countermoves are really effective.

Now, as I have mentioned in the previous section, nobody can really anticipate every compromise scenario, especially with the availability of new malware technologies and the fact that they evolve at a much faster pace than most available security tools and solutions. There will be cases where the incident responders have to face a new compromise scenario. To lessen the impact and to prepare the incident responders for something like this, solution patterns need to be identified. Solution patterns are exactly like that, patterns. They are templates that can be followed and then tweaked to solve a compromise. These patterns are extracted from solutions formulated to deal with a compromised scenario. A solution pattern kicks in when the new scenario closely resembles a known compromise scenario. For example, unknown compromise scenario (UCS) closely resembles identified compromised scenario 013 (ICS013). The solution for ICS013 is Solution 025. Solution 025 is or is part of a number of other solutions that were used to extract Solution Pattern 005 (SP005). This means that SP005 will be the solution pattern that will be applied to UCS. It will be tweaked as needed by the incident responder, and if it is successful, the UCS and new solution will be named and added to the list of identified compromise scenarios and solutions. Otherwise, the incident responder will just have to wing it and document the whole incident so the rest can learn from it. This is where experience comes in, which is why it is crucial to pick the right people for an incident response position.

Define Roles and Responsibilities

There are a few important rules that need to be followed when defining roles and responsibilities. Each of them must:

- Serve a purpose
- Have no overlap

- Be complementary
- Have a point person

Purpose

When defining roles and responsibilities, make sure that they are needed and they serve a purpose. Each of them must answer one very important question: "Will this help in or contribute to the fast and effective way of fixing a compromise?"

No Overlap

A plan must be lean and agile. Only the essential tasks must be included to avoid having a very complicated plan that will be hard to execute. If roles and responsibilities overlap, consider combining them into one.

Complementary

The whole must be greater than the sum of all its parts. Not only must the roles and responsibilities have a specific purpose, they should also complement or add value to the others.

Point Person

Things get accomplished effectively and efficiently if people know who is responsible for what. For a plan to really work, everybody needs to know his or her responsibilities and roles during the plan's execution. Everybody must understand what they are expected to do and the scope in which they are allowed to do it. It's like a basketball team. Everybody on the court plays different positions. Each position is vital to the execution of the play. If somebody messes up and forgets the play or is playing out of position, the desired result of scoring will not be achieved. The play might result in the ball being turned over to the opposing team. But if everyone knows exactly their responsibility on the hardwood floor and performs them as the play dictates, then the chances of them scoring becomes really high.

To raise the level of commitment of people involved in executing the plan, a person's name is attached to each responsibility or role. The advantage of doing this is that it establishes ownership of a process. Not only their names but also their contact information such as an on-call phone number. People who are named and are assigned specific roles and responsibilities are called the point person. They are the expert in and the point of contact for that specific task. And to ensure continuity, backups to the point persons are also named. In some cases there are also backups to the backups.

When it comes to defining responsibilities, it is not limited to what the incident responder is tasked to do, but also includes the power to decide on certain sensitive matters and to tap and command resources, including other manpower, within the company.

Tip

In a serious situation involving malware infection, incident responders sometimes need to make hard decisions. Most of the time they will make the right call, but in some isolated cases they will make mistakes. If that happens, there should be no room for blame. The decision might be applicable during that moment and the decision has to be made. It is better to be decisive and do something instead of not acting. Always foster an environment where blame is absent and where learning from failure or mistakes is encouraged.

In Actual Practice

In some incident response plans, job positions or roles, not names, are assigned responsibilities. The incident responder in that role is understood to be the one responsible for that specific deliverable.

Establish Protocols

Although some of these are common sense, it is still good to establish some basic protocols so everyone will be on the same page during the execution of the plan. This usually includes the following:

- Information source
- Communication
- Scheduling

Information Source

Everybody must be aware of and have access to where vital information is located. There must also be a place where the incident responders can collaborate on different topics relating to threats and solutions. And most importantly, everybody must know where the actual incident response plan is located.

In Actual Practice

Internal wikis are the most popular choice when it comes to information collaboration within the response team. This is also where vital information and important documents are placed for everyone to access.

A good way to ensure that the incident response plan is readily available, even during system downtime that might render any information source unavailable or inaccessible, is to have a hard copy of the plan and other important documents available to incident responders. These hard copies can be placed in each of their cubes or in a cabinet somewhere that is easily accessible.

Communication

The way to communicate with the team and the way the team communicates with each other must be established really well, especially during emergency situations.

In case a possible malware incident is discovered by someone from within the organization, that person must know exactly how to communicate the suspicious incident to the incident response team, which is why it is imperative that everyone in the organization knows how to communicate with the team. For example, an e-mail following a defined format can be used to escalate any issues to the incident response team, or an online ticketing system can be utilized. No matter what technology is used, the main goal is to have the issue communicated to the incident responders, the incident recorded, and the incident reporter updated. The incident response team should also have a backup form of communication in case other technical means are down or the incident responder has no access to any of them. For example, having a hotline that everybody can call is a good communication backup.

Aside from defining the way other members of the organization communicate with the incident response team, the team must also know how to effectively communicate with each other during a malware incident. That is designating different forms of communication to be used for a specific purpose during this circumstance—for example, designating a secure, dedicated Internet Relay Chat (IRC) channel as the main form of communication between the deployed incident responder and the rest of the team, where the deployed incident responder can consult with and update everyone on the current state of the incident and the effort to solve it.

The team must also know the different forms of communication available to them when contacting an internal expert or any external contact. For example, some contacts prefer being contacted via e-mail alone, while some would accept being phoned if the incident reaches a certain threshold or falls under a certain category.

In Actual Practice

For every malware incident, an organization usually has a group composed of some executives and key people from different teams and departments that are always informed and updated about an incident. They are usually informed via e-mail. The incident response team blasts updates to a mailing list that these people are included in.

Scheduling

Since a malware incident can happen any time, having incident responders available 24/7 is preferred. Some organizations assign a designated on-call incident responder or employ shifting. Also when it comes to personal time off (PTO), a point person and his backup are not allowed to take a vacation at the same time. This is why PTO must not only be approved by the respective managers, but must be coordinated with the team members to make sure that somebody is manning the post.

IMHO

If the organization chooses shifting as their way of covering 24/7 incident response, it is always better to change shift schedules at least on a three-month interval. This is coming from someone who has been on night shift for more than three years. This gives the incident responders on shift time to acclimate themselves to their new sleeping pattern.

Conduct Periodic Dry-Runs

Just as there are office fire drills, earthquake drills, or whatever emergency drills there are, tests are regularly conducted to check the efficiency and effectiveness of emergency responders. The same principle also applies to an incident response plan. A periodic dry-run is needed to check whether the plan works or not and to spot areas for improvement. In a dry-run, a malware incident is simulated and then the whole team goes through the process of responding to and mitigating the threat.

Also another advantage this has is that it keeps the incident responders sharp. It keeps them on their toes.

Into Action

Conduct a dry-run or a drill that is unannounced, especially during times when no one is in the office and only an on-call incident responder is available. This helps in determining whether the chosen method of 24/7 incident coverage is effective or not.

Review and Improve

An incident response plan is dynamic. It must change and adapt to the ever-changing threat landscape. It requires periodic review and improvement. It can be ad hoc and triggered by an event; scheduled on a quarterly, semiannual, or annual basis; or done during or after a malware incident post-mortem. The most important thing here is that it is done regularly.

When conducting an incident response plan review, the following are usually the focus areas for improvement:

- Compromised scenarios and solutions
- Applicability of processes and tools

Compromised Scenarios and Solutions

For every significant change in the threat landscape, new threat research findings, and encountering a totally new compromised scenario, a review and improvement of the existing compromised scenarios and solutions is imperative. This process should not end in adding new compromise scenarios or updating an existing solution alone, but also in the removal of outdated scenarios and solutions, if applicable.

Into Action

Keep the incident response team abreast of new technologies and the retiring of old ones. If old technologies will be retired and a compromised scenario is dependent on that technology, then it probably is time to retire that compromise scenario as well. For example, nobody wants a compromise scenario in a 2012 version of an incident response plan that is dependent on Windows 98.

Your Plan

A good way to improve an existing process is by going through the following checklist of basic process improvement questions:

1. What is working well in the process?

2. What is not working well in the process?

3. What new processes or tools would the team like to try?

The main goal of these questions is to retain the processes and tools that are working well for them, remove those that are not working, and have the opportunity to try new things. If they work well for the team, then these new things will appear as an answer to the first question on the next review and improvement session and will be considered a permanent process or tool; otherwise, they will appear as an answer to the second question and will be discarded.

Applicability of Processes and Tools

A process or tool that was effective before might not be as effective now because of the introduction of new methods and technologies. For example, an organization moving to pure virtualization will render processes that do not take virtualization into consideration obsolete. Another example is migrating to a different OS or upgrading to 64-bit. If the tools that the incident responders are using are applicable only to one OS or are limited to a 32-bit environment alone, then those tools will have no purpose anymore and, thus, will become obsolete.

Into Action

To get an accurate response to the three basic process improvement questions that reflects the team's views and experiences, each team member must answer these questions individually, combine all of them together, and then extract the top three answers to each question. To go about this, write the questions on a white board, an easel board, or anything that everyone can see. They can choose to name between three and five processes and tools, and write them down on sticky notes. When they are done, ask the team members to post their answers under the questions on the board at the same time to avoid other team members influencing or being influenced by others. Add up those that are the same, and then get the top three from each question.

To retain the effectiveness of the incident response plan, every process and tool must be reviewed for applicability. Those that are not applicable anymore should be updated, removed, or replaced.

Putting Everything into Action

It's now time to put everything into action. With a much better security posture brought about by the following, the organization is now ready to weather a barrage of attacks.

- Regular processes in place that includes threat modeling and system characteristics review and update

- Documented system information and other artifacts to serve as reference to current and new members of the organization

- The deployment of appropriate and well-evaluated security solutions that are both proactive and reactive

- Having a team of incident responders guided by a plan of action

Beyond Protection

Although everything we have discussed thus far requires a lot of effort, there is still more to do beyond protection. This is not the silver bullet that kills the werewolf. But it is a good and significant step in the right direction. Malware, with all its advanced techniques, still has the capability to outsmart and outmaneuver whatever protection and precaution is out there. The organization must not have only the best protection available, but also be equipped to handle a compromise. The prioritized list of systems and the incident response plan will help in allocating incident responders and other resources that deal with malware incidents much more effectively and efficiently, but it is only the beginning of the fight against malware. The incident responders must be able to not only respond quickly, but also be able to detect the threat before it poses any more danger to the organization.

We've Covered

- The value of a system as it pertains to digital threats
  - Relative value to the organization
  - Relative value to the attacker

- The value of a system relative to the organization
  - The function of the system
  - The users of the system
- The value of a system relative to the attacker
  - The operational value of a system
  - The potential monetary value of data
- The different characteristics of a system that give it its value
  - System type
  - Operational impact
  - Sensitivity of hosted data
  - Users of the system
  - Network location
  - Accessibility to the asset
  - Asset access rights
  - Recovery
  - System status
- The cost of compromise
  - Direct cost
  - Indirect cost
- The threat modeling process
  - Identify the systems
  - Map the network
  - Identify the threats
  - Rate the threats
- Basic threat modeling artifacts
  - Systems description
  - Network diagram
  - Rated threats

- Security solutions coverage
  - Before infection
  - During infection
  - After infection
- The process of choosing the appropriate solutions
  - Identify the security features
  - Research available solutions
  - Evaluate and negotiate
  - Decide, propose, and purchase
- Types of honeypots
  - Passive honeypots
  - Active honeypots
- Honeypot deployment locations
  - Production
  - Research
- How to create and maintain an incident response plan
  - Identify different compromise scenarios
  - Identify solution patterns
  - Define roles and responsibilities
  - Establish protocols
  - Conduct periodic dry-runs
  - Review and improve

CHAPTER 10

Detecting the Threat

We'll Cover

- Detecting anomalies in the network and in the host
- Pinpointing the malware by looking for suspicious behavior
- The goal of using computer forensics in malware detection
- The purpose of classifying the malware based on its attack directives

Chapter 9 laid down the foundation of protecting the organization by improving its security posture through the deployment of appropriate security solutions and having a team of talented incident responders guided by a well-conceived incident response plan to deal with a possible system compromise. But it is always a fact of life that no matter how prepared we are, or how hardened an organization's network is, things can still go wrong and we have to deal with it. As we have seen in Part II of this book, the malware technology has become so advanced that traditional solutions do not stand a chance against them. Even the most sophisticated ones oftentimes fail to detect and stop the latest threat from getting in and compromising a target. If security solutions are 100 percent effective, we will not hear any malware infection or botnet proliferation in the media. We have to recognize that there is always a chance of systems getting infected.

In this chapter, I will discuss how to detect and identify a possible threat based on anomalies in the network and in the host. And once we've identified these anomalies and isolated the systems involved, I will discuss the different tools and methods needed to identify and pinpoint the threat, so it can be classified based on its attack directive and the appropriate systems can be protected and proper mitigation techniques can be applied.

Establishing a Baseline

To identify an anomaly, a baseline must first be established. In detecting anomalies, a baseline defines what's normal. To effectively establish a baseline, behavioral data must be collected over a period of time to take into account the different network and system behavior during low, normal, or high activity in an organization. Based on this data, a baseline can be determined that reflects the normal behavior of the systems during normal operation.

Establishing a Network Baseline

To establish a network baseline, data must be recorded that will give the system administrators an idea of what normal network behavior is for an organization. A snapshot of this behavior is defined by the length of time the data is collected. The snapshot must include periods of low, normal, and high activity.

It must also be understood that a network baseline might differ from one user group to another. Some user groups might have more active network communications to unknown hosts due to research purposes, while other user groups have more active connections to controlled network resources. The most important thing here is that the network baseline represents the normal network behavior of the user groups.

Establishing a Host Baseline

To establish a host baseline is to determine what the host looks like during normal operation. The following are usually recorded:

LINGO
Golden image is another term for base image.

- Master boot record (MBR) and boot sector images
- Configuration files
- Registry files for Windows
- Startup files
- Running processes
- Open ports

In Actual Practice

Since systems in an organization are usually deployed using a golden image, this image is used as the baseline. If a suspicious host deviates from the golden image's characteristics, such as having startup files not included in the golden image and not from software that is authorized to be installed, then that's considered a deviation from the norm. Depending on the rules that are written on what constitutes an anomaly, this alone, or a combination of other deviations, will generate an alert.

Detecting Anomalies

Anomaly detection is the identification of unusual patterns of behavior that do not conform to the norm or significantly deviate from an established baseline. Usually when something fishy is going on in your network or in the host because of an infection, this leaves lots of traces that can be classified as anomalies.

The best way to detect anomalies in the enterprise or in an organization is by employing solutions that have central monitoring and control. The often-used way to detect anomalies is through network behavioral analysis (NBA) and network behavior anomaly detection (NBAD) solutions. These solutions are in addition to, or a complement to, the traditional security solutions of what most organizations currently have. Most security solutions, such as network antivirus (AV) scanning and intrusion detection system/intrusion prevention system (IDS/IPS) solutions, are signature based and only protect the perimeter of a network. They will only detect and prevent what they know. And we all know that given the development in AV evasion techniques, most of these solutions can be thwarted. Anomaly detection based on network behavior is more suited to identifying zero-day threats.

Note

Some organizations employ different AV and IDS solutions at different subnetworks that protect not only the network's perimeter but also the most important systems. Some standards, such as Payment Card Industry Security Standards Council (PCI SSC) data security standards, are required to protect certain hosts with a combination of the aforementioned solutions as a minimum requirement to pass the standard.

NBA enhances the security of a network by continuously monitoring network activity and logging anomalous actions inside the network for analysis at a later time. Think of NBA as a hall monitor and the internal network is the school. The hall monitor knows that during class, there should be no one outside of the classroom unless they are authorized or have a hall pass. The hall monitor also knows that during recess and lunch, the hall is crowded with students. This is the hall monitor's baseline. So if there are lots of students in the hallway during class hours, this is considered an anomaly. It means there must be something going on. There might be an emergency in that classroom, or the students were just asked to leave early because of some unplanned situation. In any case, the hall monitor will take note of this event to be submitted to the school staff for review later. Another thing is that the hall monitor does not care about the security outside the school; there are security guards for that. This is especially true in schools where the students are frisked and pass through a metal detector before entering school premises. Same with the

NBA solution—it does not care about the network's perimeter. The perimeter network security is being handled by other solutions such as firewalls, IPS, and IDS.

NBAD, as with NBA, also enhances the security of a network by continuously monitoring network activity for anomalies. The main difference is that instead of just logging the event for offline analysis, it generates an alert as soon as an anomaly is detected. Let's go back for a minute to our hall monitor. This time, he is equipped not only with his trusty pen and paper but also with a whistle and a walkie-talkie. And he is tasked to blow the whistle or use his walkie-talkie to call the principal's office as soon as he sees something outside the norm.

Note

NBA and NBAD both rely on having a baseline. NBA logs anomalies, while NBAD generates an alert.

There are lots of NBA/NBAD solutions available out there that will help in detecting anomalies. The solution or combination of solutions must be able to, at least, do the following:

- Continuously monitor network events
- Log anomalous events
- Generate an alert for anomalous behavior
- Pinpoint offending hosts

Basically, anomaly detection can be broken down into two parts:

- Detecting network anomalies
- Detecting host anomalies

Detecting Network Anomalies

Let's take a network-scanning incident as one example. In this scenario, a host is actively scanning the local network for the presence of other hosts. This behavior, if it is not defined as a normal baseline behavior for this host, must raise an alarm. Once an alert notification is generated, the following use-cases must be satisfied:

- Identify, log, and display the source of the scanning
- Identify who is logged in to that system
- Identify whether that host has successfully identified, is attempting to, and is connected to, another internal host

- Identify whether that host is attempting to and has connected successfully to an external host

- Identify whether that host is pulling data from an internal or external host

- Identify whether the host is pushing data up to an internal or external host

A solution that can identify these use-cases is already enough to detect the threat. With all this information available to the incident responder, it will be easy to determine whether the anomaly alert is indeed a possible malicious activity or not.

This scenario shows how an NBA/NBAD solution can be used to gather evidence that will help in determining whether a breach is happening in the system. And if a breach is really happening, the incident responder can pinpoint the compromised host where the breach might be emanating from.

Detecting Host Anomalies

There will be instances where the complaint of anomalous behavior will be coming from the user and not as a result of the NBAD solution. A user might complain of a slow machine and/or a slow Internet connection. In this instance, the solution must be able to satisfy the following use-cases:

- Identify possible interface congestions from the system of the complaining user

- Identify the network session emanating from the host to see if there is something fishy going on there

  - What systems is the system connecting to?

  - Are there large amounts of data being downloaded or uploaded?

  - What's the bit rate of the data transfer?

  - What's the server response time?

  - Is the user connecting to systems he should not be connecting to?

The satisfaction of these use-cases can help in identifying a possible malware infection that reaches out to other hosts to infect them, downloading data from external hosts that can be commands or updates of the malware, and uploading stolen data to external hosts. With this determination, the incident responder can pinpoint the offending host and also gather data about internal hosts that might already be infected and external hosts, which can include command and control (C&C), server malware, and other malware network resources, and use it to pinpoint the malware.

The preceding scenario shows how the solution enables the incident responder to gather evidence on a host suspected by the user to be infected. In this example, the compromised host does not need to be pinpointed because it is already brought to the attention of the incident responder. The incident responder simply needs to verify whether indeed it is compromised or not.

Isolating the Source of the Anomaly

The end result of anomaly detection should always pinpoint the compromised system so that it can be isolated. Once the compromised system has been identified, the incident responders must have the ability to isolate the system or the host from the network. Take note also of assets that the compromised host has successfully connected to. These assets have to be investigated for possible compromise. There is always the possibility of these assets being infected, so they must be checked for any host anomalies and isolated as well if needed.

Diving into the Compromised Asset

After the compromised system or systems have been identified and contained, the next step in detecting the threat is to dive deeper into the system to find the specific threat. Remember the main objective of this task is the following:

- Pinpoint the malware
- Classify the malware based on its directive

Pinpointing the Malware

Usually, the first thing that an incident responder determines is whether the AV product installed in the host detected anything. Most of the time, this will yield no results, so it is really not that helpful to the incident responder.

The challenge here is to know where to start looking. The information the incident responder already has that enabled him to identify and isolate the compromised system will be a guiding factor.

Typically, a telltale sign that generated an alert is an unauthorized or an unknown network communication originating from the compromised asset. The network communication can be an attempt to connect to a Universal Resource Locator (URL) or a name resolution request for a domain. This network communication can be your starting point in identifying the specific malware threat.

With a domain or URL on hand, the incident responder can start looking for processes that initiated the connection to this domain. Several tools can be used to do this. One of them is TCPView by Microsoft. TCPView is a good monitoring tool to determine which process initiated a network communication. But since TCPView is a monitoring tool without logging capabilities, the incident responder has to sit there and actively check for any connection to the offending domain. This is not effective, since some connections happen too fast for the connection to be written down or the tool's monitoring result to be saved in a text file. TCPVcon.exe, as seen in Figure 10-1, solves this. TCPVcon.exe is the command-line version of TCPView.exe.

This tool can be used to capture to a log or comma-separated value (CSV) file all information found in TCPView regarding network communication. The incident responder can simply create a batch script that will execute the tool in a continuous loop to capture the information to a CSV file, as seen here:

```
@echo off
:loop_here
tcpvcon.exe -a -c >> tcp.csv
::insert delay here
GOTO loop_here
```

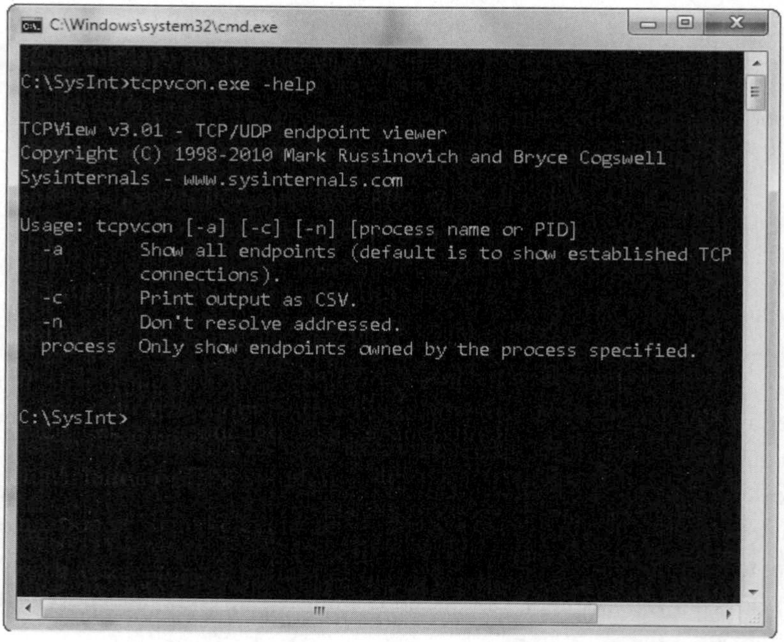

Figure 10-1 TCPVcon.exe command-line tool

The code is a simple batch loop that can be terminated using CTRL-C. Also, a delay can be inserted into the batch script. The delay command will depend on the resource kit that is available in the host.

The CSV or log file can then be collected at a later time and then a search performed on the offending domains. If they are present, take note of the process and process ID (PID) of the process initiating the communication. This file, or sets of files, will then be flagged as possibly suspicious. Collect these files and subject them to analysis by using free tools (VT, Anubis, CWS) in house (if you have your own sandbox), or submit them to AV companies for detailed analysis.

In Actual Practice

Files that are sent out for analysis are screened for confidential information to avoid it being divulged to a third party.

But there will be instances when there is no information like suspicious domains or URLs available, especially if the report is from the user. This means that the compromise was not detected by any of the monitoring systems. The user who is seeing weird stuff happening in the system raised the concern. The challenge here is not only where to start but also what to look for.

Computer Forensics

This is where computer forensics comes in. The appropriate solutions that have been deployed are there to solve an attack or threat that they already know. Computer forensics, on the other hand, comes into the picture if the security solutions failed to prevent an attack, which resulted in the organization's system or systems being compromised.

Computer forensics focuses on the gathering and analysis of evidence after an attack has occurred. In this context, we will be applying the discipline of computer forensics to pinpoint the malware. The main goal is to identify the following:

- Timeline of the attack
- Components of the attack
- Motive of the attack
- People behind the attack

Due to the complexity and sophistication of malware, some of these goals will not be achieved due to lack of evidence as a result of the malware covering its tracks. The important thing is that everything that can be gathered as evidence is collected.

Timeline of the Attack The timeline of an attack should answer what happened when. It includes the following:

- When the infection vector reached the target
- When the malware was installed
- When the malware first reached out to the attacker
- When the malware first attempted to spread
- When the malware first executed its directive
- When the malware destroyed itself (if applicable)

The timeline of an attack starts from the moment an infection vector reaches the organization. It can be the date an e-mail sent out by the attacker reached the target organization or the time when an exploit-hosting website was visited by someone from the organization that resulted in the installation of malware. This is referred to as time zero. It is also important to record, if possible, when the malware was actually installed. In some cases, this happens later. For example, a malware sent out via e-mail reached a target on time zero, but it took a user three days after that to read the e-mail and eventually install the malware unknowingly. This is a good way to determine why a malware carrying e-mail stayed undetected in the mail server or local mail storage for three days.

The timeline can also include the malware's behavior timeline that focuses on the timing of its system level and network behavior. For example, the malware checked for connectivity first by connecting to www.yahoo.com before it connected to any of its resource domains. Since this happens in a microsecond, it is impractical to put the exact time when each occurred—a simple flow of the behavior will do, as seen in Figure 10-2.

A timeline usually ends when the malware achieves its directive or when it destroys itself. Malware that has achieved its goal usually just sits on the system quietly until the next round of its payload execution, while some malware kills itself after achieving its directive. This is especially true for malware that does not want to leave a trace of its presence. In some cases where the motive is system destruction, usually by a Trojan, the directive results in the malware being destroyed in the process.

Components of the Attack The different components of the attack are enumerated and characterized to better understand its behavior and how it became successful in

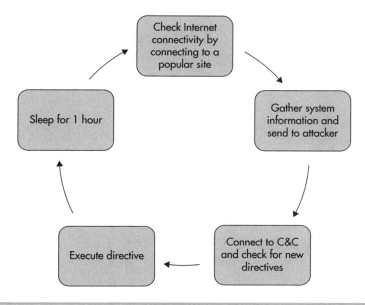

Figure 10-2   An example of a simple malware behavior flow

compromising the system. The components include the deployment technology, the malware installer, and the malware components that are installed in the system.

Motive of the Attack   This answers the question why the attack was waged against the organization in the first place and how it benefits the attacker. Understanding the motive leads to enough information that the organization can protect some of the assets that might be enticing the attacker to achieve his directive.

People Behind the Attack   This is the most challenging part of forensics, unless the attackers are stupid enough to leave digital trails that will lead to them. The people behind the attack are usually unmasked through a series of attack attributes that are collected during an attack. For example, e-mail addresses used by the attacker to register domains and handles used in hacker forums can be collected from different attacks. Different attacks are usually tied together using these attributes.

The next best thing that results from gathering enough information or evidence that will point to the people behind the attack is that the incident responder can profile the attacker. Having an attacker profile also enables the incident responder and the organization in general to anticipate the attacker's next move.

Simple Malware Discovery

Given that computer forensics can be tedious and a whole book can be dedicated on the subject alone, sometimes it is enough to simply verify the presence of malware and then extract it for further analysis.

The usual route in identifying whether malware is present in a system is by looking for the following:

- Suspicious network behavior
- Suspicious host behavior

Looking for Suspicious Network Behavior   Chances that a malware will communicate back to the attacker or to its network resources are very high, especially if it is a targeted attack. There is always that need to phone home, as it offers several advantages as we have seen in previous chapters. Unfortunately for the malware, this advantage is also its weakness. Once it reaches out to the attacker, it is exposing itself to detection. Although the malware utilizes certain techniques to conceal its network communications, the best it can do is hide what's being communicated; however, the communication itself is easily detected.

The most commonly used tool in detecting malware network behavior is Wireshark. Figure 10-3 shows a captured packet of Zeus communicating back to its C&C.

Typically, the malware can be identified just by the network communication alone. The communication is tied to the process initiating it, and the program associated with or that injected itself into that process is most likely the malware.

Looking for Suspicious Host Behavior   Malware writers invest most of their time in finding ways to hide their creation in the host. By utilizing the different obfuscation techniques and rootkit technology discussed in previous chapters, looking for malware can be quite challenging for the incident responders.

Looking for malware in a host is similar to identifying the telltale signs of infection. To spot these, certain tools are used—mostly monitoring tools that show running processes, input/output (I/O) operations, and registry writes among others. The incident responder must be able to collect data from these tools and correlate this information to determine whether there is an infection in the host. The most popular set of tools in Windows when it comes to scrutinizing the host for telltale signs of infection is Microsoft's Sysinternals Suite. Another is Trend Micro's HijackThis tool as seen in Figure 10-4.

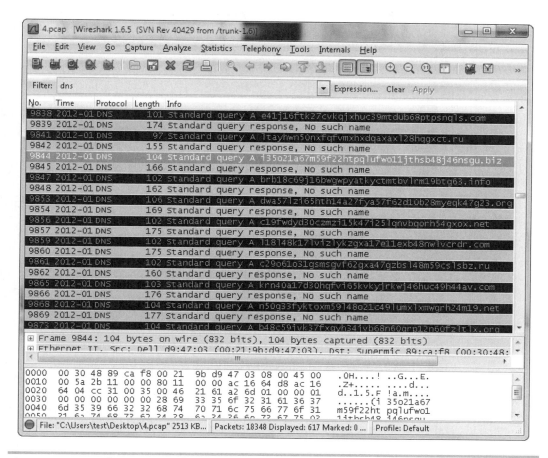

Figure 10-3   Packet capture of Zeus communicating back to its C&C

In Actual Practice

Some AV vendors provide a tool that will collect information from a suspected infected host. The resulting log file is then submitted to the AV researchers to determine whether there is a possible infection in the system. HijackThis, which is now owned by Trend Micro, is a free tool that can be used to gather host information.

Most of the time, these methods do not work, especially if the malware utilizes advance rootkit technology. In cases like this, tools that specialize in detecting rootkits are utilized. Sysinternal's RootkitRevealer and GMER from www.gmer.net are among the

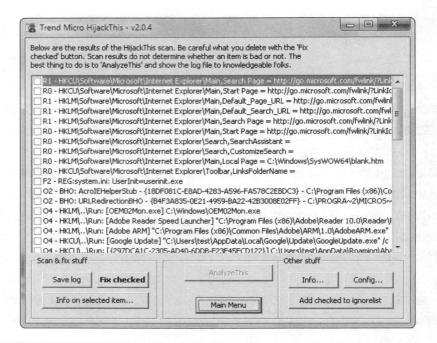

Figure 10-4   Screenshot of Trend Micro's HijackThis tool

more popular ones. AV vendors also have their own rootkit detection technology that is embedded in their product or offered as a stand-alone tool, such as F-Secure's Blacklight and Trend Micro's RootkitBuster, among others.

If the rootkit technology is hard to beat, especially if it is new or unknown to the rootkit detection tools, an offline analysis of the system is done. This means that the system's OS is not running or active during analysis as a result of booting from another device or attaching the hard drive of the compromised system to an analysis system. In this situation, the incident responder can either go the computer forensics route, as discussed in the previous section, or the easier snapshot route.

In Actual Practice

Some organizations have their own analysis system where hard disks of infected systems are plugged in for offline analysis.

In the snapshot route, a snapshot of the system or hard disk is taken. This includes the MBR, the boot sector, the file system, configuration files, registry in Windows, and any other system areas that a malware might utilize to hide and become persistent. The purpose of the snapshot is to give the incident responders an idea of the current state of the system. This snapshot can then be compared to the base snapshot of the system or to the golden image to determine the difference. Identifying what changed will give the incident responder information on where to start investigating.

Note

Oftentimes there is no need to compare to a base snapshot, especially if the current state of the system or its snapshot already reveals telltale signs of an infection. For example, a number of files and registry entries related to them become visible now that the rootkit is not running as a result of offline analysis.

A good place to start is to find out what autostart programs were not part of the original host baseline. From a list of newly identified autostart programs, the list can be narrowed further by eliminating those that the user installed, as approved by IT, in their computer systems. The remaining ones will be investigated one by one. From here, each file that autostarts will be collected and subjected to scrutiny to determine whether any of these files are malware.

Tip

Use Microsoft's Autoruns tool to determine the different programs that start up in your system. This is only applicable during live analysis when the OS is active.

In Actual Practice

Some organizations have their own in-house malware expert as a technical reinforcement to their incident response team. This person focuses on analyzing or even reverse engineering files to determine malicious intent. For those organizations that do not, the suspected malicious files are sent to AV vendors for analysis. Depending on the support tier the organization has access to, the turnaround time of analysis can be hours or days.

If malware is identified in any of these files, the appropriate information must be gathered to help the incident responders understand fully the malware's behavior and enable them to act appropriately to protect the organization's digital assets. And the best way to determine which assets to protect is to classify the malware based on its directive.

Classifying the Malware Based on Its Attack Directive

As we have seen in previous chapters, malware can be classified in different ways. It can be based on behavior, target OS, and many more factors. But in this section, we will classify them based on their attack directive. We all know by now that malware is just a tool of the attacker to achieve his directive. It is not the alpha and the omega of the attack. It is just one component—albeit a very important component, if I may say so.

Classifying malware based on its attack directive serves two purposes:

- It is the key to protecting the organization's assets.
- It is the key to mitigating the compromise.

Protecting the Assets

One purpose of classifying malware based on its attack directive is to determine what assets need to be protected so that appropriate action can be taken immediately. As we have discussed previously, an asset's value to the attacker is dictated by the attack directive the bad guys are trying to accomplish.

To determine which assets to protect, the following information needs to be extracted from the malware:

- The malware's payload
- The malware's spreading mechanism

In Actual Practice

AV researchers often accomplish both of these tasks. Organizations without any personnel with malware analysis skills rely on the expertise of their security providers. This information is critical, in that some AV vendors offer a service level agreement (SLA) in which they agree to provide not only detection but also information about the malware so the client organization can take the appropriate measures to protect their other assets—especially if the assets host intellectual property and sensitive data that is vital to an organization's operation and success. This makes an agreement of this nature very important.

The Malware's Payload   The malware's payload determines how the malware is utilized. For example, an information stealer calls for securing data hosts and sensitive data traveling through the organization's network, while a Trojan targeting to cripple the organization calls for the protection of operational critical systems.

The Malware's Spreading Mechanism   If the malware possesses a spreading mechanism, it is important to determine how it spreads. Does it spread via e-mail, via network share, or through a vulnerability found on nearby systems? Knowing the spreading mechanism enables incident responders to block resources needed by the malware to spread or to perform some necessary adjustments to systems and the network to avoid a malware outbreak and to check assets that could have already been compromised by the malware.

Mitigating the Compromise

Another purpose of classifying the malware based on its attack directive is to understand the motive behind the attack. This usually reveals the dependencies it needs to be successful. Blocking access to these dependencies impedes the malware from executing its directive. For example, if an organization that is compromised is to be used as a staging for DDOS attack by using a specific port, knowing what this port is will enable the incident responders to close it preventing any distributed denial of service (DDOS) attack emanating from the organization. This simple mitigation technique effectively thwarts the malware's directive, rendering it useless—at least until the next malware update.

We've Covered

- Detecting anomalies in the network and in the host
- Pinpointing the malware by looking for suspicious behavior
  - Looking for suspicious network behavior
  - Looking for suspicious host behavior
- The goal of using computer forensics in malware detection
  - Map the timeline of the attack
  - Identify the components of the attack
  - Identify the motive of the attack
  - Identify the people behind the attack
- Classifying the malware based on its attack directives
  - Key to protecting the organization's assets
  - Key to mitigating the compromise

CHAPTER 11

Mitigating the Threat

We'll Cover

- What is threat mitigation

- The stages of malware threat handling

- How to immediately and proactively mitigate a threat

- Common policies included in a safe computing process

- The importance of conducting a periodic security audit

- Who are the insider threats

- How to mitigate insider threats

Let's put into perspective what we have covered in this part of the book so far. Chapter 9 introduced the importance of prioritizing the different systems within an organization to efficiently manage resources used for malware incident response. Chapter 9 also took a look at the security posture of the systems to determine how prone they are to an attack and to help in determining the appropriate security solutions that will help in minimizing the likelihood of a malware incident from occurring. While some of the solutions presented in Chapter 9 help in securing the network perimeter of an organization to prevent any incident of system compromise, Chapter 10 introduced solutions to detect anomalies within the network to isolate, quarantine, or contain possible infected assets. Chapter 10 also discussed how to pinpoint the malware that is used in the attack and is responsible for carrying out the attacker's directive in the compromised assets. Once found and fully analyzed, the malware is classified based on its attack directive so other assets can be protected from compromise and the appropriate steps can be taken to remediate the compromised assets.

In this chapter, the discussion will focus on threat mitigation: the immediate and proactive response an organization can take to mitigate a threat. The immediate response concentrates more on handling a malware infection, while the proactive response delves more into the different preventive measures available to the organization. The chapter then concludes on the topic of security audits to stress the importance of evaluating the different solutions, processes, and procedures that are in place, which are all designed to mitigate a threat.

Threat Mitigation

First, threat mitigation is not equivalent to threat remediation. Threat remediation is the removal of a threat, while threat mitigation is making the impact of a threat less severe.

It's like getting ready for rain. A man knows that it will rain and that means there is a chance that he will get wet. To lessen the impact of getting wet, he brings an umbrella. But based on his past experiences, an umbrella cannot ensure that he will stay 100 percent completely dry. Depending on the wind and how the rain is falling, his head and upper body might still stay dry but his lower body might get wet. To decrease the chances of this from happening, he also decided to wear a raincoat that covers him to his ankles. He also anticipated that it might be windy and the umbrella might break under this condition so he also brought a hat or made sure that the raincoat he brought has a hood, so in case the umbrella breaks, his head won't get wet. By bringing these things he has mitigated getting wet. He will still get wet a little, but not as much. The impact is so negligible that he won't need to spend a minute drying himself. But what if, through some twist of fate, he still got wet. How would he respond? Good thing he has a towel in his backpack. He was able to dry himself as soon as he got wet and minimize the risk of getting sick.

This is similar to threat mitigation. Again, threat mitigation is the process of making the impact of the threat less severe. It pertains to actions an organization takes to weather the storm of threats, just as the man brought rain gear to prepare for rain. It must be understood that an organization will be subjected to an attack, or a barrage of attacks, depending on what type of organization it is. It will rain and it will rain hard. To lessen the impact, the organization has its own umbrella, hat, and raincoat in the form of preventive measures. As the man learned from his experience during rainy days, by using more than an umbrella to brave the rain, the organization must also assess and continuously improve the preventive measures it has in place.

But as discussed in previous chapters, given the sophistication and continuous evolution of malware technology, malware will always find a way in. The organization will still get wet. When this happens, the organization must be ready to respond and treat the infection, just as the man was equipped with a towel so he could dry himself immediately if he gets wet. This results in a more manageable malware infection situation that has less-to-negligible impact. Failure to respond to a compromise carries the risk of it spreading, which might result in an internal outbreak, or worse, a worldwide malware outbreak. If this happens, the negative impact will be great. Therefore, it is imperative that the organization have the capability to respond to threats.

So, in essence, threat mitigation boils down to two types of responses:

- Immediate response
- Proactive response

Immediate Response

The previous chapters set the stage to improving an organization's security posture. Among them is having a team of incident responders guided by a well-thought-out incident response plan to effectively deal with threats that have successfully found their way inside an organization. This is the organization's towel—its immediate response to threat. A well-executed threat response lessens the impact of a malware infection that already found its way inside the organization.

As previously stated in Chapter 9, an incident response plan can cover everything from malware infection and system breaches through hacking to system crashes. But in this discussion, our concentration will be more on responding to incidents involving malware, aka malware threat handling.

Malware threat handling focuses on responding to system compromise as a result of malware infection. It is divided into the following stages:

- Containment
- Verification
- Threat detection and classification
- Remediation and restoration

Containment

When an alert regarding a possible threat has been raised and the compromised system or systems have been identified, the first step an incident responder takes is to isolate that single or those multiple systems from the network. Containment has to happen quickly to avoid a network-wide infection internally, or worse, a worldwide malware outbreak.

Typically, a system is quarantined immediately if it is identified through network and host anomaly detection.

Verification

Once the compromised systems have been contained, they are subjected to verification and investigation. The anomalies that contributed to the alert being raised are verified. Is it really an anomaly, or is it part of a daily operation that was not taken into consideration during the establishing of the baseline for network and host? Or is it a one-off anomaly that is not malicious but triggered by a special task initiated by the user? These have to be verified first before jumping to any conclusions. This is also a good step in refining the organization's anomaly detection solutions.

Threat Detection and Classification

After it is verified that the alert is indeed anomalous and not a false alarm, investigation of the cause of the anomaly is the next course of action. The offending systems are investigated for a possible infection. Threat detection techniques, as discussed in Chapter 10, are performed to pinpoint the malware and its components plaguing the compromised systems.

Note

There are cases where no malware will be found even if there is strong evidence that there was malicious activity in the system. This is normal and is indicative that the malware might be active only in memory because of certain software vulnerabilities, e.g., SQL Slammer, or the malware already achieved its directives and deleted itself to hide its tracks as discussed in previous chapters.

And once the behavior and directive of the detected malware found in the compromised system is understood, the incident responder gains not only the needed knowledge to stop the threat but to also identify other digital assets or systems that are possibly compromised as dictated by the malware's directive or as a result of the malware's spreading mechanism. If specific data targets are identified, the data hosts are doubly protected and verified for a possible breach, while the data itself is checked for integrity to avoid any form of data manipulation and sabotage. Then other systems that are possibly targeted for compromise are also quarantined and investigated to avoid any unwanted malware outbreak.

Remediation and Restoration

Remediation is the process of removing malware from the compromised systems. In most cases, remediation is provided by antivirus (AV) vendors in the form of clean signatures used by the product's scan engine or as a stand-alone fix tool. There are also clean tools provided by hobbyists or the open-source community, especially if the malware is hot or noteworthy.

LINGO

Hot malware is malware that is spreading rapidly or has caused a worldwide outbreak of infection, while **noteworthy malware** is malware that possesses new and interesting features and technology.

In Actual Practice

Given the complexity of malware today, remediation is not always provided at the same time as detection signatures by AV vendors. Most AV vendor service level agreements (SLAs) only mention the provision of detection and malware reporting but no remediation.

Into Action

Exercise caution when using clean tools from unverified or untrusted sources, as they may cause more infection. Remember that rogue file shares exist that are ripe with malware, as discussed in Chapter 7. One technique that can be applied immediately to make sure whether a clean tool is benign is to submit it for verification to AV vendors.

Remediation is not a trivial task. There are instances wherein the changes the malware makes to the system cannot be reversed without risking damage to the operating system. For cases like this, restoration is the only way to go. Restoration can be full or partial.

A full restoration is rebuilding the compromised system from scratch as if it was a new system. This takes more time and effort, but is the safest bet when it comes to the malware being completely eradicated from the system.

A partial restoration, on the other hand, is the quickest but it carries the risk of reinfection, especially if the malware's behavior and regeneration techniques have not been fully understood. This is especially true for stealthy malware with hidden components that have not been analyzed fully. A partial restoration can include reinstallation or repair of damaged software or components of the operating system that was caused by the removal of the malware and its components. It can also include a restoration to a known good point in time when the system was not yet compromised, similar to what Microsoft's System Restore has in its Windows systems.

Proactive Response

Fixing a compromise by following the stages of malware threat handling does not stop the attacker or other groups of attackers from waging another campaign. The threat is always there. It is persistent. Think of a tidal wave that is always there. It varies in size and strength. It can be a small wave that has virtually no effect on the beach, or it can be a big wave that pushes swimmers to shore or sucks them farther into the ocean. And once in a while, a tsunami takes place that leaves a path of destruction and flooding that can overwhelm rescue personnel. Same with attacks—some are small or simple and can be easily thwarted with the security solutions in place, while some are big or a little bit complicated and might require a little bit of effort to stop. And once in a while, a tsunami of orchestrated attack campaigns is waged against an organization that renders existing security solutions useless and overwhelms the organization's malware incident responders.

In short, another attack is bound to happen, if it is not happening already, again and again and again. It can range from the simplest to the most advance attack waged by a group of highly skilled, highly motivated, and well-funded cybercriminals. So the organization has to be vigilant and be prepared for any attack that will come its way no matter how trivial or how serious and complicated it is.

It must be understood that the target cannot prevent an attack from happening because it does not have complete control over the attackers to compel them to stop. The one thing an organization has control over is its security posture. Improving its security posture by putting in place the appropriate security solutions is very important. But given the trend of improving malware technologies, sooner or later a compromise will happen. And the best way to deal with this is to recognize this possibility and do whatever the organization can or is necessary to prevent a compromise from happening or making its effect less severe by putting in place procedures, policies, and technical solutions that will mitigate the threat of an attack.

To effectively mitigate a threat, the organization must not only have the capability to respond to a malware incident efficiently and effectively, but it must also institute the following to help in improving its security posture. This is the organization's raingear, its proactive response to threat:

- Preventive measures
- Conducting a periodic security audit

Preventive Measures

As the old saying goes, "An ounce of prevention is worth a pound of cure." There's nothing more true than that when it comes to security. Investing in threat prevention today will save the organization time, money, and a lot of headache in the future. Having the appropriate security solutions in place to protect the organization from an attack is a good start. But the organization has to recognize that advances in malware technology render most of these protections only as good as the day they are updated. In terms of stopping a malware intruder, it can only stop those that it knows about. To prevent a compromise resulting in an onslaught of attacks, the organization must do more than just buy and implement security solutions. A very well-conceived combination of procedures, policies, and technical solutions must be put in place that will contribute to having an effective preventive measure against a compromise, the most common of which are the following:

- Implementing a company-wide safe computing process
- Building a culture of security awareness
- Going beyond security solutions for added protection

Safe Computing Process

Implementing a safe computing process is vital to every organization today. This is usually made up of policies and procedures aimed at fostering safe, secure, and responsible computing. Depending on the individual policies contained in the safe computing process, it can be enforced technically or through an advisory that the users of the systems must adhere to. The latter depends on the users policing themselves and being honest that they are conforming to the process in place.

The most common policies included in a safe computing process are as follows:

- Password policy
- E-mail policy
- Host policy
- Network access control policy
- External storage policy
- Information control policy
- Social media policy

Password Policy   Having a password policy in place is the first step to security. The main purpose of this policy is to make sure that passwords used to access the network are strong enough to thwart any password guessing or stealing methodology.

This policy will likely contain rules on the following:

- Password construction
- Password uniqueness
- Password shelf life

The password construction includes the length and the character requirements needed to construct a password. For example, a password must be at least ten characters long, containing at least one number, one capital letter, and one special character.

The password uniqueness rule prohibits not only the use of any user-identifying passwords, such as family name or birthday, but also the reuse of old passwords. For example, a password that has been used the previous year cannot be used anymore.

The password shelf life is the duration of the password's validity. For example, a user needs to change the password every six months.

A password policy can be enforced either through a guideline that is mandated to be followed by everyone within the company or through technical means. For example, a user that does not change a password upon its expiration will not be able to log in to the network. Another example is having a password checker that checks a password's strength.

In Actual Practice

To ensure password security, one university employs brute-forcing student account passwords. And if the result is successful, the student's account is disabled until a discussion between the student and the university's system administrators takes place.

E-mail Policy   Understanding how e-mail is used as an infection vector helps in coming up with a secure e-mail policy. The policy usually covers rules governing the following:

- Attachments
- Universal Resource Locator (URL) links
- E-mail format
- E-mail location
- E-mail communication

Typically security policies regarding *attachments* revolve around the attachment's nature. It has to be among the approved file types before it can be sent into an e-mail. Typically, these are plain text files or document files with no macros. Executables, scripts, and other file types of the same nature and have the ability to execute code are blocked. Most policies also dictate that all attachments must be compressed and password protected or encrypted with a key. An e-mail policy governing attachments is technically enforced. If an attachment does not conform to the policy then the e-mail is dropped.

Most rules regarding attachments were a reaction from the mass-mailing worms that sent themselves as attachments. Limiting and putting controls on attachments was believed to be an effective way to stop malware delivery through this vector. The only way an attachment will go through is if it is compressed and password protected, but some organizations have the password protection optional but highly encouraged. However, it

Into Action

Do not send out bouncing e-mail notifications. Information from this is used by attackers to gather information about mail servers. Simply dropping an e-mail that is sent to an invalid address in the organization is enough.

did not take long for the malware to adapt. Most malware that uses e-mail as a vector is compressed and even password protected. Since the e-mail conforms to the attachment policy, there is a high chance that it will be delivered to its target.

Tip

Sending files via e-mail should always be a last resort. Utilizing other file sharing resources is always better. It's safer, plus it saves on bandwidth.

URL links are popular infection vectors, as discussed in previous chapters. To avoid a clickable URL in an e-mail message, a URL links policy dictates that all URLs that will be transmitted via e-mail be "neutered." A neutered URL is a nonclickable URL. It is now just common text. Replacing characters in or putting spaces between the characters of "HTTP" or "WWW" achieves this. For example, "h t t p://www.baddomain.org," "hxxp:// www.baddomain.org," and "www . baddomain . org" are not clickable.

The safest *e-mail format* is text. You are free from malicious macros and scripts that thrive on other formats. Even if the links are not malformed, they are still unclickable. The drawback is that the e-mail's aesthetics take a back seat. No fancy fonts, no colors, and no graphic logos.

The *place* where e-mail is stored is important. Some organizations prefer e-mails backed up regularly in the local system or automatically delivered to the host, while some prefer the e-mails to stay in the server. But if an organization needs to comply with some data protection laws, such laws usually dictate the location of where the e-mail is to be stored.

Those that prefer e-mails automatically delivered to the recipients locally do it because of fear that any e-mail that stays in the server is open to being accessed by an attacker if ever that attacker successfully gets the right credentials to access the e-mails. This policy is usually strengthened by host encryption.

When it comes to policy that governs *e-mail communications,* some of the things that are covered include:

- Automatic deletion of spam and junk mails
- No outgoing mail to nonbusiness contacts
- Monitored e-mail communication between competitors

Host Policy   Any system that is connected to the network must conform to a set of rules. Some of the rules include the following:

- Presence of a security solution
- Only authorized software is installed

- Updated software and patches
- Encrypted local storage
- Host settings that are security-centric
- Secure browser settings
- Remember only authorized wireless networks

Network Access Control Policy   Before a system is permitted to connect to an enterprise network, it has to comply with the existing host policy. This ensures that there is minimal risk posed by connecting hosts to the network. Nobody wants an internal malware outbreak to occur as a result of joining an infected host to the network. This is especially true for mobile devices, such as laptops, that often connect to public networks.

To be able to connect to the network, a host must comply with existing policies. When a host is attempting to connect to the organization's network, access must not be granted immediately unless an automatic, thorough check of the host is conducted. In some implementations, a preinstalled agent in the host determines whether it is compliant or not. If the host is compliant, access is granted immediately. If not, the necessary changes needed to make the host compliant are made. Achieving compliance can be done automatically or manually. If the only option is manual, the user or someone from IT must do the necessary things to make the host compliant, like updating an operating system patch or uninstalling unauthorized software. While the system is being made compliant, either automatically or manually, certain network resources are already available to the system. Usually, these network resources contain the latest AV product and signature, updated software and patches, or any resources needed to make the system compliant. Once the system is compliant, as checked by the preinstalled agent, the host is granted access to the network.

External Storage Policy   Unauthorized external storage must not be allowed to be used in any systems connected to the organization's network. Only those that are encrypted and can be tied to a specific user or system are allowed. This policy is a byproduct of data leakage prevention and the rampant abuse of Universal Serial Bus (USB) as a malware infection vector.

Into Action

Disabling the autostart feature of inserted storage devices is the easiest solution to mitigate malware-laced external storage. This can be done immediately with little effort.

Information Control Policy Information flow must be controlled. Unfortunately, a data leak prevention (DLP) solution cannot be installed in humans to prevent them from leaking data verbally or through their writing. Situations vulnerable to information leakage must be identified and then addressed. Some of these situations are the following:

- Interviews
- Job postings
- Public postings

During *interviews,* the interviewer must not divulge any information about what the team is currently doing, such as what invention or research project they are currently busy with. An interviewee does not need to know this.

In Actual Practice

Some organizations have job applicants sign a nondisclosure agreement (NDA) before an interview is conducted. The NDA covers nondisclosure of what the candidate sees inside the company and the topics talked about during the interview.

Job postings are a gold mine of information for attackers during the reconnaissance stage of an attack, as discussed in Part II of the book. When posting for job openings, do not describe or put any information in the posting that reveals information about the organization's critical systems. For example, a posting for an open system administrator position can simply limit the qualification section to "knowledge in Unix and Windows systems" instead of a detailed description of the systems.

A general rule of thumb when *posting something publicly* is to use no identifying company and user information. However, work e-mails still find themselves in public forums, especially tech support forums. This is a no-no. When joining a technical forum, even if the information gathered from the forum will be used for something job related, nonwork-related e-mail must be used. Strictly adhering to this practice will render the attacker's search on public forums and other postings to gather information about a target organization fruitless.

Social Media Policy Social media is becoming very popular and is now a primary mode of keeping in touch with family and friends.

A social media policy includes provisions such as

- Be socially responsible
- Do not divulge information about work
- No work-related postings

Security Awareness Culture

The weakest link in the security chain is often identified as the one between the chair and the keyboard. It is always expected that the people within an organization are well informed when it comes to their roles and goals. But when it comes to security, they are scarcely informed. To bridge this gap, building a culture of security awareness is key.

Building a culture of security awareness instills the needed knowledge and the right attitude when it comes to information security to all the people within the organization. The main goal is to enable everyone to be aware of the security risks, both externally and internally, that may result in a system breach and having them act appropriately to minimize the risk or to prevent the occurrence from happening at all.

Organizations with a strong culture of security awareness have the following characteristics:

- People who are well informed on security trends and the threat landscape
- A positive attitude toward restrictive security rules and policies
- Sees the safe computing process not as a burden but as an added layer of protection

IMHO

Having support from the top or having a top-to-bottom initiative when it comes to building a culture of security awareness exponentially increases its chances of success.

To get things rolling, two important things must be implemented that will serve as the seeds of security awareness:

- Security awareness briefing for new hires
- Periodic security awareness briefing

Security Awareness Briefing for New Hires   Security must be part of all new employee orientation. The new hire must be familiarized not only with his job roles and goals, but also with the safe computing process the organization has put in place. Having this as part of a new hire's orientation requirement shows the organization's commitment to security.

Your Plan

The following checklist can be used to supplement a new hire's checklist:

1. Read security basics at <insert wiki page here>

2. Must read security topics
   <enumerate topics here>
   2.a. <Topic 1>
   2.b. <Topic 2>

3. Attend scheduled security awareness training as required

Bringing in a new hire takes a lot of effort. To make the process easy, the manager and the new hire must have their own respective checklists of things to do. The manager accomplishes a manager's checklist even before the new hire's first day. It usually contains items such as "approve purchase of hardware," "approve new user account," and "goal setting meeting." As for the new hire, the checklist contains items such as those he needs to do to set up his equipment, human resource (HR)-related tasks, and a list of topics he needs to familiarize himself with, the most important of which is security. The checklist should point specifically to where security-related information could be found and a list of core security knowledge that he must read and understand.

Periodic Security Awareness Briefing   Technology changes fast, and so does the threat landscape. The attackers are finding new and clever ways to infiltrate a target organization. They look for weaknesses not only technically but also in members of the organization that they can take advantage of. Because of this, any policy included in a safe computing process is considered dynamic. It must adapt to the changing technology and threat landscape so it remains relevant on the fight against any persistent threat. To maintain the users' security awareness, they must be kept abreast of any of these changes.

Into Action

Having a one-stop shop of information or a dedicated intranet or internal wiki page about changes in the safe computing process and the developments in the field of security in general is good way for people in the organization to keep abreast of the latest in security.

A periodic security awareness briefing serves as an update to everyone and ensures that everyone is aware of what's the latest in security. This can be done as frequently as quarterly or annually. This depends on the organization's assessment on how fast the technology changes and how many changes have occurred during the last security awareness briefing.

Protection Beyond Security Solutions

As we have previously discussed, protecting an organization must not rely solely on security products alone. The organization must do more. Having a safe computing process in place and starting an initiative of building a culture of security awareness goes a long, long way. But there are still things that can be done to protect an organization against an attack that goes beyond having security solutions in place.

The following are some of the things that can be done to reinforce an organization's security posture:

- Key personnel protection
- Secure network designs
- One-off protection

Key Personnel Protection   As we have discussed in previous chapters, people holding key positions in the company are often targeted for social engineering ploys that will result in the attacker gaining information that can be used to infiltrate the target enterprise. We can see this trend in spear e-mail infection vectors. When it comes to security awareness, these key people are often briefed differently. In some cases, even their family is briefed. For example, the mom who is a top-level researcher for a government contractor is attending a confidential research summit. Since the mom is trained in security awareness and practices common sense, no word of this will ever get out. But what if the son left at home tweeted, "Mom is again in VA attending one of her secret summits, FREE AGAIN :-p" This piece of information can be used by an attacker to add the best social engineering ingredient to an infection vector. An envelope with a USB drive can be sent to the mom's office with a note thanking her for attending the summit and to please accept the USB as a token of appreciation and that it contains vital information about the summit. Or instead of a mail carrier–delivered USB stick, e-mail about the summit is sent to the mom. This e-mail can be carrying the malicious file, a mail client exploit, or a link claiming to be pointing to more information about the summit. And since the mom knows that the summit is confidential and no one knows about it except the organizers and the attendees, chances are the mom will believe that the USB and e-mail came from the summit itself.

These scenarios are just a couple of ways how the information from the tweet will be used by the attackers. There are still more ways to leverage this information, and they are only limited by the attacker's imagination.

Also, in this case, any external information released by key personnel must be known to the organization's security team. This will enable the organization to tackle social engineering attacks that take advantage of the released information. For example, information released about a speaking engagement someone from the company is attending should expect socially engineered infection vectors using that topic to come their way.

Secure Network Designs   The threat modeling session should reveal whether the existing network design is secure or not. A poorly designed network can spell disaster for an organization. Imagine an open wireless network connection to the organization's production network that anybody can connect to because of an absence of authentication or because it uses technology that can easily be broken. Couple that with a signal so strong that every office in the building can detect the Service Set Identifier (SSID) broadcast. This virtually gives everyone access to the organization's production network. Threat modeling will bring security issues like this to light so they can be solved, and once all issues are fixed, the organization's network would have achieved a secure status.

Even with a secure network design but with no strong security policies in place, the network might still be open for attack. Going back to our previous example, what if the open wireless network is a wireless router connected to a local area network (LAN) port by a user who wants the convenience of connecting his wireless devices such as mobile phones and personal laptops to the organization's fast Internet connection. There must be a policy that prevents this. Otherwise, it defeats the purpose of having a secure network.

One-Off Protection   There are certain steps an organization needs to take to protect itself that are one-offs or a one-time procedure—for example, registering multiple domains that are homographic or a common fat-finger result of the organization's domain name to protect from it being used in typosquatting attacks. This is especially useful for financial organizations whose domain names are often used for phishing attacks.

Budget Note
When proposing a budget for security, also include the cost of one-off protections.

Your Plan

One of the often-used methods for assessing security risks is penetration testing. When contracting a team for penetration testing, make sure the following are done or covered:

1. External penetration testing

2. Internal penetration testing

3. Social engineering proneness

Conducting a Periodic Security Audit

The effectiveness of appropriate security solutions installed in the organization, the safe computing process in place, and the culture being fostered by continuous security awareness must be measured to determine whether the desired end result is being achieved. This is accomplished by having a security audit.

A security audit is the process of evaluating or checking that all the procedures, policies, technical solutions, and controls are working as expected and whether they are still relevant. Having something working but not relevant anymore is equivalent to it being useless. A technical solution, even if it is working perfectly, but is not applicable anymore or has been left behind by the ever-changing threat landscape must be replaced. A security audit will also identify policies that need to be retired or revised.

An external provider or a group of chosen individuals within an organization can do a security audit. But no matter who does it, the end result must be that the security risk of the organization has been assessed effectively and that vulnerable points and opportunities for improvement have been identified.

Into Action

A very simple security audit can be done through e-mail. A socially engineered e-mail mimicking that of potentially coming from an attacker containing a link or a file can be sent to everyone in the organization. If a number of users, as defined on the organization's unacceptable threshold, click the link or execute the file, this means that security awareness is lacking. These users would be good candidates for retraining on security awareness.

A security audit must be well documented. It must include the expected and the current state of what is being audited. If there is difference between the two wherein the current state is not satisfactory, a corrective and preventive action plan must be created and included in the report. This plan must include a detailed breakdown of executable tasks, an estimated timeline, and the name of the point person. The auditors must do a follow-up on every corrective and preventive plan until the expected state has been achieved.

The Threat from Insiders

An organization faces not only attacks from the outside but also from the inside. An attack emanating from within the organization is called an insider threat. This is probably the most difficult threat to detect and prevent since an insider threat is someone who already has access to the organization's network. In other words, the attack is coming from a supposedly trusted source.

Who Are the Insider Threats?

When we think of insider threat, the first thing that comes to mind is a rogue employee. But we have to bear in mind that insider threats include not just employees but anyone who has some level of access to the organization's network and has a malicious intent against the organization. It can be a business partner, a privileged client, or a contractor. In short, an insider threat is someone who

- Has access to the organization's network
- Causes damage to the organization

Has Access to the Organization's Network

One advantage an insider threat has over conventional attackers is that he already has access to the organization. There are no hoops to jump through and no elaborate socially engineered or technically powered infection vector needed.

Causes Damage to the Organization

An insider threat's action always causes damage to an organization, either through unauthorized information leakage or sabotage.

Mitigating the Insider Threat

As previously mentioned, it is hard to detect or prevent an insider threat, but certain steps can be taken to lessen its impact or at least impede the action an insider threat might take.

The following are some ideas that serve as a good starting point in mitigating an insider threat:

- Full background check of employees
- Antiinsider threat policy enforcement
- Employee exit checklist
- Implementation of network tiers
- Restriction of access to least privilege
- Detailed auditing of user sessions
- Anomaly detection tuned to detect insider threat
- Implementation of a DLP solution
- Elimination of shared credentials
- Network access control to limit devices

Full Background Check of Employees

All employees must undergo background checks. Although this is not a foolproof mitigation technique, it's still a good first step in weeding out the undesirables.

Tip

Background checks must not be limited to employees alone. They must include entities the organization wants to engage in business with.

Antiinsider Threat Policy Enforcement

There must be a policy that clearly addresses insider threats. It must be specific on the criminal liabilities and penalties an alleged insider threat activity entails. The policy must also include the proper way of reporting a suspected insider threat without divulging the identity of the reporter. In other words, it must reward the whistleblower and punish the offender. This policy can be a separate document or part of the employee handbook to be read and signed by the employee so it forms a binding contract between the organization and the employee.

Employee Exit Checklist

Just as it is helpful to have a new hire checklist, it is also helpful to have an exit checklist for departing employees. An exit checklist is a list of items that must be accomplished when either party terminates employment. This is designed to make the parting of ways go smoothly. To ensure that the exit checklist covers the organization's security bases, it must contain items such as removing all access the user has on the organization's digital assets and revoking all user names, login credentials, and Secure Shell (SSH) keys the user has.

Implementation of Network Tiers

Redesigning the organization's network to implement network tiers or network compartmentalization ensures that an infection will not go beyond the tier or zone where the compromised machine is located. This controls the spread of malware to a single network tier.

Restriction of Access to Least Privilege

The user must have no admin access to workstations that enables him to install or modify anything. Access to any resource must be limited to the least privilege level and should only be elevated if necessary and with the supervision of an IT personnel.

Detailed Auditing of User Sessions

There must be a digital trail of which users access which systems, what privilege level they had, what was the nature of the session, and the changes resulting from the session. This enables the organization to record historical user activity to help in spotting suspicious activity.

Anomaly Detection Tuned to Detect Insider Threat

Anomaly detection solutions can be tuned to cover real-time monitoring of user sessions to detect possible malicious activity. For example, an alert must be generated when a user who does not have access to a specific resource has an active connection to the location where that resource resides and is continuously attempting to gain access to that resource.

Implementation of Data Leakage Prevention Solutions

Although there is nothing a DLP solution can do to stop users from verbally transmitting information or writing about it, it is still good to have it in place so the technical options of insider threats that are stealing sensitive information are limited.

Elimination of Shared Credentials

Some organizations have a single login to a resource used by many individuals. For example, a website login that everybody uses to post blogs uses a single login credential shared by

Into Action

There will always be a need for an admin account in workstations. The best way to achieve this is to have an admin account that only IT have the credentials for and access to. This ensures that if any admin task needs to be done, IT is the only one that can do it.

all bloggers. What if one blogger leaves the company and the company did not change the shared login credential? The result is that the ex-blogger will still have access to the blog site using the shared login credential and can post unauthorized blogs with no one really knowing who it is because auditing of a shared credential is useless even if it has IP source logging. The offender can simply anonymize his session. But if everybody has their own user credentials to access even common resources, monitoring user sessions and revoking the credentials upon termination of employment will be easier.

Network Access Control to Limit Devices

There is a reason why server rooms have physical security. Imagine a rogue employee getting access to a server room and planting a box on a high tier or sensitive network. This would give that rogue employee access to the sensitive network through the unauthorized and strategic placement of the box. A simple SSH login to the box is all it takes. But with a network access control policy in place that checks for host conformity and adds more control and restriction to adding new boxes to sensitive networks, this method of connecting an unauthorized device can be thwarted.

Be Vigilant

Threat mitigation is a continuous process. It requires continuous improvement of existing mitigation techniques and staying abreast of the ever-changing threat landscape. The attacker never sleeps and neither can you. Stay vigilant and be prepared to strike back.

We've Covered

- What is threat mitigation
- The stages of malware threat handling
  - Containment
  - Verification
  - Threat detection and classification
  - Remediation and restoration
- How to immediately and proactively mitigate a threat
- Common policies included in a safe computing process
  - Password policy
  - E-mail policy
  - Host policy

- Network access control policy
- External storage policy
- Information control policy
- Social media policy
- The importance of conducting a periodic security audit
- Who are the insider threats
  - Has access to the organization's network
  - Causes damage to the organization
- How to mitigate insider threats
  - Full background check of employees
  - Antiinsider threat policy enforcement
  - Employee exit checklist
  - Implementation of network tiers
  - Restriction of access to least privilege
  - Detailed auditing of user sessions
  - Anomaly detection tuned to detect insider threats
  - Implementation of DLP solutions
  - Elimination of shared credentials
  - Network access control to limit devices

PART IV

Final Thoughts

CHAPTER 12

The Never-Ending Race

We'll Cover

- A brief summary of the book

- A glimpse into the future of malware, rootkits, and botnets

- How to follow current antimalware research works

The fight against malware is a never-ending race. A new malware technology comes out, the researchers will find ways to defeat it, and another one comes out. A new antimalware technology is developed, the malware writers find ways to defeat it, and the researchers will come out with a new one. This is how it was and this is how it will be. While we have covered mostly advances in malware technology in this book, there is lots of research going on to tackle them. The race is always on and it will never end.

In this chapter, we will take a look back at what we have discussed throughout the book; my take on the future of malware, rootkits, and botnets; and how you can hook up with the latest research works being conducted to address the malware problem.

A Short Review of the Book

The book begins by getting ourselves in gear to start our journey into the interesting world of malware, rootkits, and botnets. In Chapter 2, we went through a brief history of malware from its humble beginning as a proof-of-concept, self-propagating program into more sophisticated malicious software. Chapter 3 then introduced us to the different techniques malware uses to gain control of the operating system to achieve invisibility in the target system. Then in Chapter 4, which concluded Part I, we looked at a more sophisticated type of threat called botnets, which can be actively controlled by an attacker to launch coordinated attacks against a target.

Part II delved more into how malware is being utilized by cybercriminals. Chapter 5 focused on the technical and human elements of the threat ecosystem, enumerating and discussing the different technical elements that enable attackers to conduct an attack against a chosen target and identifying the different roles of the cybercriminals behind the attack. In Chapter 6, we narrowed our discussion to the most important technical element of the threat ecosystem: the malware. This chapter discussed the different antivirus (AV) evasion techniques utilized by malware to protect itself from security products and from the prying eyes of AV researchers. Aside from the armoring techniques described, Chapter 6 also introduced us to the reality of automated malware production and how it virtually rendered AV host solutions obsolete. Chapter 7 then discussed how these newly created or recycled malware are being deployed by the attackers to reach their target of choice by using whatever technology that can be leveraged as an infection vector. The successful deployment of malware results in a compromised machine, which is discussed in Chapter 8. The discussion also included how malware establishes its foothold in the system and the common attack directives malware is tasked to accomplish.

If there is darkness, there is light. Part III discussed how to address the malware threat. Chapter 9 established the foundation of how to prepare and protect an organization from malware threats through the introduction of practical concepts that aid in improving an organization's security posture. But as previous chapters showed, there is no silver bullet against malware. This is why Chapter 10 focused on detecting a possible malware infection within an organization through the use of anomaly detection and, once identified, isolating the infected assets so the malware can be retrieved, analyzed, and classified based on its directive. This then brings us to Chapter 11 where the concentration was on threat mitigation. In this chapter, both preventive and immediate responses to threats are discussed.

The book then concludes with this chapter, which includes my final thoughts on the topic of malware, rootkits, and botnets.

Predictions

Every year, the public is bombarded by security companies and their designated spokespersons with end-of-the-year malware reports and predictions for the following year of how the threat landscape will change. Most of the predictions are based on trending data that each company has seen, and they serve as useful information from different perspectives. Although most of them use different data as the source, there is one recurring theme: malware will continue to thrive and it will only get worse before it gets better. Some will find the predictions useful and use them to protect digital assets under their control, while others might think this is fear mongering devised to sell products. My take on this is simple. Keep an open mind, absorb the information, process it, and act upon those that make more sense to your situation.

So what does the future bring for malware, rootkits, and botnets? Let's take a more general look not just based on these threats' past developments.

The Future of Malware

Malware will always be around. We have seen it survive the ever-changing technology landscape. The introduction of new devices, new operating systems, more secure ways of developing software, and new security products and features did not slow down the development of malware. In some cases, the advances in technology even made malware more dangerous. For example, the fact that people are more connected today than a couple of decades ago makes it possible for malware to reach hundreds of thousands, even millions, of targets in seconds. This just goes to show that as the technology evolves so does malware.

The future of malware, as I see it, will be influenced by the following factors:

- Popularity of devices
- Information content of devices
- Cross-platform programming
- More kits and armoring tools
- Ignorance of users
- Computerization of critical infrastructure

Popularity of Devices

As devices become popular, they will become prime targets for attackers because this means more attack coverage. Different devices will have different hardware structure and different operating systems. This means the development of malware technology will be anchored to these. As was discussed in the book, a malware written for DOS will not work for Windows because the operating system internals are significantly different. The intention and end goal are still the same, and that is to compromise and control the target system, but the means of getting there varies depending on the hardware and the operating system of the target device.

The popularity of mobile devices such as the iPhone and Android-powered devices is giving mobile malware writers a boost. Almost everyone in the world uses mobile devices and some of these devices are even able to connect to an organization's production network. It has become a necessity. Because of this popularity and their adoption into corporate networks, mobile malware is starting to flourish once more. Expect a steady rise in the number of mobile malware, especially now that these mobile devices are like mini-computers that run software for word processing, data storage, Internet browsing, and even online banking. As these devices develop, the mobile malware will also evolve, resulting in a more complex and sophisticated new generation of mobile malware than what we see today. This may take some time, but it is bound to happen.

In a nutshell, the more popular a device becomes, the greater the likelihood of it becoming a target of choice for malware. Did I just hear Mac?

Information Content of Devices

A device that is popular and runs software, which is one requirement for the possibility of malware to be written on the device, but that does not contain information that is usable or that can be monetized by the attacker might get its share of malware but not so much that will actually garner attention. Consider mobile devices again. Aside from the rising popularity of these devices, they also hold information such as contacts, sensitive notes, saved documents, and other data cached or saved by the software installed in the devices. These kinds of information can be useful to attackers or their sponsors.

A device or system can also be a prime target even if it does not contain the desired information but instead processes it. Processing information means access to that information. The access privilege of the machine makes it a high-value target. From this device, malware can simply sit and intercept information as it passes through and is processed in the device, or it can actively access the information storage using the access privilege of the compromised machine. Expect malware targeting more of these systems. And to increase the success of the attack, malware will be developed that will continue to utilize stealth techniques and rootkit technology. And in terms of malware behavior, expect more data exfiltration to drop zones. Therefore, malware will leave traceable network footprints that can be used to identify an infection.

As more information is stored in or processed by a device, the more attractive it becomes to attackers, especially if the information being held is liquid or can be easily monetized.

Cross-Platform Programming

With the introduction of new devices and operating systems, the attackers must learn the internals of these devices to create malware for them. Since malware is also software, the same problem malware writers face with having their creations run in different platforms is also the same problem for software developers. If software developers want their software to run in new devices, they must learn the platform. One way of solving this is through cross-platform programming. A program is considered cross-platform if it is able to run or execute on more than one operating system platform. For example, an application that can run in Windows can also run in Linux or Mac. But in the case of malware, instead of it running in all of its desired target platforms, it uses third-party software that runs across or is used across multiple platforms. We saw this when we discussed Office macro viruses. Since Office macro viruses rely on macro language specific to Office products, the macro virus is able to function no matter what OS the Office product is installed in. The only time the virus will not function is if it executes code that is dependent on a specific operating system. This is also true for malware written in Java. The malware executes inside a Java Virtual Machine. As long as the operating system supports Java, the malware will run in that operating system.

Not everyone uses Office products, or even lets Java run in their systems, but almost everyone with computers or devices uses a web browser to browse the Web. And web browsers have plug-ins or extensions that can function regardless of what operating system the browser is installed in.

Although cross-platform malware is good when it comes to compatibility, it is not as powerful as malware written

> **LINGO**
> Malware that spans multiple platforms is also called **OS-independent malware**.

specifically for the operating system. So the way I see it, there will be lots of cross-platform downloaders that will serve as an initial phase of infection that will lead to the installation of a platform-specific malware. For example, the cross-platform downloader will detect what OS is running in the system, grab the malware for that specific OS from the malware-serving domains, and then install it in the system.

More Kits and Armoring Tools

Recycling old malware and creating it from kits rather than creating new malware with the same purpose as old ones is cheaper and faster. This makes malware do-it-yourself (DiY) kits a very popular and essential tool for cybercriminals. But it's not only DiY kits that are essential—armoring tools are also vital to the success of an attack, with its track record of being successful in evading host product detection. Because of the success of kits and armoring tools, it has become a very profitable gig for malware writers to make and sell them. I see more of these tools being developed with more advanced malware technology and available to anyone who has the money to buy them. Aside from the business aspect of selling malware tools, it also protects the malware writer's identity. He simply creates the tools and distributes them using different underground channels. The commoditization of skills will continue to become popular among malware writers.

With DiY kits and armoring tools becoming more advanced and sophisticated, the concept of the malware factory will never be abandoned. It will instead become more efficient in production and effective in AV evasion, resulting in a flood of undetected and hard-to-reverse malware with numbers easily quadrupling what we are currently seeing today. Since these tools add complexity to the malware, the gap between the time malware is discovered to the time a solution reaches the victim will continue to widen. As the waiting time increases, a system compromise can end up with disastrous consequences.

Ignorance of Users

The fast-paced technology will always leave some users behind. They will either be stuck in the current technology they are using or in what they perceive the current capabilities of malware to be. Because of this they fail to recognize advances in malware technology that could have helped them in choosing the appropriate security solutions or in applying basic security measures to protect the systems under their control. These users become malware carriers, especially those who own mobile devices such as laptops that join public networks or that even get plugged into a corporate network. These machines serve as infectors, a staging server for malware. Therefore, malware will still continue to wage a series of opportunistic attacks on these targets with ignorant users. They will need these as zombies and pawns in their other attack campaigns. These machines become unwitting participants in a botnet that can use these machines in a variety of ways, such as a spam relay, distributed denial of service (DDoS) attacker, or a flux agent. But most important of all, these machines can serve as the main botnet infrastructure that can and will be used in targeted attacks.

The good thing about ignorant users is that they can learn and improve, unlike those who are hopelessly stupid. The main difference between ignorance and stupidity is that ignorance is unaware or lacks knowledge of something and, therefore, can be made aware or knowledgeable through education, while stupidity, on the other hand, is the inability to learn no matter what.

Computerization of Critical Infrastructure

As mentioned in the first chapter of this book, malware is already considered by the Federal Bureau of Investigation (FBI) to be a threat to national security. And as more critical infrastructure comes online and is automated, the risk of it being attacked is higher. The possibility of specialized malware targeting critical infrastructure, like Stuxnet coming out of the woodwork, is very likely, especially if more state-sponsored attacks are waged against another state or nation.

The FBI must be seeing something that is leading them to believe that cybercrime will eclipse terrorism. Whatever data they have on this, one thing is certain and that is continuous attacks on critical infrastructure can cripple a nation.

The Future of Rootkits

For malware to survive it must remain hidden; therefore, malware, especially one that is commissioned for a targeted attack, will carry with it some sort of rootkit technology. Again, the purpose is the same; the only difference is the *how*. Rootkits will be around; the only difference is the technique, because as new devices are introduced and new operating systems powering those devices implement new methods of controlling the underlying hardware, the malware writers need to find ways to achieve control and subvert these new devices and operating systems.

The different rootkit techniques will continue to evolve together with new devices. How fast the development is will depend on how fast the malware writers learn the internals of the upcoming devices and operating systems.

The Future of Botnets

The malware component of the botnet was already covered in the discussion on the advances in malware and rootkit technology. Therefore, I believe that the main advances in botnets will be mostly on the command and control (C&C). Bulletproof hosting will continue to prosper and protect C&C servers. C&C resiliency will continue through fluxing and decentralization. But one growing trend I see is the utilization of online resources or services such as social networks as the command and control. For example, Twitter can be used as command and control. I demonstrated this concept in several talks I gave in the summer of 2011. However, Twitter, or any social network for that matter, is not the only one that can be abused by the attacker. Any online resource, such as simple webpages, can be used for command and control. The main reason for using social networks in this way is that these resources will have information on them that will serve as input to the botnets that their malware component can process and then act upon in a coordinated manner.

A botnet monitoring a certain webpage for a specific string for its command and control suddenly sees that string appear. It will immediately function as intended based on the command interpretation it has for that string. Let's say, for example, botnet acting as a spam relay is monitoring several websites for an announcement of the release of a new phone. An announcement is posted that contains the magic string the botnet is looking for. It then triggers the sending of millions of spams with the subject: "You Just Won the Newly Released iPeach Phone."

The Good Guys Are Busy Too

While the malware writers are busy beefing up their creation with new malware technologies, figuring new ways of penetrating well-protected target systems, and finding novel techniques to protect and enhance the technical elements that serve as the backbone of their attack, the good guys are also busy working on groundbreaking stuff that tackles the malware challenge head on. Experts from both industry and academia are hard at work discovering new ways to fight malware, rootkits, and botnets. Research is being conducted at a furious pace; proof of concepts are being developed; ideas are being patented; antimalware working groups are being formed; information is being shared among researchers; and new products and features are introduced periodically, all aimed at addressing the malware problem.

A good way to keep updated on current research work is to read security research papers and white papers. If you have budget to spare, attending talks or conferences on security is also a good way to keep abreast of what's going on in the security space.

Tip

An expensive conference does not mean it is the best or is always better. There are less expensive or even free conferences, such as B-Sides, that showcase lots of high-quality talks from industry experts. Also, be wary of attending conferences that choose speakers based on company sponsorship rather than on the merit of the paper. The website http://faculty.cs.tamu.edu/guofei/sec_conf_stat.htm is a good resource by Guofei Gu on security conference ranking.

The Adventure Has Just Begun

I hope you enjoyed reading this book as much as I enjoyed writing it. It has been a great pleasure for me to share some of the knowledge I have learned through years of experience, research, and conversations with industry and academic experts in this book. I do hope you come away from this reading experience armed with the knowledge to take on the digital threats that are plaguing us today and those that will in the future, and with the desire to learn more beyond the information presented in this book.

Although this is the book's final chapter, it is not the end. It is just the beginning of an exciting journey into the realm of malware, rootkits, and botnets. Wherever your adventures will take you, there will be defeats, but mostly there will be victories. Let the quest begin.

We've Covered

- A brief summary of the book
- A glimpse into the future of malware, rootkits, and botnets
  - Malware will continue to evolve as technologies evolve
  - Rootkit techniques will vary depending on new platforms that will be introduced, but the end goal of gaining administrative privileges will remain the same
  - Botnets will utilize legitimate online services more to hide its C&C
- How to follow current antimalware research works
  - Read security research papers, white papers and blogs
  - Attend quality security talks and conferences

The Bootup Process

The Windows Bootup Process

To better understand how malware autostarts in Windows, let's take a quick look at how Windows boots up. Depending on whether the system is BIOS-based or EFI-based, the bootup process differs up to the point of passing control to the kernel (see Figure A-1).

BIOS-Based system

On a BIOS-based system, the bootup process begins with the BIOS. The BIOS code selects a boot device and loads that device's Master Boot Record (MBR) into memory. The MBR is 512 bytes in size and is located at the first sector of the device. It contains the boot code and the partition table. The partition table contains the location of the primary partition in the disk. After the MBR is loaded, the BIOS passes control to the MBR boot code. The boot code parses the partition table and looks for a bootable partition. This is also called a system partition. After it is found, the MBR boot code reads the system partition's boot sector, which is found at the system partition's first sector. The MBR then passes control to the boot sector code, which informs Windows on the nature of the volume and loads the Bootmgr file from the volume's root directory, after which, control is passed to the Bootmgr.

Bootmgr operates in real mode. This means that what's on disk is what's in memory. There is no virtual-to-physical translation of memory. But the first thing it does is switch the operational mode of the CPU to protected mode. As a result, the full 32 bits of

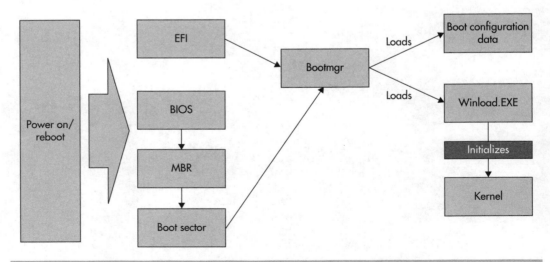

Figure A-1   A simplistic view of the bootup process

memory become accessible, enabling the
Bootmgr to access not just the first 1MB
(20 bits) of physical memory, a limitation
in real mode, but all of them. For

LINGO
A **system partition** is also known as a system volume.

Windows to operate normally, the system must be running in protected mode with paging
enabled. So after switching to protected mode, the Bootmgr also enables paging.

Note

For BIOS-based systems, the Bootmgr briefly switches back to real mode to execute
BIOS functions, especially if Bootmgr needs to access the computer display and
integrated development environment (IDE) disks.

Once the system is running in protected mode with paging enabled, the Bootmgr then
loads the Boot Configuration Data (BCD) store in the Boot folder located on the root
directory of the system volume. As defined by Microsoft, the BCD store contains boot

configuration parameters and controls
how the operating system is started in
newer versions of Microsoft operating
systems, starting with Microsoft Vista and
Microsoft Windows Server 2008 operating
systems. Once the BCD is loaded, it
directs the Bootmgr to the partition where
Windows is located. This is also known
as the boot partition or the boot volume.
From here, the Bootmgr loads Winload
.exe, which is Windows' boot loader.

LINGO
As Microsoft puts it, the **system partition** contains
the hardware-related files that tell a computer
where to look to start Windows. A **boot partition**
is a partition that contains the Windows
operating system files, which are located in
the Windows file folder. Usually, these are the
same partition, especially if you have only one
operating system installed on your computer.
If you have a multiboot computer, you will have
more than one boot partition.

Note

The BCD can have multiple boot-selection entries that can include other operating
systems. If this is the case, the Bootmgr displays the OS choices to the user and the user
decides which one to boot. If the user does not choose anything within the time limit,
Bootmgr loads the boot loader of the default OS.

Now that control is passed to the Windows OS loader, Winload.exe, it gathers
hardware description about the system and then loads the files needed to initialize the
kernel. It loads Ntoskrnl.exe and Hal.dll and their dependencies. Winload.exe then reads
the SYSTEM registry hive located in \Windows\System32\Config\System. The SYSTEM

registry hive contains the boot device drivers that must be loaded to boot the system. The registry path that contains the subkeys of the boot device drivers is HKLM\SYSTEM\ CurrentControlSet\Services. It contains not just the subkeys of boot device drivers, but subkeys of all device drivers. To differentiate which is which, Winload.exe identifies boot device drivers through their start value. Boot device drivers have a start value of SERVICE_BOOT_START(0). Once they are identified, Winload.exe loads these drivers and then prepares the CPU registers for Ntoskrnl.exe. It then calls KiSystemStartup, the Ntoskrnl.exe's main function.

EFI-Based System

EFI stands for Extensible Firmware Interface. One of the differences it has over BIOS-based systems is that it does not rely on MBR boot code. The EFI has its own boot manager that can read the partition table to determine which partition is bootable. This means that the boot code itself is in the firmware. Once the EFI's boot manager loads into memory and executes, the succeeding steps are similar to the BIOS-based startup process.

LINGO
A **registry hive** contains a registry subtree.

APPENDIX B

Useful Links

Vulnerability Information

- **National Vulnerability Database**   http://nvd.nist.gov/
- **Open Source Vulnerability Database**   http://osvdb.org/
- **Vulnerability Notes Database**   http://kb.cert.org/vuls/

Free Online Security Products

- **Trend Micro's Housecall**   http://housecall.trendmicro.com
- **F-Secure Online Scanner and Health Check**   http://f-secure.com/en/web/home_us/ protection/free-online-tools/free-online-tools
- **Norton PC Checkup**   http://us.norton.com/nortonlive/free-pc-checkup.jsp
- **Secunia Online Software Inspector**   http://secunia.com/vulnerability_scanning/online/

Free File Scanner and Analysis Tools

- **VirusTotal**   http://virustotal.com
- **Multi-Engine Antivirus Scanner**   http://vscan.novirusthanks.org/
- **Anubis**   http://anubis.iseclab.org/
- **GFI ThreatTrack**   http://threattrack.com/

Web Security

- **Malware URL**   http://malwareurl.com/listing-urls.php
- **McAfee SiteAdvisor**   http://siteadvisor.com/sites/
- **Norton Safe Web**   http://safeweb.norton.com/
- **F-Secure Browsing Protection**   http://browsingprotection.f-secure.com/swp/
- **FastFlux Tracker**   http://dnsbl.abuse.ch/

Malware Trackers

- **Zeus Tracker**   https://zeustracker.abuse.ch/
- **SpyEye Tracker**   https://spyeyetracker.abuse.ch/

Other Important Links

- **Malware Platform Names**   http://caro.org/naming/officialplatforms.html
- **Conficker Working Group**   http://confickerworkinggroup.org

Tip

Read the terms of use and privacy policies of these services carefully and ensure that all files submitted for analysis to these services do not contain any sensitive information. Make sure you understand the repercussions of using these services, giving your information, and submitting files for analysis. The author and the publisher are not liable for any of them.

GLOSSARY

acceptable use of computers   Defines what activities are acceptable on computer systems owned by the organization.

access attack   The attempt to gain information the intruder is not authorized to see.

access control   A mechanism used to restrict access to files, folders, or systems based on the identification and authentication of the user.

accountability   The process an organization uses to account for an individual's activities and to assign responsibility for actions that have taken place on an information system.

address resolution protocol (ARP) spoofing   A tactic whereby the MAC address of a system is forged to get packets directed to the attacking computer.

administrative practices   Practices that fall under the areas of policy, procedure, resources, responsibility, education, and contingency plans.

agents   The people or organization originating a security threat.

anomaly   Something that is out of the ordinary or unexpected.

antimalware system   A system designed to detect and remove malicious software.

application layer firewall   A firewall that enforces policy rules through the use of application proxies.

APT   (1) A well-thought-out targeted attack that effectively utilizes the threat ecosystem. (2) An ever present attack, backed by highly organized, well-funded, and motivated criminal elements, that is made up of a broad spectrum of infection vectors and malware technologies that are available to the attackers blended together to result in a successful compromise of a system. (3) Generally considered to be a hacker or group of hackers with significant resources and who are targeting specific enterprises. The APT uses exploits that may never have been seen before and compromises systems with the intent of keeping control of them and making use of them for some time.

audit   (1) A formal check to determine policy compliance, typically performed either by internal auditors at a company or organization or by an independent third party. (2) A function in an OS that provides administrators with a historic record of events and activities that occurred on an information system for future reference.

availability   The degree to which information is available when it is needed by authorized parties. Availability may be measured as the percentage of time information is available for use by authorized websites. For example, a business website may strive for availability above 99 percent.

backup   The copies of critical information that are archived in the event of a system crash or a disaster.

backup policy   The policy an organization has in place documenting how backup operations will be conducted.

Balanced Scorecard (BSC)   A performance measurement framework that is intended to enrich traditional financial performance measures with strategic nonfinancial performance measures, thereby giving a more balanced view of organizational performance. Developed in the 1990s by Drs. Robert Kaplan (Harvard Business School) and David Norton. (For additional information, see www.balancedscorecard.org.)

best practices   A set of recommendations that generally provides an appropriate level of security. A combination of those practices proves to be most effective at various organizations.

biometrics   The use of something related to the human body—for example, fingerprints, retina/iris prints, palm prints, hand geometry, facial geometry, or voice recognition—to authenticate an individual's access.

black swan event   An event that is highly improbable and therefore likely to end up at the bottom of the list of priorities to address. See *The Black Swan: The Impact of the Highly Improbable* by Nassim Taleb (Random House, 2007) for further reading on the Theory of Black Swan Events.

bootstrapping   A process of P2P clients joining a P2P network.

bot   Short for robot. This is a generic term for automated programs that execute tasks without user intervention.

bot agent   The host component of a botnet that communicates directly to the command and control channel.

botnet   A botnet is a network of compromised computers that can be coordinated remotely by an attacker to fulfill a malicious directive such as transmiting stolen information, sending spam, or launching distributed denial-of-service (DDoS) attacks. Essentially, a botnet is a collection of compromised machines controlled and managed by a hacker, fraudster, or cybercriminal.

brute force attack An attempt by a hacker to gain access to a system by trying to log on to one or many accounts using different combinations of characters to guess or crack a password.

buffer A contiguously finite space in memory.

buffer overflow The process of overwriting memory in such a way as to cause an attacker's code to be executed instead of the legitimate program with the intent of causing the system to be compromised or allowing the attacker to have elevated privileges to the system.

bulletproof hosting A hosting service provided by unscrupulous webhosting companies that allows account users to do virtually anything they want with no fear of takedown or identity exposure as long as the bulletproof provider gets paid.

certificate authority A central management entity that issues or verifies security credentials.

change control procedure The process used by an organization to verify the current system configuration and provide for the testing and approval of a new configuration before it is implemented.

charter A document that describes the specific rights and privileges granted from the organization to the information security team.

ciphertext Information that has been obfuscated by an encryption algorithm.

cloud computing As defined by the National Institute of Standards and Technology (NIST), a model for enabling ubiquitous, convenient, on-demand network access to a shared pool of configurable computing resources (e.g., networks, servers, storage, applications, and services) that can be rapidly provisioned and released with minimal management effort or service provider interaction. This cloud model promotes availability and is composed of five essential characteristics, three service models, and four deployment models.

command and control channel An online resource that changes or influences the behavior of bots. It is the means by which a botnet is controlled.

command and control server System or systems that host the command and control channel.

command and control traffic Data flowing between the bots and the command and control channel.

communications security   The measures employed to secure information while it is in transit.

compliance   Adherence to a set of policies and standards. Two broad categories of compliance are compliance with internal policies (specific to a particular organization) and compliance with external or regulatory policies, standards, or frameworks.

computer forensics   The process of gathering and analyzing evidence collected after an attack has occurred.

computer security   The means used to protect information on computer systems.

computer use policy   Specifies who can use the organization's computer systems and how those systems can be used.

confidentiality   The prevention of disclosure of information to unauthorized parties.

consultant   A subject matter expert who is contracted to perform a specific set of activities. Typically, a statement of work outlines the deliverables to be completed by the consultant and the deadlines for each deliverable.

core competencies   The fundamental strengths of a program that add value. They are the primary functions of a program and cannot or should not be done by outside groups or partners.

countermeasures   The measures taken by an organization to address the identified vulnerabilities of the organization.

critical systems   Systems performing critical functions vital to the operation of an organization.

cryptanalysis   The art of analyzing cryptographic algorithms with the intent of identifying weaknesses.

cryptographer   An individual who practices cryptography.

cryptographic checksum   A binary string created by running the binary value of the software through a cryptographic algorithm in such a way as to create a result that will change if any portion of the original binary is modified.

cryptography   The art of concealing information using encryption.

data cleansing   The actions performed on a set of data in order to improve the data quality and achieve better accuracy, completion, or consistency.

data encryption standard (DES)   A private key encryption algorithm developed by IBM in the early 1970s that operates on 64-bit blocks of text and uses a 56-bit key.

data leakage prevention   A mechanism for examining network traffic and detecting sensitive information.

decryption   The process used by encryption systems to convert ciphertext into plaintext.

default allow   A policy where any traffic is allowed except that which is specifically denied.

default deny   A policy where any traffic is denied except that which is specifically allowed.

defense in depth   An architecture where multiple controls are deployed in such a way that weaknesses in one control are covered by another.

denial of access to applications   The tactic of denying the user access to the application that displays the information.

denial of access to information   The tactic of making information the user wants to see unavailable.

denial of access to systems   The tactic used by an attacker to make a computer system completely inaccessible by anyone.

denial-of-service attack   The process of flooding a server (e-mail, web, or resource) with packets to use up bandwidth that would otherwise be allocated to normal traffic and thus deny access to legitimate users.

deperimeterization   The current state of most perimeters—that is, full of holes that reduce or eliminate the effectiveness of the perimeter.

Diffie-Hellman key exchange   A public key encryption algorithm developed in 1976 to solve the problem of key distribution for private key encryption systems. Diffie-Hellman cannot be used to encrypt or decrypt information, but it is used to exchange secret keys.

digital signature   A method of authenticating electronic information by using encryption.

digital signature algorithm   An algorithm developed by the U.S. government as a standard for digital signatures.

dirty data   Data that has unacknowledged correlation or undocumented origins or that is biased, nonindependent, internally inconsistent, inaccurate, incomplete, unsuitable for integration with data from other important sources, unsuitable for consumption by tools that automate computation and visualization, or lacking integrity in some other respect.

disaster recovery   The processes and procedures to protect systems, information, and capabilities from extensive disasters such as fire, flood, or extreme weather events.

disaster recovery plan   The procedure an organization uses to reconstitute a networked system after a disaster.

DMZ   A network segment containing systems that can be directly accessed by external users.

DNS spoofing   A tactic used by attackers that allows them to intercept information from a target computer.

domain fluxing   The ability to generate unique domain names on a regular time interval.

domain generation algorithm (DGA)   The algorithm that enables an executable to generate unique domain names.

drop zone   An online resource that serves as the attacker's repository of stolen data.

dumpster diving   The act of going through a company's trash to find useful or sensitive information.

dynamic domain name service (DDNS)   A service that links a domain name to a dynamically changing IP address. This means that a domain name will keep on pointing to the same host, regardless of its constantly changing IP address.

dynamic network address translation   The process used to map multiple internal IP addresses to a single external IP address.

eavesdropping   The process of obtaining information by being positioned in a location that information is likely to pass.

egress filtering   Filtering traffic that exits through a perimeter.

Elgamal   A variant of the Diffie-Hellman system enhanced to provide encryption, with one algorithm for encryption and another for authentication.

elliptic curve encryption   A public-key encryption system based on a mathematical problem related to elliptic curves.

e-mail policy Governs employee activity and use of the e-mail systems.

emissions security The measures used to limit the release of electronic emissions.

encryption The process of changing ciphertext into plaintext.

encryption algorithm The procedures used for encrypting information.

event In the context of security risk, this is the type of action that poses a threat.

failover Provisions for the reconstitution of information or capability. Failover systems are put into place to detect failures, and then to reestablish capability by the use of redundant hardware.

false negative A result that indicates no problem exists where one actually exists, such as what occurs when a vulnerability scanner incorrectly reports no vulnerability exists on a system that actually has a vulnerability.

false positive A result that indicates a problem exists where none actually exists, such as what occurs when a vulnerability scanner incorrectly identifies a vulnerability that does not exist on a system.

fast fluxing When a single domain name resolves to a frequently changing IP address. The result is multiple IP addresses assigned to a single domain name.

firewall A network access control device (either hardware or software) designed to allow appropriate traffic to flow while protecting access to an organization's network or computer system.

GOST A Russian private key encryption algorithm, which uses a 256-bit key, developed in response to DES.

hacker An individual who breaks into computer systems.

hacktivism The process of hacking a computer system or network for "the common good."

hierarchical trust model A model for trust in a public-key environment that is based on a chain of authority. You trust someone if someone else higher up the chain verifies that you should.

hit-and-run attack An attack campaign that happens in a short period of time and does not call for continuous access to a compromised system.

honeynet A collection of honeypots connected together to simulate a production network.

hot site   An alternate location for operations that has all the necessary equipment configured and ready to go.

honeypot   A monitored resource that serves as a trap or a decoy against an attack or threat. It is a security tool that helps prevent, detect, and gather information about a threat.

hot malware   Malware that is spreading rapidly or has caused a worldwide outbreak.

identification and authentication   The process that has a dual role of identifying the person requesting access to information and authenticating that the person requesting the access is the actual person they say they are.

incident responders   A team of skilled individuals well versed in security and information technology that provides incident response.

incident response   A well-planned, systematic approach that addresses an ongoing security threat or malware infection within an organization.

incident response procedures (IRP)   The procedures an organization puts into place to define how the organization will react to a computer security incident.

information classification standards   Standards that specify treatment of data (requirements for storage, transfer, access, encryption, etc.) according to the data's classification (public, private, confidential, sensitive, etc.).

information control   The processes an organization uses to control the release of information concerning an incident.

information policy   The policy used by an organization that defines what information is important and how it should be protected.

information security   (1) The measures adopted to prevent the unauthorized use, misuse, modification, or denial of use of knowledge, facts, data, or capabilities. (2) The protection of information and information systems from unauthorized access, use, disclosure, modification, or destruction. Also commonly referred to as data security, computer security, or IT security.

ingress filtering   Filtering traffic that enters through a perimeter.

integrity   The prevention of data modification by unauthorized parties.

intercept of a line   Identifies the point where the line crosses the vertical y-axis. An intercept is typically expressed as a single value (b), but can also be expressed as the point (0, b).

interception   An active attack against information where the intruder puts himself in the path of the information transmission and captures the information before it reaches its destination.

IPSec   A protocol developed by the Internet Engineering Task Force (IETF) to provide the secure exchange of packets at the networking layer.

IP spoofing   A tactic used by an attacker where the IP address of a computer system is forged.

ISO 27002   The document published by the International Organization for Standardization (ISO) to serve as a guideline for organizations to use in developing information security programs.

key   The data input into an algorithm to transform plaintext into ciphertext or ciphertext into plaintext.

liquid data   Data that can be easily sold or monetized.

live analysis   Analysis done on a system while its operating system is running or active.

MAC duplicating   The process used by an attacker where the MAC address of a target system is duplicated to receive the information being sent to the target computer.

malicious code   Programming code used to destroy or interfere with computer operations. Generally, malicious code falls into three categories: viruses, Trojan horse programs, and worms.

malware distribution server   An online resource that hosts malware components, including the bot agents, other important files, and the updates that the botnet needs for its operation.

man-in-the-middle attack   Also known as interception, the intruder puts himself in the middle of a communication stream by convincing the sender that he is the receiver and the receiver that he is the sender.

masquerading   Impersonating someone else or some other system.

mass-mailer   A program that has the ability to send e-mails to multiple recipients in a single instance of propagation.

metrics project distance   The amount of change you want to achieve in your target measurement by the end of the metrics project.

metrics project timeline   How long you want to spend to achieve the metrics project distance.

mission statement   Outlines an information security program's overall goals and provides guidelines for its strategic direction.

modification attack   The attempt by an attacker to modify information that the attacker is not authorized to modify.

network address translation   The process of translating private IP addresses to public IP addresses.

network behavior analysis   An anomaly detection mechanism that watches the flow of traffic on the network. Flow information is acquired from routers and switches or from a device directly connected to the network.

network forensics   A monitoring mechanism that collects all traffic that flows across the network in front of the collection point.

network intrusion detection system   A monitoring system that sits out of band and watches network traffic, looking for indications of an attack.

network intrusion prevention system   A layer 2 network control that sits in line with traffic and watches for indication of an attack. When an attack is identified, the traffic can be blocked.

network-level risk assessment   The assessment of the entire computer network and the information infrastructure of an organization.

network security   The measures used to protect information used on networked systems.

noteworthy malware   Malware that possess new and interesting features.

objective desired direction   The direction in which you want the metrics project measurement to go to achieve the benefits of an information security metrics program, especially the benefit of improvement.

offline analysis   Analysis done on a system while the operating system is not running or active.

offshoring   Contracting work to resources in a different country (either third party or in-house).

one-time pad (OTP)   The only theoretically unbreakable encryption system, this private key encryption method uses a random list of numbers to encode a message. OTPs can only be used once and are generally only used for short messages in high-security environments.

online analytical processing (OLAP)   A specific type of data storage and retrieval mechanism that is optimized for swift queries that involve summarization of data along multiple factors or dimensions.

opportunistic attack   An attack that does not have a specific target. The main goal is to have as many system infections or compromises as possible.

orange book   Also known as the Trusted Computer System Evaluation Criteria (TCSEC), this book was developed by the National Computer Security Center for the certification of computer systems for security.

orchestration   The administrative oversight that ensures the workflow is executed as specified. It includes functions such as signing off on a metric definition, deploying its implementation, scheduling its calculation at regular intervals, and executing and delivering updates. *See also* workflow.

organization-wide risk assessment   The analysis to identify risks to an organization's information assets.

outsourcing   Contracting work to a third-party vendor.

packet-filtering firewall   A firewall that enforces policy rules through the use of packet inspection filters.

penetration test   The test of the capability of an organization to respond to a simulated intrusion of its information systems.

perimeter   The boundary of a network or network zone.

pharming   An attack that redirects traffic intended for a legitimate website to a fake one through the modification of hosts files, network router compromise, or poisoned domain name system (DNS).

phishing   A scam that is accomplished through a socially engineered e-mail or webpage that attempts to fool the reader for the purpose of acquiring information.

physical security   The protection of physical assets by the use of guards and physical barriers.

ping of death   An ICMP echo-request packet sent to the target system with added data with the intent of causing a buffer overflow or system crash.

plaintext   Information in its original form. Also known as cleartext.

policy decision point   A control that determines a policy violation has occurred.

policy enforcement point   A control that performs an enforcement action.

policy reviews   The process used by an organization to review its current policies and, as necessary, adjust policies to meet current conditions.

prioritization   An exercise in determining the relative importance of tasks, projects, and initiatives.

private class addresses   Non-Internet routable IP addresses defined by RFC 1918.

private key encryption   An encryption process requiring that all parties who need to read specific information have the same key.

project management   Defining an end goal and identifying the activities, milestones, and resources necessary to reach it.

project scope   Indicates project coverage, typically by identifying the different regions, different networks, and/or different groups of people the project encompasses.

proxy   A security device used to apply policy to web traffic.

public classification   The least sensitive level of information classification; information that is already known by or can be provided to the public.

public key encryption   An encryption process that requires two keys: one key to encrypt the information and a different key to decrypt the information.

punycode   As defined in RFC 3492, this is an encoding syntax designed for use with International Domain Name (IDN) in applications. It uniquely and reversibly transforms a Unicode string into ASCII string.

quartiles   Divides all of the observations into four equal groups, which hold the lowest one-fourth of all observed values (first quartile), the highest one-fourth of all observed values (fourth quartile), and the two middle fourths, one-fourth above and one-fourth below the median value (or the value that divides the set of observations into two equal halves).

RASCI   A project management methodology for assigning roles in projects that involve many people and teams. Each letter in RASCI stands for a different type of role—Responsible, Approver, Supporter, Consultant, and Informed—and each role has corresponding responsibilities.

red book   Also known as the Trusted Network Interpretation of the TCSEC, this document provides guidelines for system security certifications in a networked environment.

regular expression   A mechanism used to match patterns within text.

remote login (rlogin)   Enables a user or administrator to log in remotely to a computer system and to interact as if they were logging in on the actual computer. The computer system trusts the user's machine to provide the user's identity.

reputation attack   Where the attacker is targeting the accountability of the information.

Request for Proposal (RFP)   A document that an organization uses to solicit proposals for a project that has specific requirements. The organization can then use the responses to the RFP to evaluate and compare the proposals of multiple vendors.

Rijndael   The algorithm used for the advanced encryption standard. This private key cipher uses blocks and keys of 128, 192, and 256 bits.

risk   The potential for loss.

rogue wireless network   A wireless network that is set up for the purpose of sniffing network traffic to and from the device connected to it to steal information. Also known as a rogue access point.

rootkit   A set of techniques coded into malware to gain root access and complete control of the operating system and its underlying hardware. A collection of tools used by hackers to cover their intrusion into a computer system or a network and to gain administrator-level access to the computer or network system. Typically, a backdoor is left for the intruder to reenter the computer or network at a later time.

router   A device used to route IP traffic between networks. While a router can be used to block or filter certain types of traffic, its primary purpose is to route traffic as quickly as possible.

RSA A public key algorithm that can be used for both encryption and decryption. RSA is based on the difficulty of factoring large numbers.

sacred cow An idiom for a practice that is implemented simply because it is "how it's always been done," without regard for its usefulness or whether it can help achieve a target goal or outcome.

scan An attempt to identify systems on a network. A scan may include actions that attempt to identify the operating system version and the services running on the computer system.

script kiddies Individuals who find scripts on the Internet and use them to launch attacks on whatever computer system they can find (considered a derogatory comment).

search engine optimization (SEO) A process of increasing a link's reputation through gaming of a target search engine, resulting in the link having a high rank and thus displayed first in a search result.

security information and event monitoring A system that gathers security logs from many sources and correlates the events so as to focus on events of importance.

security policy Defines the technical controls and security configurations that users and administrators are required to implement on all computer systems.

security posture The state of an organization's overall security health. It describes how well an organization is ready for any possible attack and how well it can withstand an ongoing attack.

separation of duties The partition of activities configuring a policy enforcement function from the activity of verifying the compliance of the function.

service set identifier (SSID) A unique name that identifies a wireless network.

single-factor authentication The process an organization might use with one authentication method to identify the person requesting access to information. Using a password is a single-factor authentication.

site events A disastrous event that destroys an entire facility.

slope of a line A value that represents how fast the y values are rising or falling as the x values of the line increase. Slope of line = $(y_2 - y_1) / (x_2 - x_1)$, where (x_1, y_1) and (x_2, y_2) are any two points on the line.

smurf attack   This type of attack sends a ping packet to the broadcast address of a large network and spoofs the source address to point the returning information at the target computer. The intent is to disable the target computer.

sniffer   A computer that is configured with software to collect data packets off the network for analysis.

snooping   The process of looking through files and papers in hopes of finding valuable information.

social engineering   The use of nontechnical means (usually person-to-person contact) to gain access to information systems.

spear phishing   Phishing that is targeting a specific individual, group, or organization.

SQL injection   An attack that targets applications that take input and use it in a SQL query.

stack   Controls switching between programs and tells the OS what code to execute when the current code has completed execution.

stakeholders   Leaders responsible for critical decision-making and key supporters who will drive change throughout the organization.

static network address translation   The process used to map internal IP addresses to external IP addresses on a one-to-one basis.

substitution cipher   One of the oldest encryption systems, this method operates on plaintext, one letter at a time, replacing each letter for another letter or character. Analysis of the frequency of the letters can break a substitution cipher.

SYN flood   A DoS attack in which the attacker sends a large number of TCP SYN packets to the target computer to render the computer inaccessible.

target   The aspect of an organization's information system that an attacker might attack.

targeted attack   An attack campaign that is designed for a specific target.

technical practices   Practices that implement technical security controls within an organization.

threat   An individual (or group of individuals) who could violate the security of an organization.

threat analysis   A systematic approach to determine whether a certain object, situation or condition is a threat through the process of collection, examination, experimentation and investigation of evidence and various data. The end result of a threat analysis should not only establish that the threat is real but also determine its severity and its impact.

traffic and pattern analysis   The process by an attacker of studying the communications patterns and activities of a target to discover certain types of activities and information.

Triple DES   An enhanced version of DES that uses DES multiple times to increase the strength of the encryption.

Trojan horse   Malicious code that appears to be a useful program, but instead, destroys the computer system or collects information such as identification and passwords for its owner.

two-factor authentication   The process implemented by an organization that employs two of the three authentication methods for identifying a person requesting access to information. An example of two-factor authentication would be using a smart card with a password.

Twofish   A private key encryption algorithm that uses 128-bit blocks and can use 128-, 192-, or 256-bit keys.

typosquatting   A process by which another entity registers a domain that is a typo of a legitimate domain for the purpose of scamming unwitting visitors.

use policy   The policy an organization develops to define the appropriate use of information systems.

virus   Malicious code that piggybacks on legitimate code and, when executed, interferes with computer operations or destroys information. Traditional viruses are executed through executable or command files, but they can also propagate through data files.

vishing   Short for voice phishing. This is a phishing attempt using voice communication either by a live person or a recording.

VPN   A communication method that uses encryption to separate traffic flowing over an untrusted network.

VPN server   A server that serves as an endpoint for a VPN connection.

vulnerability   A potential avenue of attack.

vulnerability scan A procedure that uses a software tool to identify vulnerabilities in computer systems.

vulnerability scanning The process of looking for and identifying vulnerabilities intruders may use as a point of attack.

wardialing An attempt to identify phone lines that connect to computers by dialing a large amount of phone numbers to see which ones return a modem tone.

web application firewall A security device that operates on the content directed at a web application.

web of trust model A model for trust in a public key environment based on the concept that each user certifies the certificates of people known to him.

whale phishing Phishing that is meant to target people holding high positions in an organization.

Wired Equivalent Privacy (WEP) A protocol designed to protect information as it passes over wireless local area networks (WLANs). WEP has a design flaw that allows an attacker to determine the key by capturing packets.

workflow A collection of rules that govern the relationship of steps required to complete a process. Relationships might include sequence order, branching conditions, looping, and number of repetitions.

worms Programs that crawl from system to system without the assistance of the victim. They make changes to the target system and propagate themselves to attack other systems on the network.

zombies Compromised machines that are part of a botnet. See *botnet* on page 317.

Index

333

D

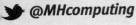